ROBERT H. FERRELL is Professor of History at Indiana University. He is the author of *Peace in Their Time: The Origins of the Kellogg-Briand Pact* and *American Diplomacy in the Great Depression: Hoover-Stimson Foreign Policy, 1929-1933,* both published in Norton Library editions; *American Diplomacy* (Norton); and *Foundations of American Diplomacy.*

AMERICAN DIPLOMACY IN THE GREAT DEPRESSION

Hoover-Stimson Foreign Policy, 1929–1933

BY ROBERT H. FERRELL

The Norton Library

W · W · NORTON & COMPANY · INC ·

NEW YORK

First published in the Norton Library 1970
by arrangement with Yale University Press

PUBLISHED SIMULTANEOUSLY IN CANADA
BY GEORGE J. MCLEOD LIMITED, TORONTO

SBN 393-00511-9

Books That Live

The Norton imprint on a book means that in the publisher's estimation it is a book not for a single season but for the years.

W. W. Norton & Company, Inc.

PRINTED IN THE UNITED STATES OF AMERICA

1 2 3 4 5 6 7 8 9 0

For Lila

Preface

THE PRESENT VOLUME is the second of a projected three-volume history of American diplomacy from 1927 to 1937. *Peace in Their Time: The Origins of the Kellogg-Briand Pact* (Yale University Press, 1952) set forth the peculiar intricacies of the most important international act of the United States in the interwar period. From this high point of policy the present book inquires into the consequent difficulties of American diplomacy from 1929 to 1933 under President Herbert Hoover and Secretary of State Henry L. Stimson. I hope to follow with a volume on the diplomacy of the New Deal.

It is at once the most pleasant task and the most difficult for an author to thank the many people who have helped him with his studies and writing. How can he say his appreciation, without resort to the usual clichés of thankfulness? Is it possible to record, without being perfunctory, that he could not have written without the help of friends?

First, my sincere thanks to the following individuals who read early drafts of the manuscript: F. Lee Benns, Dorothy Borg, Jane Carroll, Paul H. Clyde, Alexander DeConde, L. Ethan Ellis, Walter R. Fee, Arthur R. Hogue, William W. Kaufmann, Beatrice Lauter, Charles Seymour, and Robert E. Quirk. I am under similar obligation to Sir John Pratt, for many years Far Eastern adviser to the British Foreign Office; Stanley K. Hornbeck, chief of the division of Far Eastern affairs of the Department of State; the late Nelson Trusler Johnson, assistant secretary of state for the Far East and minister to China; Leon Hubbard Ellis, second secretary of the American legation in Peking; the late William H. Beck, secretary to Secretary of State Henry L. Stimson; James

Grafton Rogers, assistant secretary of state; G. Howland Shaw, chargé d'affaires in Paris in November–December 1931; and Francis White, assistant secretary of state for Latin America.

Former President Herbert Hoover most graciously allowed me to use information from his personal files housed in the Hoover Institution on War, Revolution, and Peace, at Stanford University.

Especially must I thank William R. Castle, undersecretary of state during the Hoover Administration, for the use of his diaries and for many hours of conversation. For nearly ten years, since graduate school days, I have been applying for assistance to Mr. Castle, and always he has been a constant, wise friend. Writing would have been difficult indeed without his help.

Samuel Flagg Bemis has contributed in so many ways to the present book that it is impossible to describe adequately his assistance. In the beginning, when chapters showed every error of style and organization, he tactfully pointed out elementary mistakes. Later he reread the manuscript. Rarely can one find this sort of assistance from an accomplished scholar.

I am also under large obligation to the Ford Foundation, whose generous support has made publication possible; and to the editor of the Yale University Press, Eugene Davidson, from whose keen interest in recent diplomatic history came many excellent suggestions for improving the manuscript.

Richard L. Powell expertly compiled and drafted the maps.

Lastly may I thank David Horne, editor of Yale Historical Publications, who is the best editor I could possibly have hoped to work with.

R. H. F.

Bloomington, Indiana
April 1957

Contents

Maps

Chapter One: THE GREAT DEPRESSION

1

The Great Depression was one of the most profoundly disturbing events in modern history. When it began in the United States with the stock-market crash of 1929 and spread rapidly to Europe and the entire world, it brought people everywhere to wonder about the future of life as they previously had known it. Ever since Charlemagne, Western civilization had gone from strength to strength. Though it had on occasion been in difficulty, it had always responded victoriously, and the Gates of Hell had not prevailed against it. But with the appearance of the Great Depression, wrote Arnold Toynbee, "the members of this great and ancient and hitherto triumphant society were asking themselves whether the secular process of Western life and growth might conceivably be coming to an end in their day." [1]

Before the World War of 1914–18, only a few individuals had seriously pondered such an issue. One of them, of course, was Spengler, who by 1914 had written the first draft of *Der Untergang des Abendlandes*. In the 1920's Spengler's gloomy prognostications went unnoticed by the vast majority of Americans and Europeans. Those few who read the book dismissed its thesis as one more ambitious cyclical view of history which could not stultify the continuing history of progress.

Cycles or no, the exigencies of the years after 1929 were such as to give new cogency to Spengler's argument. People began to reread Gibbon on the decline and fall of Rome. The Golden Age of the Antonines appeared to have had its modern analogue in the

1. *Survey of International Affairs: 1931* (London, Oxford University Press, 1932), p. 1.

half century ending in 1914, and the brief decade of prosperity following the World War now loomed in its true light as merely a feverish prelude to chaos. Toynbee, perhaps more inclined to such comparison than most of his countrymen, upon rereading Gibbon concluded that in both golden ages—of the Antonines and of the latter 19th century—the framework of felicity had been a world order, "an explicitly Roman world order in the one case and a virtually British world order in the other." Whereas the Roman world order was predominantly political, the British had been economic.[2] Toynbee undoubtedly was thinking of the decline of Britain in international affairs after the World War, and London's loss of much economic leadership to New York. Clearly the great Age of Britain had passed. The coming of the Depression appeared only to confirm the forthcoming decline of the West.

What could be done about it? Perhaps nothing. But for the practice of diplomacy in the Western world Toynbee's conclusions did have a special meaning: statesmen in the past decades, not realizing that the British world order and the succeeding order of the 1920's had been predominantly economic, had rather futilely occupied themselves with political solutions, which could not strike to the root of the basic economic realities. Such seemed the lesson for diplomacy of the Great Depression. No longer, then, would statesmen concern themselves so exclusively with political matters. Stanley Baldwin in 1926 had asked: "Who in Europe does not know that one more war in the West and the civilization of the ages will fall with as great a shock as that of Rome?" But after 1929 it seemed evident that Western civilization might collapse not from war, a political event, but from the awful impact of economic chaos brought on by a Great Depression.

Everywhere, in fact, the emphasis changed from politics to economics. In Britain the brilliant economist John Maynard Keynes had been writing insistently during the 1920's about the primacy of economics over politics, but Britishers although buying his books and reading them—for Keynes wrote readable prose—had not taken his warnings to heart. After 1929 he suddenly achieved a great following. In America in 1929, the year of

2. Ibid., p. 6.

the proclamation of the Kellogg-Briand Pact for the renunciation and outlawry of war, President Herbert Hoover's annual message on the state of the union began with a section on foreign relations. In 1930 the message began with the economic situation; it did not mention the Kellogg Pact. Walter Lippmann, who in many ways has proved himself a reliable barometer of American thought, was writing by 1932 that internationally the older questions of frontiers and empires and strategic advantage would no doubt remain but the chief preoccupation of the nations would be the attempt to manage politically a division of labor in the world economy.[3]

In retrospect it is obvious what this new emphasis on economics rather than politics meant for the maintenance of world peace after 1929. Statesmen doubted, as they never had before, the advantage of political solutions to international affairs. As for the peoples of the Western democratic nations, they were themselves too occupied with domestic economic matters to give much attention to international problems, political or economic. The Great Depression had, therefore, a catastrophic effect upon the maintenance of world peace. In Japan it helped to bring to power the militarist groups which, by 1941, could undertake a policy of *Hakko Ichiu,* The Eight Corners of the Universe under One Roof. In Germany it helped to bring to power Adolf Hitler, who in January 1933 became chancellor of the Weimar Republic.

Neither in the Far East nor in Europe was American policy, inhibited by the effect of the Great Depression in the United States, an effective force for peace. President Hoover and Secretary of State Henry L. Stimson made several notable public statements and engaged in a large number of diplomatic protests, but beyond that their diplomacy could not go.

In contrast to American diplomatic preoccupation with the breakdown of peace in the Far East, the statesmen of the other great English-speaking nation of the world sought to prevent the breakdown of peace in Europe. The diplomatists of Great Britain faithfully attended meetings of the League of Nations at Geneva and on other occasions maintained an apparently solicitous regard

3. "Ten Years: Retrospect and Prospect," *Foreign Affairs, 11* (1932–33), 53.

for the security of France and the small nations of the Continent against any resurgence of German power. Again, nothing concrete resulted. British interests during the Great Depression lay closer to home.

It remained for Winston Churchill, then in disgrace with the Conservative party leadership,[4] to point out the serious and immensely important position of France in Europe. The French army, Churchill said in the House of Commons in June 1931, was a "stabilizing factor. . . . The sudden weakening of that factor of stability, the unquestioned superiority of French military power, might open floodgates of measureless consequences in Europe at the present time, might break the dyke and

> Let the boundless deep
> Down upon far off cities while they dance—
> Or dream." [5]

The French army had indeed been a stabilizing factor on the Continent during the 1920's. But by the early 30's France was beginning to show the strain of her tragic ordeal in the World War. A generation of Frenchmen had died on the Marne and at Verdun, and no longer could French strength alone hold back the German tide. In the 1930's Britain and the United States might, as we see it now, have stepped to the breach, but the two English-speaking nations during the years of the Great Depression had so lost their self-confidence and their concern for international political affairs, and so come under the influence of a "depression psychosis," that at the crucial moments they stood aloof. Perhaps they would have done the same had there been no Great Depression. But event followed event, bold aggressive action led to bolder act, the Allies lacked the will and unity to enforce the great victory of 1918, and when Hitler rearmed Germany and marched into the Rhineland in 1936 the floodgates opened on the cities while the one-time victors danced and dreamed.

4. Stanley Baldwin distrusted Churchill, and throughout the 1930's Churchill remained out of office.

5. Speech of June 29, 1931, 254 *H.C. Deb.*, 5 s., c. 963, quoted in W. M. Jordan, *Great Britain, France, and the German Problem: 1918–1939* (London, 1943), p. 162.

2

More than any other single factor, the Great Depression explains the timidity of statesmanship in the crucial years from 1929 to 1933. At the end of the London Naval Conference of 1930 the Versailles settlement still prevailed in Europe, and for the Pacific and Far East there stood the general arrangement codified by the Washington Conference treaties of 1921–22. The World War had changed a good many things, but world affairs in the 1920's still seemed under the rule of law. Yet by 1933 the peace of the Far East had come apart; and in Europe the New Order in Germany was beginning to take shape. The old order was slipping sadly by 1933, if it had not yet passed, and the cause of this change was, more than anything else, the sapping of the will of liberal elements in the populations of the Western nations: beset by economic disaster, people lacked courage to stand against aggression, especially when as in the years after 1929 the forces of disorder and immorality were moving in a veiled and not yet clearly recognizable manner.

The Great Depression was perhaps the most serious economic disequilibrium in modern world history, certainly since the time in the mid-18th century when the industrial revolution first appeared in England. Between then and 1929 there had occurred many worldwide economic crises, when inflated values came down to earth and production of goods momentarily lagged or fell; but there had been nothing like the Great Depression. The latter adjustment had been long overdue, and reflected the changes in world production and trade which arose in the latter 19th century when Britain began to receive competition from other nations desiring to be workshops of the world. By 1914 the problem of competition—from Germany and the United States especially—had for Britain become serious. Edwardian England marked perhaps the last era when Englishmen could enjoy the fruits of a vast and increasing commerce.

The rise of competitors implied and necessitated, according to the classical formulas of economic thought as set forth by Britishers in the heyday of English trading dominance, that eventually many of the citizens of a nation faced by overwhelming competition would have to tighten their belts or migrate; but this proved politically impossible, and Britain after the war hopefully sought to carry on by lending old customers more money or by other devices, turning in the 1930's to tariff protection and imperial preference. The same sort of adjustments were necessary, in varying degree, for those European nations hesitating to tear down their uneconomic industrial complexes erected during the World War; and such countries, also finding adjustment under the classical forms socially impossible and militarily undesirable, even earlier than the British sought salvation through tariffs and pseudotariffs. For these nations, as for England, the readjustment posited by the classical precepts did not occur. The economies of Europe creaked along during the 1920's under an increasingly intricate load of regulations and special stipulations and agreements. In similar fashion trade and production in the Far East continued on during the 1920's without a classical reckoning.

A complicating factor in the whole situation was that, side by side with the special arrangements for trade which sprang up on the Continent and particularly in Eastern Europe—arrangements which would have horrified Adam Smith and his disciples—the nations of Europe and the world sought after the first World War to go back to the gold standard and convertibility, on demand, of their currencies. This came at a time when, because of increasing international dealings in corporate and public paper, capital everywhere was becoming more liquid and more easily convertible upon demand into gold. Hence the opportunities for panic and quick all-round deflation had grown enormously, especially since the gold cover of most of the European currencies was not large.

To discuss the workings of economies of nations is not a simple task, and the explanation here given is doubtless far from adequate. Suffice to say that superimposed upon the many rigidities and uneconomic aspects of the national economies was the complex structure of war debts and reparations, created during and after the first World War; and on top of that rickety edifice lay a complicated network of international private debts, long-term and short-term, many of them advanced to cover chronic shortages in the international balances of payments. It is easy to see that the structures of international fixed payments, the thin gold covers of currencies, the uneconomic industrial developments in many countries—all these heralded a terrific readjustment, once some single act should touch off the process of liquidation.

Such problems as the above, one should repeat, had been endemic with the industrial revolution, but in the passage of time they became more acute, and the unbalanced hot-house growth of certain parts of national economies during the War had made the situation inestimably worse. On the face of things a readjustment sounded like an aseptic sort of process, but it was by nature bound to translate itself into such human tragedies as lost savings, lost jobs, and the dangerous frustration of unemployed minds. Only great spirits can bear up under crushing economic blows, and it should have been a foregone conclusion that economic trouble meant social trouble and political trouble and probably international trouble.

Among the great nations of the world there were two national economies in the 1920's capable of precipitating the economic readjustment. Happily the first nation, Germany, got through her difficulties in the early part of the decade and settled down to an exceedingly prosperous if shaky existence in the latter 1920's; in 1929 the economist James W. Angell could publish a book entitled *The Recovery of Germany*. It remained for the United States, through a disgracefully inflated stock market, to do its share in precipitating world economic disaster.

The German economy had collapsed in 1923, when after the French invasion of the Ruhr the German government allowed the mark to soar to an astronomical figure which even today strains the eyesight: 1/43,000,000,000,000th of a British pound. Inflation had really started during the War, but the postwar German governments, either through extreme incompetence or deliberate fraud, allowed the mark to go off into the stratosphere, effectively taking up with it the savings of a once-thriving class of German rentiers and also (which to some interested individuals was helpful) the entire bonded indebtedness of German industry. As a result of this financial disappearing act it became necessary for Germany to secure liquid capital from abroad—there was hardly any left within the borders of the Reich—and in the mid-1920's there began a series of international private loans to Germany which by the end of the decade had risen to large proportions because of the high German interest rate. Foolishly, improvidently, the German bankers borrowed short and invested long (although their lending was nominally short-term, the purposes to which they devoted many of the loans were not appropriate to this type of financing, and as the event proved, the loans became "frozen" in crisis). By the end of the 1920's the German economy, bearing appearance of prosperity, was in a shaky condition. But almost all the economies of Europe were booming in the years after 1925, and no one foresaw that Europe economically was living on borrowed time. After all, by the middle of the decade the nations had achieved their prewar production levels, and in the subsequent five years production expanded more rapidly than American production.

In the United States the 1920's were a most happy period economically, except for certain sick industries such as agriculture and coal. Production increased and Americans set Europeans agog by conspicuous consumption; European intellectuals retreated, as they had before and would again, into a half-envious criticism of "American materialism." American capital by the billions went out to Europe and South America, and no enterprise seemed too large for investment; American brokerage agents camped at the doors of the world's governments, ready in an instant to take up and sell bond issues, be they ever so worthless. And never in the history of the United States had the businessman surrounded himself with such an aura of prestige; Wall Street seemed more than ever the axis on which America turned, and bankers and brokers walked the earth like kings.[6] Unfortunately there was great fraud and dishonesty rampant not only on Wall Street but throughout the nation, as insiders of the business world pumped up stock values, sold underwater real estate in Florida, and built fantastic pyramids of holding companies cemented together with virtually bogus issues of stocks and bonds. Not that these practices were entirely new in American economic history; in the years after the Civil War investors had gambled recklessly

6. Frederick Lewis Allen, *The Big Change* (New York, 1952), p. 144.

time after time, and although some on occasion found themselves caught and squeezed, the majority made their fortunes and went on to larger schemes. The difference was that in the 1920's the practice of piling holding companies on holding companies had reached such proportions that the businessmen themselves had lost all perspective. Samuel Insull in 1929 was chairman of the board of directors of sixty-five different concerns—most of them holding companies—and president of eleven others.[7] The greed of such members of the business community eventually proved the undoing of themselves, their confreres, and much of the American economy, for the structure of payments became so artificial that it had to collapse.

Perhaps the Great Depression would have come anyway, even if the Wall Street disaster of late October–early November 1929 had not precipitated it. But when the Depression arrived it was like a global tornado that sucked up everything in its track. The weakness of the German economy soon became evident when American bankers began frantically calling in their short-term loans, and the resulting debacle in Central Europe in the spring of 1931 [8] caused untold repercussions throughout the world, eventually opening the way in Germany for the coming to power of National Socialism. Seldom if ever has one disaster, a great economic readjustment and liquidation, led to so many other calamities, the effects of which have not even yet received full appraisal.

3

It was indicative of the businessmindedness of the United States in 1929 that Herbert Hoover, who had never before run for public office but had served with success as secretary of commerce, should have become president. He gained office with the slogan "Four More Years of Prosperity," which was no more foolish than the slogan of 1924, "Coolidge or Chaos," nor more misleading than Wilson's slogan of 1916, "He Kept Us Out of War," nor the

7. The holding company was not peculiar to the United States. The Swedish financier Ivar Kreuger constructed an enormous empire of match companies stretching all over the world.

8. See below, ch. 7.

later election promises of Franklin D. Roosevelt that American boys would never be sent to fight in foreign wars. In his inaugural Hoover spoke of "our abounding prosperity," and what was later a subject of much ridicule—the imminence in the United States of complete abolition of poverty.

Hoover intellectually was an extremely able person, and in his economic views and opinions he represented some of the best-informed thought of his time. He was the individualist par excellence in a nation of individualists. There can be no more instructive view of his mind than to read his little book *American Individualism,* published in 1922 and reprinted in 1928, in which he advised his fellow citizens to "stand up to the emery wheel of competition," whilst the government modestly ensured equality of opportunity at the wheel.[9] As time went on, Hoover's views of the role of government in this matter became more sophisticated, but his prescription for success in the United States of the 1920's was really just a compendium of the homely maxims which countless American boys have learned as children and in part unlearned as adults—honesty, thrift, hard work. It is a fine question whether either Hoover or his principal assistants, such as Stimson, understood the crude methods by which in 1929 some wealthy men, with whom Hoover and Stimson personally had been associating for years, were getting hugely rich in Wall Street. Neither Hoover nor Stimson, though both millionaires, were stock plungers, and it is fair to believe that both men, brought up in and still cherishing the rigorous principles of their youth, did not realize that times had changed, or at least that new and less restricted business methods had come into fashion. Hoover later would become justly bitter at many of the leading bankers of New York. The nation's "rotten banking system," he believed, was one of the two causes of the Great Depression in America.[10]

9. Garden City, N.Y. (Doubleday Doran), pp. 9–10. It is of interest that this program of a Republican president was identical with Woodrow Wilson's New Freedom.

10. The other was the collapse of the financial systems of Europe, stemming from the difficulties of the first World War. *The Memoirs of Herbert Hoover: The Great Depression, 1929–1941* (New York, Macmillan, 1952), pp. 21, 26, 107.

President Hoover had been in office barely a few months when—on Thursday, October 24, 1929—the ridiculous inflation of stock values collapsed.[11] Preceding smaller drops had cleaned out marginal operators, and the cascade of selling orders which flooded the exchange in New York on the twenty-fourth was the result of brokers' sales to redeem their forfeited loans. On Tuesday, October 29, the avalanche reached its maximum force, with more than 16,000,000 shares sold. Losses in value were enormous. Liquidation continued until November 13. In a few short weeks the market disaster blew $30,000,000,000 into thin air—a sum almost as great as the entire cost to the United States of its participation in the first World War and nearly twice as large as the national debt in 1929.

There followed a rally in values, and quotations moved up and down uncertainly for several months. Indeed, some upward movements were of considerable strength, and stock values in the spring of 1930 on occasion compared rather favorably with the peak values of September–early October 1929. This is not the place to chronicle the successive movements of prices and confidence, or to repeat the now time-worn statements of encouragement made by business and government leaders. Edward Angly collected the foolish remarks in a little volume, *Oh Yeah!,* published in 1931. Suffice to say that Hoover—as was true of almost everyone else, including respected domestic economists like Yale's Irving Fisher and foreign observers such as Maynard Keynes—believed that the market liquidation was in some ways a healthy development and that after the return to reasonable values the nation's business would proceed as usual. Shortly after the turn of the century, in 1903 and 1907, there had been sharp liquidations, and although the latter "panic" had proved especially sharp and its effects endured over a period of some years, in neither case did deflation give a serious set-back to the economy. Congress had passed the Federal Reserve Act of 1913 to eliminate panics like that of 1907, and in 1929 the business community simply could not believe that a truly enormous liquidation was in progress. In November there

11. For a recent reappraisal of the crash see the witty book by John K. Galbraith, *The Great Crash: 1929,* Boston, 1955.

appeared a little tune entitled "Happy Days Are Here Again," written for one of the new talking pictures appropriately named "Chasing Rainbows," and this together with "singing in the rain" and keeping one's "sunny side up" suggested the returning confidence of the time.

The last day of the fateful year 1929 was in no sense a day of mourning. Happenings at home and abroad indicated that life went on much as it always had. Looking at random into the New York *Times* for January 1, 1930, one can see that in New York City, Mayor James J. ("Jimmy") Walker took the oath of office for his second term; Admiral Byrd was on his post at Little America; Secretary of the Treasury Andrew W. Mellon predicted that in 1930 the nation would make steady progress; and Secretary of Commerce Robert P. Lamont forecasted "over the long run" a continuance of prosperity. Will Rogers saw hope for "us Democrats" in 1930. Dr. Ernest H. Cherrington, general secretary of the World League against Alcoholism, beheld the world turning to prohibition (Nadir Khan, the new king of Afghanistan, had established prohibition in his kingdom). France, Britain, Germany, and Italy looked to the new year with courage and confidence. In Belgium the lingerie of Princess Marie Jose's trousseau was on display, but there was some question as to whether photographers would be allowed to take pictures. Despite muffled despair in Wall Street, 1929 went out with a normal amount of human trivia and of solemn traditional resolves and pretty predictions.

American diplomacy (and American citizens) did not at first feel the effect of economic liquidation. But in May 1930 the market collapsed again, and presently the Depression entered a much grimmer second phase—the long grinding disintegration of late 1930 and 1931 and 1932. This was the period which crushed men's souls, crippled the world's diplomacy, and presented to aggression and aggressors what seemed to be a golden opportunity.

4

President Hoover, speaking in October 1930 before the American Bankers Association, took a radically new view of the Depression—which, he now said, was worldwide, with causes and effects that lay only partly in the United States. It was, he had come to believe, the product of some American misdeeds, but in the main the Depression was the penalty of a great war and its aftermath in Europe. Hoover was in part correct. That the Depression was worldwide there could be little question, and there never was any doubt that the maladjustments of the World War had played a large role in bringing on the collapse of 1929. In putting the blame on Europe, however, he was attempting to get it off his own administration before the November congressional elections. His effort was unsuccessful: a Democratic landslide resulted in a majority in the House of Representatives and also in control of the Senate. Fortunately for Hoover, by an ancient quirk of the Constitution going back before the horse and buggy age, before the days of railroads, steamboats, and canals, back to the 18th-century stagecoach, the new Democratic Congress would not assemble for another year.

The president's original thesis that the Depression came out of Europe eventually joined another thesis in retrospect—that the American difficulties were largely the result of "our rotten banking system" [12]—and these two arguments explain the course of action which Hoover followed as the Depression deepened during the remainder of his administration. He attended to the European factor in the collapse by the famous Hoover Moratorium on intergovernmental payments of war debts and reparations, which he proposed and persuaded the nations to adopt in the summer of 1931.[13] The rotten nature of the American banking system became apparent during the same year, and in January 1932 Hoover carried through Congress a bill for a Reconstruction Finance Corporation which would rescue the nation's banks by lending them government funds. In these two solutions, domestic and international, Hoover found answers to the twin devils of the Depression. It is interesting that both of the president's solutions lay outside the customary laissez-faire horizons of his economic thought.

12. *The Great Depression,* p. 107.
13. See below, ch. 7.

When the president at the outset of the Depression had talked to his elderly secretary of the treasury, Andrew Mellon, the latter had advised no action at all in the crisis, letting affairs run their course. Hoover conceded to Mellon that the Depression at first afforded certain analogies to the long depression of the 1870's after the Civil War; but, he added, in the 1870's an untold amount of unnecessary suffering took place; moreover the American economy had been far simpler when the nation was 75 per cent agricultural, for agriculture now occupied only 30 per cent of the nation's workers. Mellon shook his head, with the observation that human nature had not changed in sixty years and that the Depression should run itself out, purging the economic system of impurities.[14] This was the method Hoover followed from about the middle of 1930 to the spring of 1931; earlier he had sought to encourage businessmen not to lay off employees; but when this voluntary program failed he did virtually nothing until he proposed the moratorium for Europe and the RFC for the United States. In this inaction he reflected his own upbringing of American individualism and his life-long disdain for any program of experiment, particularly with "collectivist ideas gleaned from the Socialists, the Communists, and the Fascists." [15] As president he steadfastly refused to pursue a policy of "squandering ourselves into prosperity," or to bring out the "Trojan horse of Emergency." [16] By executive order he did stop virtually all immigration. There was considerable precedent for such action in the restrictive legislation of the 1920's; he acted under a law permitting temporary suspension of immigration which Congress had passed during the Coolidge Administration.

There was a limit, though, beyond which the natural liquidation recommended by his secretary of the treasury could not go, and Hoover came gradually to understand that social pressures if not

14. *The Great Depression,* pp. 29–31.

15. Ibid., p. 36. Hoover deplored the New Dealers, especially Keynes' bright young disciples who came "from the colleges mostly around Boston." Ibid., p. 482.

16. Frederick Lewis Allen, *Since Yesterday* (New York, 1939), p. 53; *The Great Depression,* p. 357.

political expediency forbade allowing liquidation to run its natural course. The inflated debt structure had linked itself inseparably to the economic fabric of the country, and too drastic a liquidation would have brought economic chaos. When Stimson in 1931 also suggested to Hoover that the Depression should run itself out, the president foresaw such social troubles that he told his secretary of state he was going to do his best to shore up the situation.[17] The pressures for government action became overwhelming. Even those Americans who hitherto had been most insistent that the government keep its hands off business were blaming the government and the president now that business had gone wrong. Hoover had to buttress the economy by devices such as the RFC. Unfortunately, in undertaking his program of support he insisted upon indirect action—aiding the banks, which in turn would aid the people—rather than a more direct approach which would have had political results, as his successor, Franklin D. Roosevelt, was to try in "quarterback" fashion.

Hoover, of course, received no credit for his change of tactics toward the Depression, and the president indeed found himself blamed for everything that had happened to the American economy beginning with the market crash. The Hoover Administration had started out in 1929 as a business administration, for this was what the country then wanted, and it could not protect itself later when the Depression had removed the shine from the businessman's shield. Hoover writhed under the attacks of the Democratic party's skillful publicity chieftain, Charles Michelson, who with a large corps of helpers from an office in New York propagated descriptions of old newspapers as "Hoover blankets," jack rabbits as "Hoover hogs," and the shanties of starvation rising on the outskirts of cities as "Hoovervilles." He took great annoyance from the "constant parrot-call" of the Democrats that he was the sole creator of the world depression,[18] a call which rose to a deafening

17. Stimson diary, Sept. 29, 1931; microfilm deposited in the Yale University Library.

18. *The Great Depression,* p. 103; Charles Michelson, *The Ghost Talks,* New York, G. P. Putnam's Sons, 1944. "The battle of 1932," Michelson wrote, "has frequently been referred to as a smear campaign. In looking back over

roar when in December 1931 the new and hostile Congress assembled and began campaigning irresponsibly for the next presidential election.

The Depression was now entering its worst phase. Many Americans did not really feel it until 1931–32, when after months of increasing uncertainty liquidation gathered momentum, reaching almost rock bottom by the middle of 1932 when industry was operating at less than half its 1929 maximum. According to the Federal Reserve Board's adjusted index of industrial production the figure had fallen from 125 to 58. National income dwindled from $81,000,000,000 in 1929 to $41,000,000,000. Cotton was below 5 cents, wheat below 50, corn at 31. On November 13, 1929, the New York *Times*' industrials closed at 224; on July 8, 1932, they were at 58. Unemployment reached the large figure of about 7,000,000 heads of families. *Iron Age* announced that steel operations had reached 12 per cent of capacity. This was the time when reporters asked the once rapturous optimist of the business world, Charles M. Schwab, about the state of business affairs, and found that Schwab had lost all confidence: "I'm afraid," he responded, "every man is afraid. I don't know, we don't know, whether values we have are going to be real next month or not." Between July and September 1932 there was an upturn in business activity—though apparent only in the realm of cold statistics, lost in the overwhelming human tragedy of personal insecurity [19]—but after the national election everything slumped toward the grand debacle of February–early March 1933, when in spite of a whole year's activity by the RFC the nation's banking system collapsed at the moment Hoover was leaving office and Roosevelt was taking over. In the following years, business activity picked up to a considerable extent, but despite the New Deal the Great Depression did not really end until involvement in the second

---

the files, I find little of personal attack on President Hoover. The pamphlets and speeches that emanated from headquarters at the Biltmore Hotel in New York were practically all devoted to the various acts and omissions of his administration to which we traced the causes of the depression . . ." Ibid., p. 41.

19. Harvey Wish, *Contemporary America* (New York, 1945), p. 437.

World War effectively brought the economy to a state of prosperity.

To adjudge the effect of the Great Depression upon any one segment of American government activity in the period 1929–33 is at best difficult, and it is no easy task to say precisely how the Depression affected American diplomacy. That it had a great effect is beyond doubt. The personal diaries of Secretary of State Stimson, Undersecretary of State William R. Castle, and Ambassador Dawes are full of references to the Depression, and it was frequently Stimson's lot to talk foreign policy to Hoover when the latter was disconcerted and "blue" over some new economic deterioration. Apparently, economic difficulties did not have much if any effect upon American diplomacy until the end of the London Naval Conference of 1930. For another year there were no important diplomatic developments. But the Hoover Moratorium in the summer of 1931 was itself a diplomatic manifestation of the Depression, and there could be no doubt from then on that economic problems had captured the attention of peoples and governments everywhere in the world. The Far Eastern Crisis in Manchuria, beginning in 1931, had its roots in the dire effect of the Depression upon the poverty-stricken Japanese proletariat and farm workers. The nations of the world took a timid attitude toward the crisis, and though timidity might well have appeared had there been no economic troubles, it is certain that the Depression restrained all thought of drastic action. In the other principal diplomatic effort of Stimson's last two years in office, the disarmament discussions early in 1932 when the World Disarmament Conference assembled, the Depression played a mixed role: while arms reduction would have been welcome to the nations, most of which were having budget difficulties, the armament industries had the virtue of offering employment which was politically difficult to curtail.

The coming of the worldwide Great Depression should have brought home to the American people the close interrelations of the various nations of the world. To some Americans it did; but to many the economic blight on the world seemed only additional proof of the folly of participation in the World War in 1917–18, and the desirability, indeed necessity, of detaching the United States from further vicissitudes of Europe. This latter view—that the Depression stemmed from Wilsonian internationalism—was not an intelligent view, but it offered a scapegoat for economic distress and was more soothing to the mind than the hypothesis that the Depression showed only the need for more internationalism.

The Great Depression underlay the deterioration of American foreign relations during the years 1929–33. If there had been no Depression, it is quite possible that world peace would not have broken down in the Far East in 1931 and that Hitler in 1933 would not have achieved power in Germany. The Depression was the principal reason for the international tragedy of the 1930's—the loss of all gains of the Allied victory of the first World War.

What other factors explain the course of American diplomacy during the Great Depression? There was the special nature of American diplomatic principles and policies, the intellectual heritage of assumptions and practices that guided the actions of all American statesmen of the time. There was the personal ability, or inability, of American diplomatists—the manner in which native intelligence, upbringing, formal education, and experience had loosened or hardened their minds and wills. Each international event also had its own peculiarities, making American diplomacy easy or difficult as the case might be. The way in which all these elements of American foreign relations—the Great Depression, the heritage of diplomatic principles and policies, personal abilities, events themselves—combined during the several diplomatic crises of the era is the subject of the chapters that follow.

Chapter Two: AMERICAN DIPLOMATIC PRINCIPLES AND POLICIES IN 1929

Because of the peaceful state of American foreign relations in the latter 1920's one would not have thought that American diplomatists concerned themselves much over diplomatic principles and policies. When Henry L. Stimson became secretary of state in the spring of 1929, he began his term with fewer worries about American foreign relations than almost any of his predecessors, certainly his successors. In international as in national affairs, the end of the Golden Twenties was a wonderful, carefree time. Germany had lost the Great War and with it her military power, Japan in the Far East seemed peacefully inclined, Russia was a backward agricultural nation still weakened by revolution. Peace prevailed throughout the world. "It seems to me," Hoover wrote to Stimson on September 17, 1929, "that there is the most profound outlook for peace today that we have had at any time in the last half century . . . it occurs to me that the dangers of war during the next six or ten years . . . are inconceivably less than they have been at any period since the Great War." [1]

Was American diplomacy in 1929, in the midst of such profound peace, operating without any fixed points whatsoever, other than a glib belief in the continuance of peace? There was some truth in such a suspicion. To an extent more than one would have assumed, however, American diplomatists during the 1920's had thought out their diplomatic position toward the world. They had arrived at certain views of the world, certain basic assumptions, from which in turn they constructed the specific policies of American diplomacy. That these basic assumptions happened to indicate a con-

1. *Papers Relating to the Foreign Relations of the United States: 1929* (Washington, 1943), *I*, 241 (cited as *FR*).

tinuation of world peace, as they did, was perhaps incidental to their formulation.

The first of these assumptions of American diplomatists during the 1920's was in regard to the meaning of the World War of 1914–18. This war, American diplomatists believed, was an aberration of European and world history, a departure from the normal course of human events which, once brought to a successful conclusion by the force of Allied arms in 1918, would not—indeed, could not—happen again.

Second, the diplomatists believed that in the post-Versailles world the nations of Europe, now dominated by the victorious allies, Britain and France, could take care of themselves.

Third, they believed that Eastern Asia, where lived the hundreds of millions of Chinese, and the scores of millions of Japanese, could likewise get along, albeit with occasional suggestions from the United States.

Fourth and last, during the 1920's they had convinced themselves that the real force for peace in the world was moral, not military. The old system of military force, they held, had brought on the World War. They believed that out of the horrors of the war there had been born a new interest in foreign affairs on the part of people everywhere; that the day of public opinion, in the largest sense, had dawned; that the moral force of world public opinion would guard the world's peace in the postwar years with an effectiveness that military force could not possibly hope to achieve. They believed, further, that the Republic of the United States of America, having stood free of most of the antagonisms that had beset Europe in the prewar and war years, was a natural leader of the world, the "great moral reserve" [2] of the new postwar era.

1

Were these assumptions of American diplomacy valid? Was there any body of experience, diplomatic and otherwise, to which Americans could have gone in the 1920's and ascertained the truth

2. Herbert Hoover to Woodrow Wilson, Apr. 11, 1919, William Starr Myers, *The Foreign Policies of Herbert Hoover: 1929–33* (New York, Scribner's, 1940), p. 17.

of their assumptions? Was there any test that Henry L. Stimson, encountering these beliefs in 1929, could have applied to them?

Take first of all the assumption that the first World War was a departure from the traditions and general course of European and world history. There was much in the history of Europe since, say, the year 1870 that had pointed steadily in the direction of such a war: the hardening of alliances in Europe in the 1890's and after, the intensification of national pride that accompanied this alliance-making, the widening differences between European nations because of the rivalries of imperialism, the growth of armaments, the pandering of the European newspaper press. Sidney B. Fay set down these developments in his two thick volumes on the *Origins of the World War* published in 1928. Fay's colleagues, such scholars as Bernadotte Schmitt and William L. Langer together with a host of other individuals, were all working on books during the 1920's that showed the historical probability if not inevitability of the first World War. To have believed that the war was a strange sport or freak of European history that happened to appear in the world in the summer of 1914 was to ignore the conclusions of an impressive postwar array of American scholars during the 1920's, not to mention their European colleagues.

On the other hand it was possible to argue with equal conviction that the World War had been neither necessary nor probable. If certain conditions of European international relations had been otherwise, it was pointed out, the war would never have come. Scholars in the United States, studying assiduously the origins of the war, were themselves supporters of this latter view. Each scholar was seeking to ascertain exactly where the world went wrong, in the tragic years between 1870 and 1914. Although scholars knew that the War was a natural result of European and world conditions, of the processes of history for at least fifty years before 1914, they knew also that at various points along the way there had been choices, and that if prewar statesmen had taken those choices with due consideration for the values of Western civilization, with a sense of the far higher importance of those values than any strictly national gain, the War would not have occurred at all.

It was possible, therefore, to conclude that the War had not been necessary, and that it had come because statesmen made the wrong choices. It was possible to assume that the wrong choices, on so grave a question as a world war, would not be made again. It was possible to assume that the course of Western civilization would encounter no more of such interruptions, and that it would go on from strength to strength as it had in the past. There surely was no inclination on the part of American diplomatists to accept such predictions of the future of Western civilization as Spengler had made in *Decline of the West.* Spengler wrote gloomily that he had seen the World War "in a quite other light. It was no longer a momentary constellation of casual facts due to national sentiments, personal influences, or economic tendencies endowed with an appearance of unity and necessity by some historian's scheme of political or social cause-and-effect, but the type of *a historical change of phase* occurring within a great historical organism of definable compass at the point preordained for it hundreds of years ago." [3] No American diplomatists would have seen in Western civilization, as did Spengler, "a conclusion, a thing-become succeeding the thing-becoming, death following life, rigidity following expansion, intellectual age and the stone-built petrifying world-city following mother-earth and the spiritual childhood of Doric and Gothic . . . an end, irrevocable, yet by inward necessity reached." [4]

This was the first assumption of American diplomatists in the 1920's: that the World War was an unnecessary part of European and world history and that, since the war was finished, history could go back to its ordinary and usual course.

Stemming from this assumption was a second tenet, namely that Europe in the postwar era could take care of itself, without assistance from the United States. Here, of course, was a belief that went back to the foundation of the Republic: the United States should eschew permanent alliances with Europe, remain apart from the Continent's *ordinary* combinations and collisions, and trust to temporary alliances for extraordinary emergencies. The World War had been no exception to this historic American belief

3. *Decline of the West* (trans. by Charles Francis Atkinson, 2 vols. New York, Knopf, 1926–28), *I*, 47 (italics in original).

4. Ibid., *I*, 31.

in abstention from European affairs. An extraordinary emergency had been the reason for American intervention in Europe in 1917. President Wilson had intervened because German measures of submarine warfare threatened one of the most cherished principles of traditional American foreign policy, freedom of the seas. Wilson later came to see other reasons for American intervention, such as making the world safe for democracy; but the American people, while momentarily accepting such reasons, in the end rejected them; in the postwar years it was evident to most Americans that they had gone to war in 1917 to preserve American rights on the seas, a traditional policy of the United States, threatened by *extraordinary* combinations and collisions of the powers of Europe. Once the United States had set the world aright, restored European and world politics to their ordinary ways of peaceful behavior, there was no longer any need to participate in European affairs. As Hoover wrote to Wilson in April 1919, before signature of the Treaty of Versailles, "I am convinced that there has grown up since the Armistice the policy, perhaps unconscious, but nevertheless effective, of dragging the United States into every political and economic question in Europe." The United States, Hoover believed, could not afford to be "dragged into European entanglements." [5]

To American diplomatists in the 1920's it seemed certain that the two leading victor nations of Europe, Great Britain and France, could maintain peace on the Continent without any American help whatsoever. The War had brought home to Americans the dangers involved when a general war convulsed the European nations. Even so, the balance of power in Europe during the 1920's seemed so securely in favor of the two wartime Allies, the power of the postwar French army appeared so overwhelming, the strength of the British fleet so dominant, that there was no danger of war anywhere in Europe that Britain and France could not put down. Why, so it seemed, should the United States meddle in a situation already under control? The Europeans could take care of themselves.

It is a fine question whether American diplomatists in 1929

5. Hoover to Wilson, Apr. 11, 1919, Myers, *The Foreign Policies of Herbert Hoover,* pp. 16–17.

realized the shaky and uncertain basis of European peace. They tended, one must conclude, to see the appearance and fact of Anglo-French strength without understanding that the will to use that strength was rapidly ebbing away. Americans knew that both Britishers and Frenchmen in the postwar years had no desire again to go to war against Germany, but they had little understanding of how far the British and French were willing to let the Germans go in a policy of "revision" of the Treaty of Versailles. For that matter, Americans had little understanding of how far the Germans themselves wished to go in revising the Versailles Treaty, of how an adventurer such as Hitler could achieve power in Germany on a program of revision. Such eventualities were hidden from Americans during the 1920's, and only a few small signs of the future appeared from time to time. American diplomatists did not give much attention to those signs. They saw them as the usual alarums of European international politics, and continued to believe that Anglo-French power on the Continent was sufficiently strong to take care of all difficulties.

A third assumption of American policy during the 1920's concerned Asia rather than Europe. In the notion that Eastern Asia, like Europe, could take care of itself was one more indication that Americans expected no more trouble in the world after the Armistice of 1918 and the Paris Peace Conference. In the Far East, as in Europe, American diplomatists saw equilibrium, and they believed there was little they needed to do to preserve it. Still, in the Far East, Americans felt that on occasion they should offer advice to the Chinese and Japanese governments, for those governments were of fairly recent origin—the Chinese more so than the Japanese—and stood in need of more advice than did Europeans.

A propensity to give advice had always conditioned the American view of Eastern Asia. Such advice was always well-meaning, and at times it had stood the Japanese and Chinese in good stead. The Chinese especially, Americans thought, appreciated advice from the United States. At the turn of the 20th century Americans had undertaken a large missionary program in China, under the magical words "The Evangelization of the World in This Generation"; and there had been much American educational and technical assistance to China as the Chinese in the 19th and 20th centuries strove to Westernize and democratize their country. As far as concerned the Japanese, Americans in the 1920's were less certain of the receptivity and appropriateness of advice. At the Washington Naval Conference of 1921–22 American advice to Japan had blended with a threat to outbuild the Japanese navy. The arrangements of that conference had not been altogether to Japanese tastes. There had followed the Japanese Exclusion Act of 1924, and this legislation incensed Japan to a point where there was a very real question of the future of American-Japanese relations. Happily, in the years between 1924 and 1929 relations with Japan proved unexpectedly easy. Especially did Japan cooperate—with almost no American advice—in the important matter of Far Eastern peace. The Japanese governments of those years were peacefully disposed and worked with the United States and other Western nations during the disturbances in China incident to the unification, by 1928, of that country.

There were, then, these major assumptions by American diplomatists during the 1920's pertaining to relations of the United States with the powers of the world: that the World War had been a transitory phenomenon of European and world history; that Europe in the postwar years could care for its own problems; that Eastern Asia likewise could maintain peace of itself and required no serious worry on the part of the United States, although it might occasionally use some American advice. Last was the American belief that moral force, rather than military force, was the leading force for peace in the world—because of the newfound strength of world public opinion, as a result of the political awakening of peoples everywhere during the World War.

This notion of the power of public opinion, of moral force, greatly attracted American diplomatists during the 1920's and 1930's, even when during the latter 30's it became evident that military force was doing rather well for itself. The best one could say for this American diplomatic belief, as it stood unchallenged in the 1920's, was that it was a noble conception and deserved judgment on its nobility rather than its impracticality. But the idea of moral force never had a chance to function: it presumed some imaginary world where there was no nationalism and where there was complete literacy, so that every move made in international politics would automatically find acceptance or rejection by world public opinion acting intelligently and impartially. There could be no complicating factors, if world public opinion were to be a really strong force in international affairs.

Look at statements of this belief by American presidents and secretaries of state during the 1920's. There are few easier tasks of research than to take the writings and public utterances of American statesmen during the 20's and cull out impressive utterances about the moral force of public opinion. "My ambition in our foreign policies," Hoover wrote, several years after he left office, "was to lead the United States in full co-operation with world moral forces to preserve peace." [6] Secretary of State Stimson, despite a lifelong belief in soldierly solutions and the utility of military force, became completely enamored of the possibilities of public opinion, which in 1929 he thought would be the greatest single force in the world for international peace. As he wrote to his friend Walter Lippmann (who also was enthusiastic about public opinion), public opinion was the sanction that lay behind the judgments of the Supreme Court in its decisions between the States and the Union, and it could support the law of nations in international controversies. "It is a sanction which is growing stronger every day where public opinion is growing more enlightened." The "surest way" to increase the efficacy of the Kellogg-Briand Pact, the great multilateral antiwar treaty signed by the United States at Paris in 1928, was "not by seeking to add extraneous sanctions of force, but by providing the machinery for enlightening and strengthening the present sanction of public opinion." [7] President Hoover in public speeches in 1929 and following years constantly drew pleasing analogies between munici-

6. *Memoirs of Herbert Hoover: The Cabinet and the Presidency, 1920–1933* (New York, Macmillan, 1951), p. 330.

7. Stimson to Lippmann, Jan. 7, 1930, 711.0012 Anti-War/1060 (citations followed by file numbers refer to the unpublished records of the Department of State, in the National Archives at Washington).

pal and international law, seeing consent rather than force as the basis of both. President Coolidge had done this before him, and so, earlier, had Presidents Harding and Wilson. The latter, indeed, had based his whole system of the League of Nations on the support of world public opinion. Wilson during the drafting of the Covenant attacked the idea of collective security based on armed force as only "substituting international militarism for national militarism." [8]

Did this belief of American diplomatists in the moral force of public opinion in international affairs only camouflage an intense desire of all Americans not again to go to war? Had Americans, not desiring to fight again in Europe, simply attached their hopes to this new doctrine of nonviolence? Such a view would overlook the conviction with which American leaders and citizens alike discussed the influence of moral force in world affairs.

The large annual appropriations for the American navy during the 1920's were not necessarily proof that Americans did not trust their own doctrine of moral force. The navy, they believed, was an essential part of American defense. When President Coolidge told them that it was a small navy, in view of the length of coastline that it had to defend, Americans accepted Coolidge's explanation with full appreciation of the sincerity in which he offered it. When President Hoover said that the American navy needed to be the same size as the navy of Great Britain, there was no feeling that any disparity in size could as easily be made up in moral force, but rather that both navies, being navies of defense, should be equal. To a later and perhaps more cynical generation this easy compartmentalization of the navy and moral force might seem a little ingenuous and simple-minded. The diplomatists of the 1920's did not consider themselves ingenuous or simple-minded. They were dealing in terms of two different propositions, national defense and a program for international peace.

2

What were the concrete policies of American diplomacy, as apart from its more basic assumptions, during the 1920's and in

8. David Hunter Miller, *The Drafting of the Covenant* (2 vols. New York, 1928), 2, 294.

1929? Those policies, most of which had originated during or after the World War, were: disarmament, the Kellogg-Briand Pact, the Nine-Power Treaty, the World Court, arbitration and conciliation, and collection of war debts and reparations.

Disarmament was perhaps the leading diplomatic policy of the United States during the decade of the 1920's. It was a legacy of the War—many people believing that the War had come because of the enormous piling up of weapons in Europe prior to 1914. Because weapons were available in 1914, so the argument ran, the "militarist" generals and admirals of Europe took advantage of a relatively small diplomatic crisis to begin a great war. The compulsions to use the armaments stacked up in Europe in 1914 were so overwhelming, people afterward believed, that war became inevitable. Even Sir Edward Grey, who knew something about the origin of wars, succumbed to this belief, and wrote in his memoirs published in the mid-1920's that "great armaments lead inevitably to war. . . . The enormous growth of armaments in Europe . . . made war inevitable." [9]

In the postwar years a belief in the necessity of disarmament prevailed in most of the nations of the Western world, but it received especial support from citizens of Great Britain and the United States. In both nations the pressures of public opinion had been such that, at the end of the war, the national armies were reduced to a fraction of their wartime strength. Navies in the two Anglo-American countries remained at a high level of size and efficiency, and it became the task of public opinion in Britain and the United States in the postwar years to reduce the navies, or, at the very least, place a limit on their size. This movement for naval reduction or limitation was what Americans meant, in 1929, by disarmament. The American and British governments together called the Washington Naval Conference of 1921–22, where Britain, the United States, Japan, France, and Italy limited the numbers of their battleships and aircraft carriers. Another conference of the "big three" maritime nations, Britain, the United States, and Japan, failed at Geneva in 1927 in an effort to limit cruisers,

9. Viscount Grey of Fallodon, *Twenty-five Years: 1892–1916* (2 vols. New York, Stokes, 1925), *1*, 89–90.

destroyers, and submarines. Stimson and his chief, President Hoover, in 1929 were thinking of calling still another conference on limitation of naval arms. Preparation for what became the London Naval Conference of 1930 took up most of Stimson's first year as secretary of state.

A second policy which Stimson would follow in 1929, one virtually equal in importance to naval disarmament, pertained to the Kellogg-Briand Pact, negotiated and signed at Paris in August 1928 by Stimson's predecessor, Secretary Frank B. Kellogg. This grand multilateral treaty for the renunciation and outlawry of war had bound all of its fifty-odd signatories and adherents to renounce war "as an instrument of national policy" and to settle "all disputes or conflicts of whatever nature or of whatever origin" by pacific means. There were, unfortunately, a number of exceptions to this wondrous international ordinance of self-denial, in particular a reservation, stipulated by Secretary Kellogg himself, of the right of self-defense. Some of Kellogg's critics had concluded uncharitably that because the Kellogg Pact had so many reservations it was nothing but an international kiss. Not so Secretary of State Stimson. When the latter came into office he determined to make the Kellogg Pact a cornerstone of American policy. Stimson aspired to "strengthen" the pact, as he put it, with additional sanctions of public opinion. He had in mind a supplementary article stipulating for consultation by the nations, in event of international aggression anywhere in the world.

Then there was the Nine-Power Treaty, another cornerstone of American policy. This treaty had promised that the signatories —Great Britain, the United States, France, Italy, Japan, the Netherlands, Belgium, Portugal, and China—would respect China's sovereignty, independence, and integrity; give China the fullest and most unembarrassed opportunity to maintain an effective and stable government; use their influence to establish and maintain equal opportunity for the commerce and industry of all nations in China; refrain from taking advantage of conditions in China that would abridge the rights or privileges of citizens of friendly states, and from countenancing action inimical to the security of such states. The treaty also pledged the signatories to "full and frank" discussion if any of them should raise the issue of the treaty's violation. No one had invoked the treaty by 1929. Indeed, in 1923, a year after the nations signed the treaty, Secretary of State Charles Evans Hughes after observing the constant revolutionary disorder and turmoil in China had undiplomatically told the Chinese minister in Washington that "it was idle for China to declaim, as she had at the Washington Conference with respect to her sovereignty and her political integrity and her rights as a nation" when the Chinese were so incapable of putting their own house in order.[10] Throughout the 1920's there was considerable sentiment, especially in Japan, that the Washington nations had concluded the Nine-Power Treaty under the erroneous assumption that China was a nation, when in reality it was little more than a geographical designation, and that because of the revolutionary disturbances in China during most of the twenties the treaty was —in fact if not in law—virtually a dead letter. After the pronouncement by Secretary Hughes to the Chinese minister the American government said no more during the 1920's on the subject of China's right to respect as a government. Hughes had said nothing in 1923 about the Nine-Power Treaty. It was an open question in 1929 whether the dubious doctrine of international law known as *rebus sic stantibus,* stipulating that treaties retained their force only as long as the conditions under which they were concluded remained the same, might reduce the Nine-Power Treaty to a nullity. The Japanese government at various times during the 1920's intimated as much, and would openly assert such a view on a later, important occasion. The American government, as events were to turn out, had in no sense accepted this interpretation of the Nine-Power Treaty, and under Stimson's direction would invoke the treaty in 1932 against the pretensions of Japan.

Disarmament, the Kellogg-Briand Pact, and the Nine-Power Treaty marked definite postwar policies of the American government. There was also the World Court. This was, perhaps, the most typical, although certainly not the most important, American

10. Memorandum by Hughes of a conversation with Sao-ke Alfred Sze, June 7, 1923, *FR: 1923, I,* 625.

diplomatic idea during the 1920's. The court was the favorite project of that distinguished American elder statesman of the 1920's, Elihu Root. Root had gone to Europe at the end of the war, to help work out the protocol for the World Court, and during the twenties it was his hope that the United States, having refused to enter the League of Nations, would enter the court. American entrance failed in 1926, although the Senate gave its advice and consent; the Senate attached to its resolution a destructive qualification that the United States should not take any part, without express consent of the Senate, in one of the Court's lesser functions, the giving of advisory opinions to the League of Nations; this reservation proved unacceptable to the forty-eight state members of the Court. The disappointed Root had to go to Europe again to work out some sort of compromise by which the United States might enter the Court. When Stimson, an admirer and protégé of Root, became secretary of state in 1929 he began a new effort to get the World Court protocol through the Senate. President Hoover was less sympathetic to this effort than Stimson, but was willing to place the Court before the Senate if only because such an action would please Stimson and Root.

Whether American membership in the Court would have accomplished anything special in the direction of ensuring world peace must always remain doubtful. The court embodied the fond American ideal of the rule of law rather than force in international affairs. Americans overlooked the extremely undeveloped state of international law and also the fact that an international court unsupported by military force could not hope for much obedience from a wrong-doer. Fortunately for the court's reputation, the problem of obtaining obedience to the court never came up in the interwar period. The court could take jurisdiction in a dispute only when asked by all the parties, and questions put to the court were seldom of much international consequence. Even the so-called "optional clause" to the court's protocol, by which signatories consented in advance to bring their disputes to the court, met frustration in a proviso that disputes be of a "legal" nature. The possibilities of deciding whether or not a dispute was of a legal nature were endless. Because of such restrictions the

court could do little for world peace, and one must therefore wonder what American membership in it could have done for world
peace.[11]

An alternative to the World Court during the 1920's was the
traditional American policy of concluding treaties of arbitration
and conciliation with whatever nations were willing to make such
treaties. The weary task of drawing up these bilateral engagements
—arbitration treaties in accord with a formula set down by Secretary Kellogg in 1927, conciliation treaties according to the pattern
established by Secretary of State William Jennings Bryan in 191
—went on throughout the 1920's, into the year 1929 and following
years. The Hoover Administration made twenty-five new arbitration treaties and seventeen new conciliation treaties. Such international promises generated little enthusiasm. Nations signed
them out of fear of displeasing the United States, rather than
from any strong belief in their importance. No adjudications eve
occurred under the arbitration treaties, nor did any nation invoke
the conciliation treaties.

The final policy which Secretary Stimson inherited in 1929 wa
collection of war debts and reparations—debts owed the United
States by the wartime Allies, reparations owed the United State
by defeated Germany. The American government had refunded
the Allied debts during the early 1920's, at varying rates roughl
according to capacity to pay. Reparations from Germany receive
adjustment by an international conference in 1924 led by Charle
G. Dawes. Another conference met in 1929 under leadership c
another American banker, Owen D. Young. This entire probler
of debts and reparations belongs properly to the diplomacy of th
1920's, for these obligations ceased to be obligations, by the simpl
process of repudiation and indefinite postponement, early in th
1930's. Debts and reparations were one of the most difficult an
politically sensitive problems with which Stimson as secretary c

11. It is not difficult to accept the view of the court held by Hoover's unde
secretary of state, William R. Castle, who in 1931 wrote in his diary that th
court was a matter of "extraordinary unimportance." Entry of Feb. 10, 193
This voluminous typescript diary is in the possession of Mr. Castle, in Washington, D.C.

state had to deal. He willingly would have written off these obligations. President Hoover refused to hear of such a course. Hoover's reasons for demanding payment of the debts were as cogent as the counterarguments of Stimson; there were many reasons why the debtors should have paid. Sometimes, however, there is also reason to make a virtue of necessity, and when it became obvious during the Hoover Administration that the debts were uncollectible it would have been better to have forgotten them with some grandiloquent gesture. Unfortunately the American people were convinced that the United States Government should collect its debts, and Stimson's desire to write them off would never have obtained public approval, even down to the end of the 1930's. The American people were more unanimous on this one question of foreign policy than on any other.

Such were the several policies of American diplomacy in 1929. They derived with fair logic from the four basic assumptions of American diplomacy—the uniqueness and transitoriness of the first World War, the equilibrium in Europe, the equilibrium in Asia, and the importance for international relations of the moral force of world public opinion rather than military force. Were these assumptions, and the half-dozen policies taken from them, suitable for the year 1929? With the advantage of hindsight it is easy to see that they were not. But in view of the information available at the time, they were, perhaps, most of them, as sensible as one could have expected. They looked forward to a world at peace. They found justification, if not their origin, in "the most profound outlook for peace . . . that we have had at any time in the last half century." [12] There seemed so little reason to believe, in the spring of 1929, that the peaceful state of world affairs, like the economic prosperity that accompanied it, would change completely in the following four years.

12. Hoover to Stimson, Sept. 17, 1929, in *FR: 1929, I*, 241.

Chapter Three: AMERICAN STATESMEN

The Department of State in Washington in 1929 was still located on Pennsylvania Avenue between Sixteenth and Seventeenth Streets, in the rambling post-Civil War structure known as the State, War and Navy Building. Generals and diplomatists shared the old structure (the navy had departed during the first World War) [1] and in the 1920's—an era of small government establishments—there was plenty of room. The building had seen its share of American history. In the 80's and 90's it had served as headquarters for the last campaigns against the Western Indians. In later years Admiral George Dewey, gleaming with gold braid, resplendent in his famous handlebar mustachios, stalked pompously down the corridors. Here, too, had labored the secretaries of state since Hamilton Fish in the time of President Ulysses S. Grant. Within that great official pile John Hay had pondered the fateful Open Door notes and the independence of Panama. Twenty-five years later Henry L. Stimson found the Department of State less cluttered with Victorian bric-a-brac, but otherwise unchanged since the times of Hay and Fish. The Department was like a large Southern law office, with its cool dark corridors, high ceilings, swinging doors, black leather rocking chairs, brass cuspidors, and a grandfather's clock in the office of the secretary.[2] That office was itself one of the most interesting in the capital—a large rectangular room on the second floor, lighted by ample windows, looking south across the Mall to the Washington Monument. The

1. To a temporary building on Constitution Avenue. The navy was still there in 1957.

2. George F. Kennan, *American Diplomacy: 1900–1950* (Chicago, University of Chicago Press, 1951), pp. 91–2.

secretary sat at a huge mahogany desk a little toward the outside wall from the center of the room, with his back to the windows, flanked by the flag of the United States and his own flag of office. Around the room and in the approaching corridors the former secretaries of state, among them many of the nation's greatest leaders, stared down from somber oil portraits framed in heavy gilt.

As for the actual functioning of the Department, two newspapermen in an impudent but famous book would later describe Department workings under the rubic "Pink Peppermints and Protocol." [3] So it may have appeared to outsiders, but such sticky sarcasm stood far from the truth. In the 1920's there were 600 Washington employees working vigorously and efficiently at the business of foreign policy. The Department in 1929 was nevertheless relatively small. Not until the New Deal and the Fair Deal, and the New Deal under Republican management, would the State Department grow into the great organization now so unrecognizable to old-timers, with nearly 8,000 people, housed in a large new building on Foggy Bottom with two dozen heterogeneous annexes scattered over the District of Columbia.

1

Henry L. Stimson was not too well-known a personality in Washington when he arrived in the national capital, late in March 1929, to take up his new duties. He had come from the Philippine Islands, where he had served for a year as governor general. President Hoover knew him scarcely at all, and had chosen him because, after three other men refused, Stimson seemed the only remaining prominent Republican who was politically available and had some knowledge of foreign affairs.[4] Rumor had it that he

3. Drew Pearson and Robert S. Allen, *Washington Merry-go-round,* New York, Liveright, 1931.

4. Charles Evans Hughes and Senator William E. Borah refused. Dwight W. Morrow declined after an oblique overture. Hoover in his memoirs has written that he would have given the secretaryship to Charles Francis Adams, had he known Adams better in 1929. *The Memoirs of Herbert Hoover: The Cabinet and the Presidency,* p. 220. Adams was Hoover's secretary of the navy. Hoover told Richard N. Current that he would have preferred to have kept Kellogg

was a positive, undiplomatic person, likely to carry things through with a big stick rather than persuasion. But the new secretary made a commendable first appearance. One of his State Department greeters at the railroad station afterward remembered the "determined face, but I should not think an obstinate face; a kindly smile but no twinkle of humor." [5] Stimson was a man of above-average height, with firmly set chin, stern eyes, slightly acquiline nose, and something of the military in the cut of his graying hair and mustache—both closely cropped, the hair parted down the middle in the old-fashioned way, with a few wisps drooping at the front on each side. His face, composed and severe, belied his age, which was sixty-one.

Before taking the oath of office, the secretary of state-designate spent a hectic week and a half with President Hoover at the White House. Each day began far too early for Stimson's taste—at 7:00 A.M., in the White House basement, where the president convened the Medicine Ball Cabinet. Stimson privately thought this exercise a little too severe for the president and himself. Hoover would hurl the medicine ball viciously across the net; sometimes opponents would take it, sometimes they would duck it; once in a while they could not get out of the way fast enough, taking it on the ribs, painfully reminding them for days afterward of college football injuries.[6] Breakfast at the White House the erstwhile governor general found a disorganized affair. Hoover kept two big dogs in the room and allowed them to climb all around and over everyone and even to eat from the presidential fork and plate.[7] After these ordeals Stimson would go over to the Department, to get accustomed to the routine under the tutelage of the retiring secretary, Frank B. Kellogg. Evenings he spent with the president in conference over vital problems. The discussions with Hoover and Kellogg proved extremely valuable in putting him into touch

---

rather than take Stimson. Richard N. Current, *Secretary Stimson: A Study in Statecraft* (New Brunswick, N.J., 1954), p. 43.

5. Castle diary, Mar. 27, 1929.

6. Theodore G. Joslin, *Hoover Off the Record* (Garden City, N.Y., Doubleday, Doran, 1934), p. 56.

7. Stimson diary, Aug. 28, 1930.

with international affairs, for he had been in the Philippines for a year and had paid little attention to European affairs since the World War.[8] After ten days of intimate tutelage he took the oath, on March 28, 1929. Chief Justice Taft, his old chief of nearly twenty years before when Stimson had been secretary of war in the Taft Administration, came down from the court chambers on Capitol Hill and presided at the ceremony. The two men stood before a galaxy of reporters and photographers who dictated the publicity of oath-taking in a way which, as the new secretary sharply observed, he had not been accustomed to in the Philippine Islands.[9]

Properly sworn in, Stimson took up his first task—obtaining congenial advisers, getting together what he liked to call his "team."

From the Philippines there duly arrived the handsome Captain Eugene Regnier as military aide. During the next four years "Gene" served as riding companion, social secretary, and factotum (some malevolent spirits would anger Stimson by dubbing Regnier the "Grand Vizier"). From New York City came a new undersecretary, Joseph P. Cotton, a brilliant, urbane lawyer who served until his untimely death in March 1931. Cotton would become known as the most undiplomatic man in the Department—he was given to wisecracking, and his pointed humor often proved too much for diplomatic callers. Four assistant secretaries carried over from the previous administration: Francis White (Latin America), Nelson T. Johnson (Far East), Wilbur J. Carr (administration), and William R. Castle (Western Europe). Stimson in early 1931 brought in James Grafton Rogers, a former dean of the University of Colorado Law School, to replace Johnson, who became minister to China. In April 1931 Harvey H. Bundy, a lawyer from Boston, replaced Castle, who on the death of Cotton became undersecretary. A new office, special assistant to the secretary, went

8. Ibid., Aug. 30. In his memoirs, *On Active Service in Peace and War* (New York, Harper, 1948), written with McGeorge Bundy, Stimson frankly admitted that of all assignments in his years of public service, the State Department in 1929 was the one for which he was least prepared.

9. Diary, Aug. 30, 1930.

in November 1930 to Allen T. Klots, Jr., son of one of Stimson's old Yale friends. The secretary in mid-1931 appointed as economic adviser Herbert Feis, an expert on international economics. For Far Eastern matters he retained throughout his four years Dr. Stanley T. Hornbeck, a former Harvard instructor who in Kellogg's time had become chief of the Department's Far Eastern division.

Of the members of the team "Joe" Cotton, and after his death "Jim" Rogers, stood closest to Stimson personally, although the secretary frequently consulted Gene Regnier and Allen Klots on all kinds of Department matters. Probably the most important member of the team, however, in point of influence upon policy, was Assistant Secretary William R. Castle, later undersecretary. Scion of a prominent Hawaiian-American family, "Bill" Castle had joined the government during the World War, another Department officer who gave up a promising academic career at Harvard. He became successively, in the 1920's, chief of the Department's division of Western Europe and assistant secretary for Western Europe. In Kellogg's time the latter post amounted to that of undersecretary.[10]

Seldom has the Department of State possessed more capable policy officers than during Stimson's secretaryship; yet when Stimson arrived at the State, War and Navy Building he from the outset often ignored many of the most experienced Department men, hardly speaking to them for weeks on end, not to mention consulting them. After some months, matters improved, but too often Department officers seeking to get their views before the secretary were reduced to writing interoffice memoranda. Stimson's relations with the permanent officers of the Department were never too good, and there gradually arose a considerable animosity on his part toward Castle, which became pronounced after the latter upon President Hoover's recommendation became undersecretary and thereafter supported Hoover's views at the Department. Castle and Hoover got on together personally, as Stimson never did, and the latter in writing his memoirs fifteen years afterward

10. Kellogg's two undersecretaries, Robert E. Olds and J. Reuben Clark, preferred to act as legal advisers, and left policy matters to Castle.

still showed an animus against his undersecretary.[11] Stimson was a man of strong opinions, which as his successor Cordell Hull later remarked, he held with the greatest imaginable tenacity.[12] His sometimes highhanded treatment of assistants at the State Department was unwise, and on many occasions he lost much-needed advice.

Stimson at times was inconsiderate to his assistants in small personal ways, reflecting in this respect the unattractive manner in which he could treat men of lesser position than his own. It is not beside the point to relate that his Department secretary, William H. Beck, who had faithfully served four secretaries of state beginning with Robert Lansing, found relations with Stimson so difficult that he requested a consular appointment abroad. Stimson not infrequently would fly into rages over little matters, throwing books and papers and yelling at "Bill" Beck as if he were a slave. Beck for a time managed to get along by cutting a peek-hole in the door separating his office from the secretary's, whereby he could diplomatically survey the secretary's humor before entering the presence.

2

Stimson, despite certain temperamental weaknesses, was an able and impressive individual who would have made his mark in whatever activity he undertook, as New York lawyer or secretary of state.

So also, one must add, was his superior in the government during the years 1929–33, President Herbert Hoover.

Hoover was one of the most learned and capable men ever to rise to the presidency. In sheer mental power, in administrative ability, the thirty-first president of the United States has had few equals. It was his misfortune, as we have seen, to be president during the first years of the Great Depression. His domestic policies during that saddening era proved incapable of stopping the economic decline. Hoover received much personal criticism, in

11. See *On Active Service*, p. 192.

12. *The Memoirs of Cordell Hull* (2 vols. New York, Macmillan, 1948), *1*, 160.

retrospect undeserved. He had the makings of a superb president, and he was overwhelmed by events which, given the economic knowledge of the day, were beyond his control.

In foreign affairs as in domestic matters, Hoover had had much experience when he became president in 1929. For some years prior to the first World War he had lived abroad, both in Europe and the Orient, pursuing his work as a mining engineer. During the war he spent many months in Belgium and elsewhere. It is true that after the war he did not go abroad again for nearly twenty years; but no one, surveying his foreign experiences, could say that he had not known the world. He was no provincial American, secure in the facile wisdom of a summer or two in Europe and perhaps a hurried excursion to the capitals of the Far East. He was the best-traveled American president since the time, over a hundred years before, of John Quincy Adams.

Why then did there gradually appear between him and Stimson a strained personal relation that by the end of Hoover's presidency had grown almost to the size of a gulf? Why could not this Quaker president, with his profound knowledge of foreign affairs, get along with the man whom he appointed as his agent in international relations?

One must say, first of all, that their difficulties, mainly personal, did not have much effect on the outward workings of American diplomacy, although they did at times make determination of policy unnecessarily difficult.

Perhaps a principal cause of dissension between the two men was that Hoover worked so hard. He was the hardest-working president in the history of that office—again with the possible exception of J. Q. Adams. His ways of work differed markedly from those of his easy-going predecessor, Coolidge. "Silent Cal" had taken a two-to-four-hour nap in the presidential office every afternoon.[13] Coolidge had avoided as many appointments as possible, and those which proved absolutely unavoidable he handled in a highly unorthodox (though effective) manner. The

13. In addition he slept on an average of eleven hours a day. His chief usher recalled that "No other president in my time ever slept so much." Irwin Hood ("Ike") Hoover, *Forty-Two Years in the White House* (Boston and New York, Houghton Mifflin, 1934), p. 268.

petitioner would enter the presidential office and state his case while Coolidge, feet on the desk, smoking an impossible-smelling black cigar, looked out the window. When the case was finished there would often follow a long, embarrassing silence while Coolidge thought. Frequently at this crucial moment petitioners moved for the door, only to be halted by a nasal "What're you going for?" The silence continued. Coolidge finally would make a decision in a few well-chosen words, or else refer the matter to "my secretary of the treasury" or "my secretary of state." [14]

Hoover managed matters much differently. He saw more callers than Coolidge—although not nearly so many as Harding—but his favorite method of administration was the telephone, instead of office interviews. He was perhaps the first president to realize the administrative efficiencies of the telephone. He installed in the White House a special switchboard connecting his desk by private wire to the offices of all the leaders of his administration. Stimson many times while secretary of state would answer the telephone and hear the White House operator say, "The president is on the wire."

Bearing in mind his motto, "Work is Life," [15] Hoover arrived at his desk before eight-thirty in the morning, snatched ten or fifteen minutes for luncheon brought in on a tray, and labored in the Lincoln study until the early hours of the next morning.[16]

Such was not Stimson's schedule. Two or three hours in the Department constituted a normal day's labor for the secretary of state (although he did handle some official matters at home), and he punctuated work with frequent vacations—hunting excursions in the autumn and winter, long holidays in Europe in spring and summer.

Hoover attributed this "slackness" to bad health,[17] which may have been true. Stimson complained frequently to his diary of

14. Hugh R. Wilson, *Diplomat between Wars* (New York, Longmans, Green, 1941), pp. 176–7.

15. Joslin, *Hoover Off the Record,* p. 77.

16. Hoover set a record at the White House in the speed with which he could change from business suit to formal cutaway, receive an ambassador, and change back to business suit. He once performed this stint in ten minutes. Irwin H. Hoover, *Forty-Two Years in the White House,* p. 242.

17. *Memoirs of Herbert Hoover: The Cabinet and the Presidency,* p. 336.

biliousness and indigestion, from which he sometimes gained relief through exercise. Perhaps at this time he was becoming occupied with his health as do many men who, long accustomed to a strenuous life, reach their 60's and find themselves subject to frequent petty and novel maladies. His inability to work for any long period of time may also have stemmed from his many years of successful law practice and the leisure that may be attendant upon large fees.

Hoover had had far more experience in the world than had Stimson. The latter had taken a number of vacation trips to Europe and the Far East, had served in France for a few months during the World War, had spent a short time in Latin America in 1927, and had lived in the Philippines for the year prior to becoming secretary of state.

The president was a younger man than the secretary, and this may have imparted a subtle strain on their relations.

Surely in temper the two men differed markedly. Hoover was modest and even bashful, highly sensitive, a worrier, frequently unsure of himself; whereas Stimson seldom worried, and once he had made up his mind could doggedly follow a course of action, never looking back.

Hoover was not a pacifist; he did, however, hold little love for soldiers and soldierly solutions; Stimson, on the other hand, although convinced of the desirability of pacific settlement—of the effectiveness of public opinion in international affairs, rather than military force—championed occasional use of military power. Stimson (Theodore Roosevelt once had called him "my kind of man") liked military men and admired military ways. As Hoover later wrote of him, "Instinctively, Mr. Stimson's first love was the law; and his second, the military field. Mentally, he was a mixture of a soldier and an advocate." [18]

Given such differences between the president and the secretary—Hoover's dislike of, Stimson's preference for, military men and their ideas; differences in habits of work and experience abroad—it is not hard to understand how, almost from the beginning, there began to appear small signs of friction between them. It may have

18. Ibid., p. 219.

been seldom visible to outsiders, but it increased steadily if not always discernibly during Hoover's four years in the White House. When Stimson, in part out of a sense of the dignity of his office and in part from sheer disinclination, refused to campaign actively for Hoover in 1932, relations almost snapped. Not openly, of course, nor even privately on the part of Stimson, who never fully realized the manner in which he had lost the confidence of his superior. But had Hoover won the election, he would not have kept Stimson in the cabinet.

In 1929 these personal difficulties lay in the future, and during the spring and early summer the new secretary occupied himself in becoming acquainted with his new chief and assembling his team. President Hoover spent these early weeks and months of his administration in sizing up the Government of the United States —surveying the possibilities of budget reduction, the chances of making the government a more efficient enterprise, the opportunities of cutting red tape for American businessmen in their operations at home and abroad. Fortune seemingly had smiled on the Hoover Administration, and there appeared no danger either of economic depression at home or war in distant lands.

The routine of the State Department went on from day to day. Some of the Department's business was trivial. The Spanish ambassador, Alejandro Padilla, would come to diplomatic hours every Thursday and regale Assistant Secretary Castle with the week-by-week status of corks, onions, and grapes. Sometimes there was a touch of color to Department operations, as in the early summer of 1929 when the Rumanian government decided to replace its Washington minister, and Department personnel gossiped expectantly as to whether the new envoy would wear rouge and corsets.[19] Much of the time, however, there was serious negotiation, on economic, political, and other concerns, with the ambassadors of the major world powers—Great Britain, France, Italy, Germany, and Japan. If this negotiation did not carry the risk of war, everyone rightly assumed that it held large importance for the maintenance of peace.

19. When the minister arrived in October 1929 he wore neither.

But what, one might now ask, was the Hoover Administration's first real experience with diplomacy in 1929? Was there any inkling, in early months at the White House and the State Department, of trouble to come—some small sign that American foreign relations would not for much longer be sailing a summer sea? The first sign of international trouble, of the extremely serious problems of diplomacy which were to confront the Administration in the years that followed, came from a place far removed from peaceful Washington. An issue arose in Manchuria in the summer of 1929 between China and Russia over the jointly owned Chinese Eastern Railway. This was a most intricate argument, confused and confusing, reflecting traditional Oriental maneuver; but it involved the covenants of the new Kellogg-Briand Pact, to which both China and Russia were parties, and therefore presented a challenge to one of the leading policies of American diplomacy.

Chapter Four: TESTING THE KELLOGG-BRIAND PACT IN MANCHURIA

The Kellogg-Briand Pact, signed at Paris during a solemn ceremony in August 1928, the most important international engagement—other than the Washington treaties—that the United States undertook in the first decade after the World War, was put to the test during the early months of the Hoover Administration. The test occurred, of all possible places, in Manchuria during a Sino-Soviet controversy over the Chinese Eastern Railway. In Manchuria the railway system consisted chiefly of two lines, the Chinese Eastern and the South Manchuria, the former a jointly-owned Sino-Russian venture and the latter belonging exclusively to Japan. These railways were the focal points of international conflict in the area, for whoever controlled the rail lines controlled the territory through which they passed. Manchuria was one of the most desirable portions of Eastern Asia. It was, at least by Oriental standards, largely unpopulated. It contained important economic resources, including coal and some iron ore, not to speak of a thriving agriculture. It was a place worth fighting for, and in 1929 the Chinese and Russians actually came to blows for part of it, contrary to their solemn promises under the Kellogg-Briand Pact never to use war as an instrument of national policy and to settle "all disputes or conflicts of whatever nature or of whatever origin" by peaceful means.

1

In physical contours Manchuria certainly offered no striking contrast to places with which Americans were thoroughly familiar.

Northern Manchuria, locale of the Chinese Eastern Railway, was an amazingly fertile agricultural region, quite similar to the midwestern United States. Its farm and grazing lands, its forests, and the Sungari-Amur River system reminded occasional American travelers of the region of the upper Mississippi and its tributaries, the fertile farmland and deep black soil of northern Missouri, Illinois, and Iowa. The American consul general at Harbin, George C. Hanson, told a newspaperman in 1929 that Manchuria and Inner Mongolia could produce enough corn, wheat, soya beans, and livestock to feed most of the people of East Asia. Chinese farmers who arrived destitute from China proper were able in less than ten years to purchase their farms outright and to refund loans advanced for purchase of farm machinery.[1]

What, then, of the peculiar circumstances of the Chinese Eastern Railway, the line over which China and Russia fought in 1929? The Chinese Eastern, the most important line in northern Manchuria, stretched for a thousand miles across the plains of Heilungkiang province, from Manchuli in the northwest to Harbin and Suifenho in the east, bearing to markets and the sea the produce of Manchurian agriculture. It sliced off about two days from the Trans-Siberian Railway's meandering route over the steppes of upper Asia from Moscow to Vladivostok; the Chinese Eastern was a highly convenient short cut for supplying Russian troops and ships based far to the east on the Kamchatka Peninsula.

Historically the railway's military value for Russia had been at least as important as its economic value for China, and as a military route it for many years had occupied the attention of Russian strategists and diplomats. The French Republic of the 1890's, deeply interested in Imperial Russia's military capabilities, had lent the Tsarist government funds to build the C.E.R. The French loan was one of the first fruits of the Franco-Russian alliance. Russia completed the great railroad in 1903, at a cost of two hundred million dollars. The building of the Chinese Eastern across Manchuria during the years at the end of the 19th century symbolized the growing cordiality of Franco-Russian relations, and

1. John B. Powell, *My Twenty-Five Years in China* (New York, 1945), p. 177.

was one of the factors inducing Imperial Germany to knit more closely its own system of alliances in preparation for the European and world struggle that came in 1914.

The road underwent many vicissitudes in the years after outbreak of the first World War. During the war the Chinese Eastern temporarily passed out of Russian control. The Allies landed troops in Siberia, after the Bolshevik Revolution, to prevent stores of Allied war material at Vladivostok from falling into German hands and to prevent the ambitious Japanese from seizing large expanses of Siberian territory. In the course of this protective operation an American army colonel took over and ran the C.E.R., and an Interallied Commission invested ten million dollars in the railway, in addition to a considerable amount of equipment. When the troops finally withdrew, the future status of the C.E.R. was uncertain. The railway was left to the devices of Chinese and Russian diplomatic bargaining.[2] In the years after the war the two nations, China and Russia, moved slowly and at first uncertainly. During the period just after the Bolshevik Revolution, Russian power in the Far East was at its lowest ebb; this was the time when Soviet leaders talked glibly of anti-imperialism, of allowing the various acquisitions of Imperial Russia to go their own way. But by the year 1924 Soviet power had revived sufficiently to allow a more aggressive foreign policy. A Sino-Soviet agreement of that year, concluded in this more favorable climate of Soviet power, inaugurated an assertion of prewar Russian rights under color of Sino-Soviet "equal participation" in the C.E.R. The Russians by 1929 at last had regained complete control.

It is an understatement to say that the Chinese, by the latter 1920's, were unhappy with Russia's reassertion of control over the Chinese Eastern. Chinese nationalism had been waxing mightily ever since the revolution of 1911–12, and by the late 1920's the nationalists of the Kuomintang Party burned with resentment against Russian imperialism. Still, the old status quo in Manchuria—Russian control of the C.E.R., completely reasserted by

2. Betty Miller Unterberger, *America's Siberian Expedition, 1918–1920: A Study in National Policy* (Durham, N.C., 1956), pp. 107–17, 204–29.

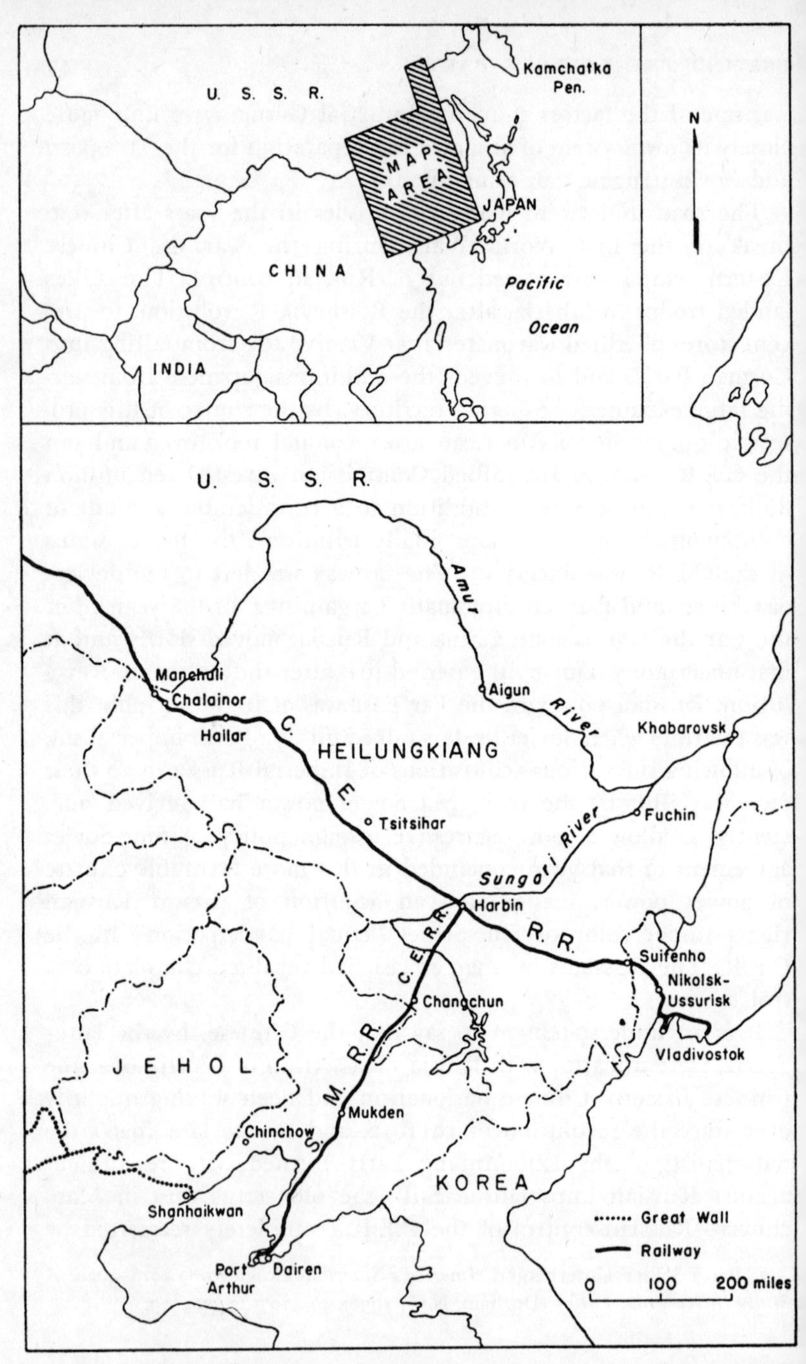

Manchuria and Its Railway System—the Chinese Eastern Railway and the South Manchuria Railway

1929—seemed difficult to challenge. The status quo appeared assured because of proximity to the Chinese Eastern of Japan's own South Manchuria Railway. Before the Russo-Japanese War of 1904–05 this line had been a part of the system of the Chinese Eastern. The Japanese, having obtained the S.M.R. as a result of the war, had extended it and made it the center of all their industry and other holdings in South Manchuria. The Japanese government by the 1920's would have frowned upon all action by China against Russia, for if the Chinese managed to assert any rights to the C.E.R. they might then turn their attention to the S.M.R. There was still another deterrent to Chinese action. The Western powers holding treaty rights of extraterritorial jurisdiction in China—France, Britain, the United States—could hardly subscribe to any drastic Chinese démarche against Russia, because the Chinese afterward might attempt to abrogate all extraterritorial concessions.

Even so, the new Nationalist government of Chiang Kai-shek, growing stronger as its powers of taxation reached out from Nanking, listened thoughtfully to the antiforeign sentiment of its supporters. The president of Nationalist China already was walking the tightrope of expediency that twenty years later would conduct him to a smaller and more manageable domain on Formosa. In the late 1920's he spent his time in Nanking buying and balancing his opponents throughout China, equating the Chinese revolution with his personal power, worried constantly about the appearance, not to mention reality, of his control over the erstwhile domain of the Manchus. The internal difficulties of the Kuomintang party were such as to encourage an adventurous foreign policy. Would it not be advisable, the politicians reasoned in Nanking, to assert Chinese rights against some foreign power, preferably a weak one like Russia, and further unite the Chinese nation? Would it not be possible to pull the tail of the harmless old Russian bear?

To some Chinese minds, alert to opportunity for intrigue, there came the special vision of allowing the independent-minded warlord of Manchuria, the so-called Young Marshal, Chang Hsueh-liang, to begin a dispute over the C.E.R. Officers of the

Japanese army in Manchuria, the Kwantung Army, had assassinated Young Marshal Chang's father, the Old Marshal Chang Tso-lin, in 1928.[3] The young Marshal, because of his understandably anti-Japanese sentiments, had been drawn to the Kuomintang. His allegiance was tenuous and uncertain. He was, moreover, too dominant a figure in Chinese politics to suit Chiang Kai-shek. The young Marshal was an easy target for intrigue. Brought up in the pleasant ways of Shanghai, he liked to live in Peking with the foreign set, playing golf and tennis, dancing, gambling, dictating letters and memoranda to his sixteen female secretaries.[4] His knowledge of military matters was, of course, nonexistent. Politically he was naive. He had inherited his warlordship from his astute father, the Old Marshal, who had ruled Manchuria with an iron hand for a quarter of a century. Perhaps, therefore, the dilettantish Young Marshal could be persuaded to begin a dispute with the Russians over the Chinese Eastern Railway. If the scheme misfired, the Nanking government could disavow its Manchurian governor, handily disposing of the blame and perhaps also of the Young Marshal; should the adventure triumph, Nanking's prestige would rise equally if not more than that of the Young Marshal.[5] Either way, would it not strengthen China's sovereignty in Manchuria?

Whatever the reasoning, trouble soon appeared in Manchuria. Consul Hanson in Harbin reported to Secretary of State Kellogg in December 1928 that General Tsan Ping accompanied by police officers had taken over the Harbin telephone service, installed and hitherto operated by the C.E.R. Local Soviet authorities, the consul

3. Paul S. Dull, "The Assassination of Chang Tso-lin," *Far Eastern Quarterly, 11* (1952), 453–63.

4. When the Young Marshal left China for Europe in 1933 he took along his polygamous household. The Shanghai papers reported that "The Young Marshal left this morning for Europe, accompanied by sixteen lady secretaries."

5. According to the pro-Soviet account by Louis Fischer, *The Soviets in World Affairs* (2 vols. New York, 1930), *2,* 797, there was another calculation. If seizure of the C.E.R. passed smoothly, there would follow a Chinese thrust toward Russian-dominated Outer Mongolia, further raising the Kuomintang's prestige, and outflanking Nanking's two principal domestic opponents, Generals Yen Hsi-shan and Feng Yu-hsiang.

added, feared that the railroad's telegraph lines would go next, and then the entire railway.[6] All sorts of rumors arose. The American consul in Mukden heard that the Chinese were considering ways and means of bringing to fruition their "pet scheme" of taking the C.E.R.[7] The able correspondent of the New York *Times,* Hallett Abend, cabled his home office that the Russian government feared, "not without reason," a Chinese move; Abend reported a rumor that Russia was seeking to dispose of the railway either to France or Japan but that there were no takers. "For who wants to buy a hornet's nest?" [8]

Early in July 1929 the Chinese took over the railroad. Russia and China severed diplomatic relations. There was talk of war.

2

Half way round the world, the secretary of state of the United States from his office at the State, War and Navy Building watched the Far Eastern fracas with increasing displeasure. As Henry L. Stimson was preparing the ceremonial proclamation of the Kellogg-Briand Pact, he grew alarmed at the distinct possibility that war between two adherents of the antiwar treaty might break out before July 24, 1929, the date for proclaiming the treaty. On the morning of July 18 he had a confidential talk with Assistant Secretary Castle. Stimson's experienced assistant secretary held out for caution. "I told him," Castle recalled afterward, "that I thought nothing would come of it but he felt that we, largely because we were responsible for the Kellogg Pact, ought to do something, and he did not know what to do." [9] Castle advised a talk with the Japanese ambassador in Washington and the Chinese minister and perhaps the French ambassador. He warned against sending indirect messages to the Soviets (the Soviet government, sensitive over American refusal to recognize its regime, might employ the occasion

6. Consul George C. Hanson to Kellogg, Dec. 24, 1928, 861.77 Chinese Eastern/4.

7. Consul Myrl S. Myers to the American minister in Peking, J. V. A. MacMurray, Feb. 7, 1929, *FR: 1929, 2,* 189.

8. New York *Times,* Feb. 24, 1929.

9. Castle diary, July 18, 1929.

to give Stimson one of the by then well-known Bolshevik harangues).

That same day Stimson conversed with the British, Japanese, and French ambassadors, and the Chinese minister, and pointed out the "grave responsibility imposed by the present situation" upon all powers signatory or adherent to the Kellogg Pact. Agreeing with the secretary, they promised to telegraph their governments.[10]

The Kellogg Pact was almost the only way the nations could approach the dispute in Manchuria.[11] It was not possible to use the machinery of the League of Nations, or to invoke the Nine-Power Treaty of the Washington Conference; Russia was not party to the latter, and neither Russia nor the United States belonged to the League. Fortunately, the Kellogg Pact proved a rallying point for the forces of peace. The nations in July 1929 fell in behind the leadership of the United States. The foreign minister of France, Aristide Briand, reminded the Chinese minister in Paris of China's obligations under the Kellogg-Briand Pact. Briand also reminded the Soviet ambassador. In Tokyo the Japanese foreign minister, Baron Kijuro Shidehara, spoke to the Soviet ambassador.[12] The acting head of the Soviet government, Commissar Jan Rudzutak, soon was saying that the interests of his government in the Chinese Eastern Railway were less important than preservation of the integrity of the Pact of Paris. "Our signature of the Kellogg Pact," the commissar avowed, "was not just a diplomatic gesture. . . . our pacific pronouncements are not just words . . . When we talk of peace we mean peace . . . No other country ever received such

10. *FR: 1929, 2,* 210.

11. Stimson could have invoked the Convention for the Pacific Settlement of International Disputes which Imperial Russia, together with the other great powers, had signed at the First Hague Conference of 1899. Article 3 pledged that powers strangers to a dispute "have the right to offer good offices or mediation, even during the course of hostilities. The exercise of this right can never be regarded by one or the other of the parties in conflict as an unfriendly act." This pledge was repeated at the Second Hague Conference in 1907. See James Brown Scott, *The Hague Peace Conferences* (2 vols. Baltimore, 1909), 2, 83, 311.

12. Shidehara did this without knowledge of Stimson's request to the powers of July 18. The American chargé in Tokyo, Edwin Neville, to Stimson, July 26, 1929, 861.77 Chinese Eastern/210.

provocation as we have received from the Chinese. But we shall not fight unless our country is invaded." [13] That same day the Nanking regime in China promised to "devote itself to the maintenance of peace." [14] For the time being the crisis had passed.[15] Representatives of nearly all the nations of the world gathered in the East Room of the White House on July 24, 1929, and President Hoover proclaimed the Kellogg Pact.

Next day Stimson called the representatives of the powers to his office and gave out an aide memoire, "Suggestions for a Commission of Conciliation." He had determined to put an end to any possible trouble in Manchuria—by an international commission.[16]

Here, and for the first time in his diplomatic career, the secretary went too far. In his suggestions for a commission of conciliation he made the mistake of taking action without first examining the difficulties of the problem involved, and without first inviting the opinions of interested governments.[17] This sort of mistake, of course,

13. New York *Times,* July 20, 1929, quoted in Pauline Tompkins, *American-Russian Relations in the Far East* (New York, 1929), p. 226.

14. *FR: 1929, 2,* 228–31.

15. Assistant Secretary Castle wrote in his diary that the Russian-Chinese "near-imbroglio" took up a considerable amount of time and an enormous amount of telegraph money: "It may have a definitely good effect if the world can be made to believe that, through respect for the Pact, war was averted. This will not be true but that does not matter if the world believes it true. It will make the Pact a real thing and something to be called forth in similar cases in the future. The only thing that worries me at all is that other nations may get the idea that we, as depository of the Pact, must act every time there is a threat of war. That would turn a strong body of American opinion against the Pact because it would be exploited as getting us entangled in foreign affairs—the very thing we have always said it would never do." Diary, July 23, 1929.

16. For the text of Stimson's suggestion, see *FR: 1929, 2,* 242–4.

17. The initial reception of Stimson's proposal by the Washington representatives of the powers was hardly auspicious, and might have brought home to the secretary of state—had he been more alert to the situation—that his proposal was maladroit. Assistant Secretary Castle recorded that "I was present at the meeting at which Mr. Stimson presented these documents [Stimson's aide memoire] to the assembled diplomats. I think they all felt that he was making too much of a matter which seems to be settling itself and should settle itself. Sir Esme [Howard, the British ambassador] was serious and a little exaggeratedly polite. Debuchi [the Japanese ambassador] was almost openly sarcastic.

was nothing new in the history of American diplomacy. In their eagerness to achieve praiseworthy goals, American "shirt-sleeves" diplomatists often had thrown caution to the winds, making suggestions which other nations, not so zealously and idealistically inclined, found completely unacceptable. The result each time had been deep embarrassment at the State Department, and such was the case in 1929. The Japanese ambassador in Washington, Katsuji Debuchi, after a few days called at the Department and presented certain opinions of his government which placed Stimson in an awkward position. The Japanese government, according to Debuchi, believed that in Manchuria neither Russia nor China would welcome help from the powers; moreover, should either or both contending parties reject Stimson's suggestion, it would place the powers in a "peculiarly embarrassing position"; the Japanese government presumed that none of the powers intended to exercise "material and effective pressure" upon the unwilling parties to force acceptance of conciliation; and if conciliaton were rejected, did Stimson have in mind further action? Much on the spot, the secretary made some lame remarks and ended the conversation. Debuchi was sympathetic. "He said he understood that perfectly. . . . He said he understood this fully. . . . He said he understood that." As for the European powers, they proved only slightly more cooperative. Briand held the secretary's proposal of conciliation "in every respect" in accord with the Kellogg Pact; its legal basis was "strong"; but the experienced French foreign minister advised waiting a while. The German government desired to refrain from diplomatic action. Great Britain took no notice of the American proposal.[18]

Martino [the Italian ambassador] was evidently surprised but glad to be here. Leitner [the German chargé] was impressed. Claudel [the French ambassador] was always chuckling to himself. [Undersecretary] Cotton said afterward he thought it was a funny meeting." Castle diary, July 26, 1929.

18. Memorandum by Stimson of a conversation with Debuchi, July 30, 1929, *FR: 1929, 2,* 259–61; the first secretary of the French embassy, Jules Henry, to Castle, Aug. 1, 1929, ibid., p. 264; the American ambassador in Berlin, Jacob Gould Schurman, to Stimson, Aug. 5, 1929, ibid., p. 271. Stimson and the British ambassador, Sir Esme Howard, had a long talk on Aug. 26. "I asked him if he could tell me what he had heard from his Government in regard to our

The dispute, Debuchi had told Stimson, should be settled by the parties. He might have added that the Sino-Soviet agreement of 1924 had stipulated that disputes between the parties should be so settled. The fact was, and Stimson had not recognized it, that the post-Versailles doctrine of collective security tended to break down in areas where the great powers had vital interests. Japan wished no international interference in Manchuria, even interference to the virtually harmless extent of a commission of conciliation. Japan as owner of the South Manchuria Railway and the many business ventures attached to the S.M.R. considered Manchuria intimately connected to the Japanese national interest, a life line for the Japanese people, one of the few places where Japan's economy could expand without stay or hindrance from Western powers. This was one place, all Japanese agreed, where there should be no Western diplomatic meddling. Although Japan in 1929 was not anxious to see Nationalist China win over Soviet Russia, a precedent which might make for difficulty over the South Manchuria Railway, it was better to allow the Sino-Russian quarrel to run its course than to support the slightest tincture of Western and especially American diplomatic intervention in Manchuria. On two previous occasions the United States had had the temerity to interfere in Manchuria. Secretary of State Philander C. Knox in 1909 had ineptly proposed the "neutralization" of Chinese and Manchurian railroads and an international loan to China which would permit the Chinese to purchase the railroads from their Western owners.[19] Then during the World War an American officer acting under the Interallied Commission had operated the C.E.R. For Stimson in 1929 to suggest a commission of conciliation at once antagonized Japan, not to mention Soviet Russia, which nation was altogether likely to rebuff any diplomatic suggestion from a government not yet recognizing the Soviet regime.

---

former discussion on July 25." Sir Esme replied that he had only a telegram to the effect that no answer to the aide memoire was necessary, because the British government feared that Stimson's suggestions might be resented in Russia and China. Ibid., pp. 303–4.

19. An alternative proposal was construction, under neutral administration, of a north-south railway through Manchuria from Aigun to Chinchow.

Prudence dictated that Stimson avoid so tender a situation, so replete with international rivalries. A few years later, meditating over the Far Eastern Crisis, the secretary would describe himself as something of an expert in Oriental matters. Had he not made several brief trips to China and Japan? Had he not served as governor general of the Philippines? [20] But his diplomatic actions in July 1929 in regard to the affair of the Chinese Eastern revealed little knowledge of Far Eastern history and politics.

Nothing of further interest occurred in the Manchurian trouble of 1929 until autumn, when the Russians suddenly began making border raids into Manchuria. Three aircraft reportedly bombed the outskirts of Fuchin on October 30, and Soviet troops seized the town for three days. There was a panicky feeling in Harbin.

Finally, on November 17, 1929, about five thousand Soviet cavalry and infantry began an attack on Chalainor and Manchuli, and took those localities without opposition from the Chinese defenders.

These "hostilities," let it be added, were rather farcical, for there seem to have been virtually no casualties on either side. The principal worry of Chinese civilians in the hostile areas in the autumn of 1929 was over looting by troops of their own country. The Russians abetted this looting, and in Fuchin they organized it: they took possession of the local bank and flour mills, confiscating both money and flour. With the money they hired the Chinese coolie population to load flour on a number of river barges, for transport to Russia. The coolies received three dollars a day, about six times their normal rate, and when these tidings reached the retreating Chinese soldiers, a number of them shed their uniforms and returned to offer their services, which were accepted.

Hallett Abend of the New York *Times* later recalled that even reports of Russian bombing in Manchuria—such as the bombing of Fuchin on October 30—were exaggerations, if not fabrications. The Russians, Abend wrote, put the Chinese to flight on the plains near Hailar by bombing them from low-flying airplanes. The Chinese complained to the world that the Soviets had used high explosives and poison gas bombs. Actually the Russian flyers

20. Stimson, *The Far Eastern Crisis* (New York, Harper, 1936), p. 6.

stampeded the Chinese by "bombing" them with heavy paper bags, some filled with soot and sand, and some with very rotten cabbage.[21]

Still, Russian troops had invaded Chinese soil, contrary to the Kellogg-Briand Pact. What would the nations, in particular the United States, do about it?

3

"The main question," Assistant Secretary Castle wrote in his diary in late November of 1929, "is what, if anything, to do about the Russian advance in Manchuria. It is making the Kellogg Pact look like 30 cents . . ."

It was possible, he thought, again to address the great powers—as Stimson had done in July—with a proposal of a neutral commission or something similar; but the July démarche had received "the cordial support of nobody," and there could be little advantage in that course. It was possible to address China and Russia directly, once more suggesting what they might do to avoid war, but the difficulty with that approach lay in treating with the Soviet government, unrecognized by the United States. A third course might be a statement to the press which would be read in Moscow and in Nanking, probably to no effect, but which might encourage American public opinion. The Department's Far Eastern adviser, Stanley Hornbeck, had drawn up a statement which Castle believed "a little too innocuous but perhaps we can jazz it a bit before it is issued." [22]

Secretary Stimson, believing that some action was essential, took the second course suggested by Castle—another formal admonition to China and Russia. On November 26 he cabled American diplomatic representatives in Paris, London, Rome, Tokyo and (on November 27) Berlin, and instructed them to call at the respective foreign offices, see the minister of foreign affairs, and leave an enclosed statement, which the secretary of state proposed to send, if approved, to China and Russia. "The American government," the

21. Hallett Abend, *My Life in China: 1926–41* (New York, Harcourt, Brace, 1943), p. 106.

22. Diary, Nov. 25, 1929.

statement concluded, "feels that the respect with which China and Russia will hereafter be held in the good opinion of the world will necessarily in great measure depend upon the way in which they carry out these most sacred promises [of the Kellogg Pact]." Stimson wished the powers to publish a similar statement and communicate it to Nanking and Moscow.[23]

As happened in July, so again in November. The Japanese government doubted the practical benefit of such a statement. The British foreign secretary, Arthur Henderson, thought one desirable but urged Stimson to collect individual statements and present them himself. The German government demurred, although "prepared to do everything in its power, in accordance with the Paris Pact, to further peace in the Far East." [24] Foreign Minister Briand of France, joint-architect of the antiwar treaty, weakly agreed "in principle" to its invocation. Only the Italian government, possessing virtually no interests in the Far East, agreed without ambiguity.

All this was embarrassing enough, when the Japanese Foreign Office allowed Stimson's proposal, transmitted in secrecy, to leak out to the Tokyo newspapers. A representative of the Associated Press telephoned Assistant Secretary of State Nelson T. Johnson and asked for confirmation of this alleged American démarche, and Johnson felt forced to give it.[25]

Undismayed, Stimson set on foot a new diplomatic effort—his

23. *FR: 1929, 2,* 350–2. "Nelson Johnson and Cotton and Hornbeck and I also discussed at some length the Chinese-Russian situation. The Secretary is eager to be the Great Peacemaker and telegraphed Japan, France, Great Britain and Italy the text of a statement he wants to issue reminding the two nations again of their obligations under the Kellogg Pact, etc. and suggesting that the other nations issue simultaneously similar statements. He omitted Germany because he thought Germany did him in the eye last July when he tried to turn a similar trick but we think him wrong in the omission. It will irritate Germany to no purpose. We, therefore, telegraphed him that unless he telephoned not to do it before 12 today we should repeat the message to Germany. Cotton said 'give him a definite time limit. That is what he does to other nations.' . . . probably the Secretary's latest demarche will be a flop." Castle diary, Nov. 27, 1929.

24. Schurman to Stimson, Nov. 28, 1929, *FR: 1929, 2,* 359.

25. Memorandum by Johnson of a conversation with Debuchi, Nov. 29, 1929, *FR: 1929, 2,* 364–5. Also Castle diary, Nov. 29, 1929.

fourth—in the matter of the Chinese Eastern Railway. He had first invited the representatives of the great powers, on July 18, 1929, to remind the Manchurian disputants of the promises of the Kellogg Pact. Then on July 25 he had proposed a commission of conciliation. Next he had asked the powers on November 26–27 to make another reminder to the disputants. Now on November 30, 1929, he imitated the diplomatic tactics of one of his most illustrious predecessors at the Department of State. Thirty years before, John Hay in 1899 had circularized the powers relative to the Open Door. The replies had been almost uniformly evasive—one, that of the Imperial Russian Government, amounting to a thinly disguised rejection. Hay then engaged in an international bluff, announcing that because all the powers circularized had favored his proposal, trade in China henceforth would adhere to the rules of the Open Door. Stimson used the same tactic in 1929, in cables to the powers announcing their approval of an admonitory communication to China and Russia. "Having received replies from all of the Governments addressed, and finding the replies in general favorable in principle to my proposal," he was transmitting directly to the Chinese government and indirectly by way of France to Soviet Russia a "statement" (not a note, for the United States had no diplomatic relations with the Soviet Union).[26] The statement invoked the Kellogg Pact.

The results of this fourth move by the American secretary of state gradually became evident. In his announcement Stimson expressed hope that all nations signatory or adherent to the antiwar treaty would themselves communicate similar statements. Out of fifty-five nations, thirty-seven took action. Some moved immediately, many acted after three or four days, some delayed more than a week.[27] Of the great powers, the French adopted the text of the American admonition; the Italian government followed suit; likewise the British. The German government chose to "reserve its decision as to the time and form of its further steps in the matter." [28] Japan sent no note at all—although when Assistant

26. For the text of the statement, see *FR: 1929, 2,* 366–7.

27. Russell M. Cooper, *American Consultation in World Affairs: For the Preservation of Peace* (New York, 1934), p. 100.

28. Schurman to Stimson, Dec. 2, 1929, *FR: 1929, 2,* 376. The German am-

Secretary Johnson gave Ambassador Debuchi a copy of Stimson's statement, the ambassador seemed pleased and said several times that Baron Shidehara wished to support the Kellogg Pact in every way possible. Seeking to allay Japanese displeasure, Stimson told Debuchi that the recent American action had not proceeded from "any desire to intrude into Manchurian affairs," but only to save the Kellogg Pact from losing its strength and force. Again Debuchi, so the secretary afterward recalled, "understood perfectly." [29]

Misfortune followed Stimson's every representation. Unknown to him when he sent his statements of November 30, private negotiations between China and Russia for a settlement of the C.E.R. dispute already had reached a final stage. Chinese and Russian representatives signed a provisional peace at the Siberian town of Nikolsk-Ussurisk on December 3, 1929, stipulating for termination of hostilities on the basis of the status quo ante. Envoys of the two nations signed a confirmatory protocol at Khabarovsk on December 22. The protocol of Khabarovsk did not mention the Kellogg Pact. Soviet forces estimated at between five and ten thousand men on December 23 began evacuating Manchuria, and had departed by January 2, 1930.[30]

There remain two episodes connected with Stimson's diplomacy over the Chinese Eastern Railway which are worth recounting. In accord with the secretary's request, the Rumanian government, not in diplomatic relations with Soviet Russia, transmitted through Paris to the French ambassador in Moscow the text of a note apropos the controversy. As he had done with Stimson's similar communication, Ambassador Jean Herbette journeyed to the

---

bassador in Washington later informed Castle that Germany, charged during the C.E.R. dispute with looking after Soviet interests in China and Chinese interests in Russia, could not send a statement.

29. Memorandum by Stimson of a conversation with Debuchi, Dec. 2, 1929, 861.77 Chinese Eastern/555.

30. The Khabarovsk protocol required that a Chinese delegation representing both Mukden and Nanking should go to Moscow to negotiate a final settlement. A delegation entrained for Moscow in May 1930. There followed months of parleying. When the Japanese began the occupation of Manchuria in Sept. 1931, Russia and China were still without diplomatic relations, which they resumed on Dec. 12, 1932.

Commissariat of Foreign Affairs and presented the note to Vice Commissar Maxim Litvinov. The vice commissar cavalierly declared that he did not care to receive it. Herbette replied that it was his duty to present it, whereupon Litvinov took the note and tore it up.[31]

The second episode concerned another request by China for action by the United States in support of the Kellogg-Briand Pact. Stimson on December 5, 1929, informed his press conference that he would not answer this Chinese invocation. Three months later the State Department's Far Eastern division drew up a memorandum addressing "future historians examining the records of this period, with a view to an analysis of the effect produced by the Treaty for the Renunciation of War in international relations." Such historians might "find it significant that the United States . . . returned no reply to a request on the part of China . . . It is impossible, of course, to anticipate the interpretation that will, in the future, be placed upon the absence of a reply . . . The truth seems to be that, owing to the lack of machinery or of established procedure under the Treaty for the Renunciation of War, there appear to be no further 'necessary and appropriate measures' to be adopted . . ." [32] Undersecretary Cotton in March 1930 cabled the American minister in China suggesting an acknowledgment of the Chinese note "for purposes of the record." [33]

4

As for the true record of Stimson's venture in Manchurian diplomacy, his invocation of the Kellogg-Briand Pact, success would seem to have implied that war threatened in Manchuria

31. Memorandum by Stimson of a conversation with Claudel, Dec. 26, 1929, *FR: 1929, 2,* 430. Litvinov did not tear up the American statement, when Ambassador Herbette delivered it on Dec. 3, 1929. There was, in fact, a formal Russian reply, transmitted through Herbette, dated the same day. The reply berated Stimson for presuming to give advice to an unrecognized government. Ibid., pp. 404–6.

32. Memorandum by the Far Eastern division of the State Department, Mar. 8, 1930, 861.77 Chinese Eastern/908.

33. Cotton to Nelson T. Johnson, the new American minister, Mar. 28, 1930, *FR: 1930, 2,* 300.

and that the American secretary of state prevented it. Stimson believed war was imminent on the Manchurian border in 1929. In this he was in error, for neither Russia nor China desired war.

Russia had engaged in military operations along the border, but it is almost certain that the Soviets in 1929 would have gone no further than a punitive operation against the Chinese.[34] Soviet Russia in the latter months of 1929 was about to begin the Second Bolshevik Revolution, the forced collectivization of agriculture. Success or failure of the first five-year plan, the grand scheme for making Soviet Russia an industrial as well as agricultural nation, depended upon this "collectivizing" of agricultural production. Between December 1929 and March 1930 millions of peasants were forced into collectives. Ardent members of the Communist party, sent out from the cities to dragoon the peasantry, pressed the campaign with such savagery that Stalin in March 1930 had to call a temporary halt to the operation, which he did in his famous letter to *Pravda,* "Dizziness from Success." The Soviet government in the autumn of 1929, anticipating at least some of the difficulties involved in collectivization, could hardly have been preparing to prosecute a war in Manchuria.

There were other considerations against war. For one, the internal situation in China in 1929 could not have borne a prolonged and costly conflict. Chiang Kai-shek was encountering severe troubles at home. "By the early autumn of 1929, the clouds of war were rolling up, high and black, across the horizon . . . and Nanking lay in the shadow before the swiftly advancing storm." [35] Chiang's political opponent in South China, Wang Ching-wei, was threatening a new government in Canton, and everywhere in China the "outs" were clamoring to displace the "ins" of Nanking. The warlord Feng Yu-hsiang was in open rebellion in the north. Feng was a redoubtable opponent; the so-

34. "So far as war was concerned, both nations were undoubtedly bluffing. This Mr. Stimson failed to see, although other foreign offices were under no illusions. He believed war to be imminent . . ." William R. Castle, manuscript book on American foreign relations, p. 199. This manuscript is in the personal possession of Mr. Castle, in Washington, D.C.

35. Hollington K. Tong, *Chiang Kai-shek: Soldier and Statesman* (2 vols. London, Hurst and Blackett, 1938), *I,* 284.

called Christian General,[36] crafty, crude, efficient, had one of the best armies in China. The confused process of revolution took only a brief if solemn pause while the body of Dr. Sun Yat-sen was removed from Peking to its final resting place in the mausoleum on Purple Mountain beyond the walls of Nanking. The grand state funeral was held on June 1, 1929. Immediately afterward Chiang went to Peking to bribe the Christian general into cooperation. Feng was to be allocated $3,000,000 silver for payment of his armies, and $200,000 silver to cover expenses of a trip abroad. Feng did not fall for either stratagem then, but late in October, Chiang took the field against Feng, only to suspend the war a month later, presumably because his bribery of Feng then was successful. Meanwhile a contumacious general named Shih Yu-san revolted at Pukow, just across the river from Nanking, after having been purchased only a few months before. This warrior moved so rapidly that he almost took the capital. And early December brought mutinies in Central China.[37]

Soviet Russia was probably responsible for at least some of Chiang Kai-shek's troubles. Russian support of Feng Yu-hsiang in 1929 appears indubitable, although difficult to prove.[38] Feng by 1929 had abandoned Christianity for Communism, and there is some suspicion that the Russian campaign along the Manchurian border in November 1929 may have been devised in part to assist Feng in his conflict with Chiang Kai-shek, by keeping the troops of the Young Marshal, Chang Hsueh-liang, occupied in Manchuria where they could not support Chiang against Feng in China Proper. Chiang Kai-shek had broken with his Chinese and Russian Communist supporters only two years earlier, in 1927,

36. During a temporary conversion to Christianity, Feng had converted his entire army of ten thousand men, baptizing them with a rubber hose. After a trip to Moscow he discarded his Christianity and turned all his men in one stroke into anti-Christians.

37. Harley F. MacNair, *China in Revolution* (Chicago, 1931), pp. 167–76.

38. Curiously, the rifles which the Soviets supplied to Feng's troops bore the trademark of the Remington Arms Company. They had been manufactured in the United States for the Tsarist forces in the first World War, and were taken over by the Bolsheviks after the Revolution of 1917. John B. Powell, *My Twenty-Five Years in China*, p. 172.

and by the latter months of 1929 his regime, struggling for its very existence against the attacks of such individuals as the erstwhile Christian General, suffered a marked decline in power and popularity. The British scholar Arnold Toynbee, then in Manchuria, encountered much popular feeling against the Kuomintang party.[39] The promises of a new era for China, apparently in process of fulfillment when Chiang as the leading disciple of Sun Yat-sen had occupied Peking in 1928, were rapidly disappearing. The dollar bonds of the Nanking government were falling in value, and the government was considering withdrawal of its authorities to the four or five provinces in the vicinity of Nanking where it was certain of its control. To the Soviet government it might have seemed that a good hard push by Russian forces in Manchuria might add enough trouble to the almost overwhelming woes of the Nationalist government to topple the anti-Communist regime in Nanking. Once Chiang Kai-shek's government had been eliminated, a puppet government subservient to Russia could take its place. It was a standard practice of Soviet strategy not to let revolutions develop into nationalist governments, but to result rather in Communist satellites.

It is altogether doubtful if Stimson in Washington realized the complexity of the rivalries in China and Manchuria, much less the practice of Soviet revolutionary strategy. No mere diplomatic note or statement of his could have resolved the Chinese rivalries or frustrated Soviet policy. Nevertheless Stimson felt that his policies in 1929 had been successful in preventing war in the Far East, and later wrote to a friend that the "pressure" of his diplomatic actions, coupled with support obtained from the "cooperative" notes of the powers, was an influence in determining Russia not to push forward to Harbin.[40]

One could argue that Stimson's diplomacy kept intact the principle of the Kellogg Treaty, so that other nations of the world, resorting to force, would have had to calculate the embarrassment of being reminded of a pledge solemnly made and attested. "If the

39. Toynbee, *A Journey to China* (New York, 1931), pp. 251–2.

40. Stimson to Charles P. Howland, Nov. 3, 1930, Stimson MSS deposited in the Yale University Library.

recent events in Manchuria are allowed to pass without notice or protests," Stimson said to a press conference, "the intelligent strength of the public opinion of the world in support of peace cannot but be impaired." [41] Still, as Assistant Secretary Castle later wrote, "There seems little doubt that this . . . move as custodian of the Kellogg Pact was unwise." Castle concluded that Stimson's diplomacy in 1929 "did not enhance the value of the Pact, but tended to make it a little absurd." [42]

It is undoubtedly true that Stimson's appeals through the Kellogg Pact to the moral force of public opinion had proved unsuccessful. Public opinion in China vociferously supported seizure of the C.E.R. Opinion in Russia, although not readily assessable, was controlled by the iron discipline of the dictatorship in defense of traditional Russian policy in the Far East.[43] In Japan public opinion seems to have supported its government's assertion throughout the course of the dispute of Japanese prerogatives in Manchuria.

The policy of Japan in 1929, if Stimson could have understood it, was worthy of his special attention. During the entire C.E.R. affair the "neutrality" of Japan, as observers described it, was disquieting, and there is some evidence that Japan had arrived at a tacit agreement with Soviet Russia. For example, the Japanese refused to transport Chinese troops over the South Manchuria Railway, making more difficult the Chinese military position, and Litvinov in a speech to the Central Commissariat of the U.S.S.R. allusively remarked: "We are glad to observe a notable stabilization of relations with our great Far Eastern neighbor Japan and the mutual loyalty observed by both governments." [44] Ambassador Debuchi in Washington at one point informed Stimson that

41. Press conference of Dec. 7, 1929, Dept. of State press release.

42. William R. Castle, manuscript book on American foreign relations, p. 203.

43. Eugene Lyons in his *Assignment in Utopia* (New York, 1937) has described how the Soviet government kept the Russian people in ignorance of developments in the Manchurian conflict. See Lyons's ch. 16, "The War Nobody Knew," pp. 250–4.

44. John W. Wheeler-Bennett, ed., *Documents on International Affairs: 1929* (London, 1930), p. 213.

Russian armed raids in Manchuria would not go so far south as Changchun, for that would bring the Soviets into the Japanese sphere of influence, and the Tokyo government "would not sit quietly by and see this happen." [45] The American minister in Riga, a well-known listening post close to the Soviet Union, reported the opinion of "some acute observers here" that Japan had determined the entire course of the C.E.R. dispute—that the governments of Japan and Russia had worked hand in glove, Japan setting the time and extent of Soviet military action.[46] It perhaps never will be known whether in 1929 there existed some sort of secret Russo-Japanese entente, similar to that of 1910–12, designed to perpetuate the respective spheres of influence in Manchuria and exclude all foreign interference.[47]

What lesson might the American secretary of state have taken to heart from his diplomatic experience with the tangled estate of the Chinese Eastern Railway in 1929? What conclusion might he have drawn from his diplomacy of invoking the provisions of the Kellogg-Briand Pact against Nationalist China and Soviet Russia?

He had wrought no appreciable change in the course of international relations in the Far East. There was, perhaps, some increase in Soviet Russia's distrust of the United States, although in

45. Memorandum by Assistant Secretary Johnson, Nov. 25, 1929, *FR: 1929*, 2, 349.

46. The minister in Riga, Coleman, to Stimson, Jan. 9, 1930, 861.77 Chinese Eastern/857. Assistant Secretary Castle, acting temporarily as ambassador to Japan, believed that Coleman's dispatch quoted some clever but unfounded speculation. Castle to Stimson, Feb. 27, 1930, 861.77 Chinese Eastern/907.

47. Dr. Hornbeck believed that there was a Russo-Japanese understanding in 1929. Memorandum entitled "Manchuria Situation," Mar. 11, 1932, 793.94/4946.

Nearly thirty years after the dispute of 1929, after the second World War had brought to light many of the secret archives of Japan, there was still no proof of a Russo-Japanese entente in the affair of the Chinese Eastern Railway. No material of any value appeared in the proceedings or exhibits of the Tokyo war crimes trial of 1946–48, although perhaps nothing should have been expected in view of the fact that Soviet Russia was one of the trial's prosecutors. Nor did anything come to light in the Japanese Foreign Office documents microfilmed by the United States Government after the war and placed in the Library of Congress.

the year 1929 this was of no special importance. American diplomacy had not endeared itself to the Nationalist government of China; still, this was only a momentary matter, for the Chinese knew that, year in and year out, their best friend among the Western powers was the United States. The American government had been acting *in loco parentis* to China since announcement of the Hay Open Door notes at the turn of the century, and the time would come after 1929, as it had before, when the United States could be of assistance. Nothing was lost in Chinese-American relations, but precious little was added to any amenity of Russian-American relations by Stimson's Manchurian diplomacy of 1929.

A disturbing aspect of the secretary's diplomatic moves anent the Chinese Eastern Railway was their impulsiveness. Stimson had displayed a tendency to act without consulting his diplomatic colleagues in other countries, a tendency to force them into policies which they themselves deemed unwise or ill-timed, too great a resourcefulness in diplomatic devices which those governments had not been willing to put to a test in calculations of their own interest. Perhaps this marked merely his apprenticeship in diplomacy, and with further experience he would become more circumspect.

Chapter Five: THE RAPIDAN CONFERENCE

Stimson's attempt to settle the Sino-Russian dispute over the Chinese Eastern Railway had been a frustrating experience. Upon entering office he had believed that problems of the Far East or even Europe were no more incapable of settlement than those of Nicaragua and the Philippines. He was certain that international problems were more subject to rational approach than the disputes of backward, colonial peoples clamouring under the irrationalities of their petty nationalisms: international affairs perforce were more manageable than the volcanic animosities of the Nicaraguan generals, Sacasa and Díaz. Not so in the tangled estate of the Chinese Eastern Railway; it did not prove amenable to settlement by a diplomatist who had lost touch with international affairs since the end of the World War. The best of intentions—preservation of peace, respect for the covenants of the Kellogg-Briand Pact—were not enough. Stimson had intervened in the C.E.R. dispute with cavalier unawareness of the historic pitfalls.

Simultaneously the secretary of state and President Hoover proceeded on another campaign where the terrain was more familiar. Stimson and Hoover together, during the first months of the Hoover Administration, prepared for a new international conference on limitation of naval armaments. One of the secretary's most illustrious predecessors in the Department, Charles Evans Hughes, had convened a successful naval conference, and Stimson in 1929 aspired to similar distinction. He trusted that the peaceful climate of world opinion, ensured by the Kellogg Pact, would make straight the way. His chief, President Hoover, was even more attracted to the idea of a new naval conference which, Hoover hoped, would resume the work of limitation of naval arms so auspiciously inaugurated at Washington in 1921–22. Though not a pacifist, the new Quaker president heartily disliked war. Disarmament, he believed, offered "the only effective way to bring militarism under control." [1] Hoover also kept in mind the large expense of naval arms—the replacement cost of an average battleship was fifty million dollars. In his inaugural address he stated that the Kellogg-Briand Pact had set an advanced standard in the relations of the United States to the world; the antiwar treaty, he said, "should pave the way to greater limitation of armament, the offer of which we sincerely extend to the world." [2]

Such were the desires and hopes of Hoover and Stimson in regard to disarmament. In the spring and summer of 1929 the problem was to translate the ideal into the real, to clothe "faith and idealism with action." [3] This involved, before any naval conference could be called, a preliminary agreement on naval limitation with the British government. Washington officials knew that cooperation from the largest naval power of the world was necessary to the success of any naval arms conference. An Anglo-American agreement was therefore worked out in detail during the summer of 1929, and was followed, as a climax to the negotiations, by the Rapidan Conference of October 1929, the famous conference held along the wooded banks of the Rapidan River in the State of Virginia, between President Hoover and his British opposite, Prime Minister Ramsay MacDonald.

1

The idea of disarmament, as we have seen, was much in vogue during the 1920's. A direct legacy of the War, it stemmed from a

1. Herbert Hoover and Hugh Gibson, *The Problems of Lasting Peace* (Garden City, N.Y., Doubleday, Doran, 1942), p. 238.

2. William Starr Myers, ed., *The State Papers and Other Public Writings of Herbert Hoover* (2 vols. Garden City, N.Y., Doubleday, Doran, 1934), *1*, 9.

3. Speech by President Hoover at Arlington on Memorial Day 1929, New York *Times*, May 31, 1929.

belief that armaments had been one of the chief causes of the War and should be limited or reduced, if not abolished. In Great Britain and the United States during the postwar period there was enormous popular sentiment in favor of limiting or reducing naval armaments, the only armaments of any size that the two English-speaking nations possessed after the demobilization of 1919, and the idea of naval disarmament had to be catered to, if not believed in, by all postwar American and British statesmen. Actually, most Anglo-American diplomatists, impressed by the singularly peaceful state of international affairs during the 1920's, did believe in naval disarmament and were sincerely anxious to achieve international agreements on disarmament. Still, statesmen knew that such agreements were not as easy a task as many of their fellow citizens believed.

The history of international efforts toward disarmament had not, until the postwar years, been encouraging.[4] When Tsar Nicholas II of Russia proposed to the great powers the first international conference on disarmament, to meet at The Hague in 1899, the German, Austrian, and French armies were equipping themselves with a new type of field gun, which faced Russia with the necessity of equipping her armies with the new weapon in quantity. For sound reasons of economy Count Witte, the Russian minister of finance, desired to prevent a further drain on the near-bankrupt Russian treasury; he did not have enough money to order the new field guns and also some much-needed new warships, and he wished to concentrate on the latter.[5] Disarmament at The Hague, inspired by this exigency of the Russian treasury,

4. For early efforts at disarmament see Merze Tate, *The Disarmament Illusion: The Movement for a Limitation of Armaments to 1907,* New York, 1942. The later history of disarmament appears in such books as Henry Wilson Harris, *Naval Disarmament,* London, 1930; Benjamin H. Williams, *The United States and Disarmament,* New York, 1931; Rolland A. Chaput, *Disarmament in British Foreign Policy,* London, 1935; Merze Tate, *The United States and Armaments,* Cambridge, Mass., 1948; Pusey, *Charles Evans Hughes, 2;* John Chalmers Vinson, *The Parchment Peace: The United States Senate and the Washington Conference, 1921–22,* Athens, Georgia, 1955.

5. E. J. Dillon, *The Eclipse of Russia* (New York, 1918), pp. 269–78; Thomas K. Ford, "The Genesis of the First Hague Peace Conference," *Political Science Quarterly, 51* (1936), 354–82.

proved a complete fiasco. Nor in following years did it appear more than a dream. An armaments race engrossed all Europe, and as Sir Edward Grey candidly informed the House of Commons in 1907, disarmament at such a moment in world history while possibly serving as an example might just as possibly have invited martyrdom.[6]

Only after the War did disarmament for the first time have any chance of being put into practice. The prospect seemed bright for limitation of both land and naval arms. The Versailles Treaty placed severe restrictions on the army of the new Weimar Republic of Germany, and with destruction of the German fleet at the end of the War it seemed possible that the wartime Allies and Associates, especially the United States and Great Britain, facing no threats from enemy navies anywhere in the world,[7] might prove willing to limit their navies in the interest of disarmament and international peace.

There followed the Washington Naval Conference of 1921–22, held at a highly propitious moment because of the peaceful state of postwar international affairs and the popular insistence on disarmament. The British government, in financial straits after the war, was happy to achieve limitation of battleships and aircraft carriers through a naval conference. So also was the American government, for despite postwar resumption of the great building program set down in the Naval Act of 1916, there was serious doubt that the American people through their congressional representatives would support financially any further expansion of naval power. Then there was a technical naval reason for placing limits on battleships during the conference of 1921–22: the powers would be limiting a category of vessel which in the opinion of at least some naval experts of the time was of doubtful utility in war; during the World War, battleships had not proved especially valuable.[8]

6. E. L. Woodward, *Great Britain and the German Navy* (Oxford, 1935), p. 134.

7. The Japanese navy at this time did not seem to be a real threat to Anglo-American naval supremacy throughout the world.

8. Admiral Sir Herbert Richmond asserted after the war that battleships were not worth their expense. At Jutland both Germany and Britain used

Another reason for the success of the Washington Conference was the special diplomatic arrangement made on that occasion with Japan. The conference sought to stabilize at a level acceptable to the Western naval powers the strength of Japan in the Far Pacific, namely at the level at which their navies had emerged from the War. In return for promises of good behavior the Japanese received superiority of naval strength in their own waters, through a pledge by the United States not to build new fortifications in the island possessions west of Hawaii, and by Britain not to fortify Hong Kong. Japan in the Nine-Power Treaty promised to respect henceforth the sovereignty, independence, and territorial and administrative entity of China, a promise attested and likewise agreed to by France, Britain, the United States, Italy, the Netherlands, China, Portugal, and Belgium. The Japanese government during most of the 1920's, perhaps as a result of these political arrangements, was peaceably disposed.

After the Washington Conference there continued throughout the 1920's the widespread popular interest in disarmament, which reflected itself in a considerable amount of diplomatic activity, although no diplomatic results. Limiting auxiliary naval categories —cruisers, destroyers, submarines—was a far more difficult matter than limiting battleships. The auxiliary categories, especially cruisers, seemed highly useful types of warships, and although Britain and the United States and, to a lesser degree, Japan, France,

---

battleships, but Jutland in a technical sense was an indecisive engagement, and for most of the war the battleships did little but lay up in harbor or make an occasional unimportant coastal sally. Considering the hundreds of millions of dollars gone into their construction, the performance of the monsters of the sea had not lived up to the promise. The historian Arnold Toynbee expressed a growing conviction when at the close of the 1920's he wrote that battleships probably would have no more future than had the *Victory* after Trafalgar. The future, Toynbee believed, lay with cruisers, destroyers, submarines, and airplanes. *Survey of International Affairs: 1929,* p. 21.

Battleships found little employment during the second World War. There were a few actions, such as the *Bismarck-Hood* encounter in 1941, but although Britain and the United States continued to build battleships during the war it was the carrier that became the capital ship of the Anglo-American navies. In the years after 1945 almost all battleships have gone into "mothballs."

and Italy favored an across-the-board limitation, there was difficulty in elaborating its details. President Coolidge proposed a technical naval conference for the summer of 1927 in Geneva, in hope of achieving some agreement on the unlimited categories. Japan, Britain, and the United States attended this Geneva Naval Conference (the French and Italian governments refused to attend because of a political rivalry in Europe).[9] The conference closed after a few weeks of discussion, apparently because technical naval discussion had proceeded nowhere without such accompanying political pourparlers as had occurred at the Washington Conference.

Political discussions looking toward naval disarmament were then taken up by the governments of France and Britain, resulting by the summer of 1928 in a tentative Anglo-French agreement upon a basis for naval limitation which in effect proposed to limit only those classes of auxiliary categories—large cruisers and large submarines—which interested the United States. The sole effect of this ingenious proposal, made under color of the idea of disarmament, would have been to reduce the power of the American navy: large cruisers, capable of sailing long distances without refueling, were essential to a nation such as the United States which, unlike Great Britain and France, possessed few bases located at strategic points around the world; likewise the American navy, with its home base in the Western hemisphere, had need of large, ocean-going submarines. The Anglo-French tentative agreement on disarmament understandably enjoyed slight favor among officials of the American government and quickly disappeared from view. For the remainder of the Coolidge Administration little was accomplished in the way of disarmament. Coolidge was so peevishly irritated at the British and French proposal of 1928, following hard upon the failure of his conference at Geneva, that he could scarcely bear mention of the word "disarmament." This was the status of disarmament when Hoover came to the presidency in 1929.

With inauguration of Hoover the prospect quickly changed.

9. The Mussolini regime during the 1920's was constantly sparring politically with France, hoping thereby to obtain Tunis, Nice, and Corsica.

Ambassador Hugh Gibson, the American representative at the preparatory commission for a world conference on disarmament then being planned by the League of Nations, spoke at Geneva in April 1929 in favor of limitation of naval arms.[10] Hoover on Memorial Day remarked that if the Kellogg Pact were to fulfill its high purpose, the United States and the other nations would have to clothe faith and idealism with action. He was directing his overtures at Great Britain, and Congress barbed his proposals by passing a bill for fifteen heavy cruisers and an aircraft carrier. The Cruiser Bill, if not the Kellogg Pact, most assuredly created a new international atmosphere for naval limitation.

The response of Downing Street was immediate. Prime Minister Stanley Baldwin came out in favor of naval limitation. The Conservative government was putting out additional feelers when it went out of office in early June 1929, but Baldwin's successor as prime minister, the Laborite Ramsay MacDonald, evinced an even stronger desire for disarmament. Hoover had sent an unofficial disarmament emissary to London in the spring of 1929, the Chicago journalist Edward Price Bell, who sounded MacDonald, and on June 4 cabled the president that HAVE AUTHORITY MACDONALD STATE THAT IF YOU INVITE HIM VISIT YOU WASHINGTON CANVASS WHOLE QUESTION BRITISH-AMERICAN RELATIONS HE WILL ACCEPT WITHIN TWENTY FOUR HOURS.[11]

10. For the preparatory commission, and the World Disarmament Conference of 1932–34 see below, pp. 194–214. Hoover had met Gibson in Washington before the inauguration, and together the two men had drafted the Geneva speech. *Memoirs of Herbert Hoover: The Cabinet and the Presidency,* p. 340.

11. 033.4111 MacDonald, Ramsay 1/2. According to the Castle diary for June 5, 1929, Hoover at once forwarded this private cable to the State Department.

The course of Edward Price Bell's unofficial mission to London in 1929 can be traced in the Bell MSS deposited in the Newberry Library in Chicago, the Dawes MSS in the Charles Deering Library of Northwestern University, the archives of the Department of State, and the Stimson MSS. Bell carried no credentials, a fact which considerably hampered his mission. Hoover had met him during a pre-inauguration voyage of good will to Latin America, when Bell was one of the newspapermen accompanying the president-elect. Hoover had not given Bell a "scratch of the pen," but only asked if Bell and his newspaper, the Chicago *Daily News,* could assist in dissipating the ill-feeling be-

Washington now grew cautious at such disarming enthusiasm, and it was decided that matters should first be explored between MacDonald and the new American ambassador to Great Britain, Charles G. Dawes, who at that moment was crossing the Atlantic to take up his post.

2

No American of the 1920's was better known, at home or abroad, than Charles Gates Dawes. When he died in Chicago in 1951 at the age of eighty-five, he for many years had been forgotten; but there had been a time when he was known everywhere. In photographs of the 20's he appears jauntily in a high Hoover collar, a roundish head topped with a shock of black-gray hair parted down the middle; on each side of a wide, straight mouth prominent lean jowls hang down slightly over the collar; there are the rather large Dawes ears, an underslung pipe, and the mussed clothes looking (according to one critical friend) as if they had been purchased at Montgomery Ward's.

Dawes's great-great-grandfather, William Dawes, had helped begin the American Revolution by riding from Boston to Concord with Paul Revere.[12] His father fought as a Union general in 1861–65. Beginning his own career as a small-town lawyer in Lincoln, Nebraska, Charles G. Dawes took an office in the same building as

---

tween the United States and Great Britain (Bell to Charles G. Dawes, June 17, 1929, Dawes MSS). As late as July 10, 1929, Bell's mission was not known to the American embassy in London (the first secretary, Ray Atherton, to Castle, July 10, 1929, 500.A15a3/84). During the London Naval Conference of 1930, Bell remained in the British capital, but Stimson virtually ignored him. Hoover had to write the secretary of state personally advising of Bell's reliability and usefulness (Hoover to Stimson, Feb. 25, 1930, Stimson MSS). There is a detailed account of the Bell mission in George V. Fagan, "Anglo-American Naval Relations, 1927–37," an able doctoral thesis (1954) at the University of Pennsylvania.

12. Perhaps the only ill luck in the history of the Dawes family was when Henry Wadsworth Longfellow in a memorable poem made Revere a historical figure, rather than William Dawes, because "Paul Revere" was a metrical name. Paul R. Leach, *That Man Dawes: The Story of a Man Who Has Placed His Name High among the Great of the World in This Generation because He Ruled His Life by Common Sense* (Chicago, 1930), p. 18.

another obscure lawyer, William Jennings Bryan. The two men occasionally lunched together with the young instructor of cadets at the state college, Lieutenant John J. Pershing.[13] Dawes later left Nebraska for Chicago, and took over and managed McKinley's first presidential campaign in Illinois. At the age of thirty-two he became comptroller of the currency in the McKinley Administration. Later he organized the Central Trust Company of Chicago and made a large fortune. When the United States entered the World War he joined the army and rode to his first army post at Atlanta, Georgia, in a private railway car to take up his important duties as major of engineers. The end of hostilities found him brigadier general in France in charge of all supply of the American Expeditionary Force. After the war he organized the Minute Men of America to search out Communists and assist Attorney General Harry M. Daugherty in deporting them. Off to Europe in 1924, he scaled down German reparations with a new plan of payment. Back in the United States fresh from constructing the Dawes Plan, he ran for vice-president on the Republican ticket with Calvin Coolidge. The next four years he spent presiding over the Senate loudly rebuking senators who wasted too much time talking. Tiring of this, he turned over his duties in 1929 to the new vice-president, Charles Curtis, and jubilantly set out for new activity as Ambassador to the Court of St. James'.

Upon arrival the American ambassador rushed from Southampton to London, presented his credentials to the King, and took the next train for Forres, Scotland, where Prime Minister MacDonald was vacationing. The prime minister, unaccustomed to foreign ambassadors seeking him out in such haste, naturally gathered that

13. Pershing, thirty-five years old when at Lincoln, still a second lieutenant, reportedly broached the subject of a law partnership with Dawes. "I'd try the Army for a while yet," the latter answered. Bascom N. Timmons, *Portrait of an American: Charles G. Dawes* (New York, Holt, 1953), p. 28. Dawes was a charter member of the Lincoln Round Table, a local discussion club, but he and Bryan and Pershing used to hold debates at the "Square Table" in Don Cameron's Restaurant. The cost of lunch—called dinner in those days—was fifteen cents. A rather large supper could be had in the evening for twenty-five cents, which satisfied even the ravenous Bryan. Ibid., p. 25; Leach, *That Man Dawes,* p. 39.

Dawes had something important to say—perhaps that MacDonald could come to visit the United States. Instead Dawes discussed naval affairs in general, and departed.[14]

Meanwhile the American government, as had been somewhat obscurely reflected in the activities of its representative in England, was in no hurry to further negotiations for a naval conference. Hoover and Stimson believed that the ground should be carefully prepared in advance, to block off all possible pitfalls. Price Bell from London cabled that MACDONALD HAS NO INTENTION REOPENING DEBT QUESTION.[15] Assistant Secretary Castle conferred with the Italian ambassador and gave assurance that MacDonald's visit would not be for the purpose of drawing up any Anglo-American agreement on navies "to upset the world as the Anglo-French agreement had upset it some time ago." [16] The French ambassador, Paul Claudel, asked assurance that an Anglo-American agreement would not prejudice France's international position. Claudel feared the results of "amateur diplomacy." A Department officer informed the ambassador that the United States could not object to MacDonald's visit any more than if the premier of France, M. Poincaré, wished to come to the United States. There arose the possibility that the press would expect too much from a journey by the prime minister. Secretary Stimson discussed this problem with the British ambassador, and it was agreed that for the prime minister and the president to settle everything at their meeting "would of course be quite impossible"; Sir Esme Howard

14. The reason which Dawes gives in his diary for the hurried trip to Scotland was that President Hoover had asked him to show MacDonald a speech which he was to make at the Pilgrims' dinner in London. On the ship he had learned that the prime minister was leaving London for a rest and would not return until after June 18, the date Dawes was to speak. "This was the reason for my hurried movements." Charles G. Dawes, *Journal as Ambassador to Great Britain* (New York, Macmillan, 1939), p. 14 (diary entry for June 23, 1929). And again: "This trip [to Scotland] was absolutely necessary. It was in no wise taken for publicity purposes as a few have maintained." Dawes diary, June 23, 1929, manuscript deposited in the Charles Deering Library of Northwestern University.

15. Bell to Hoover, June 8, 1929, 033.4111 MacDonald, Ramsay/2 1/2.

16. Memorandum by Castle of a conversation with the Italian ambassador, Nobile Giacomo de Martino, June 12, 1929, 033.4111 MacDonald, Ramsay/18.

believed that the two executives might announce agreement in principle and leave details for others (this would "take the sting out of the press").[17]

MacDonald in London elaborated carefully his own position. He affirmed that the Kellogg Pact should be a "vital and controlling fact" in Anglo-American relations, a "starting point" in negotiations.[18] This did not mean that disarmament would be drastic and unconditional. The prime minister noted a "tremendous tide of opinion here in favor of agreement," but, he added, the British people would not permit friendship for the United States to leave England exposed to any "mischief-maker" in the rest of the world. The Pact of Paris, MacDonald was certain, had crippled the mischief-makers, but in the transition period public opinion would be "tender" and Britain and America would have to act in a statesmanlike way.[19] (Perhaps in referring to mischief-makers he had in mind Japan; reports already were coming from Tokyo that the Japanese government, anticipating Anglo-American harmony and a new naval conference, had decided to ask for a ratio of 5-5-3.5 in auxiliary ships, as opposed to the 5-5-3 Washington Conference ratio.)[20]

Still, despite most detailed exchanges of views between London

17. Memorandum by Stimson of a conversation with Howard, June 20, 1929, 033.4111 MacDonald, Ramsay/8.

18. MacDonald to Dawes, in Dawes to Stimson, July 9, 1929, *FR: 1929, I*, 140–1.

19. MacDonald to Dawes, in Dawes to Stimson, Aug. 1, 1929, *FR: 1929, I*, 171–4. In similar vein MacDonald on Sept. 23 remarked that everyone in England was anxious to reach an agreement with the United States "on the assumption that there will be no war and no interference in which our fleets are involved. But I am not justified in making the same assumption as regards the rest of the world, and Mr. Kellogg himself used language which justifies that. He referred to the possibilities of wars of defense. I may regret it, but he did it, and if I am to get Parliament to agree to our programs I cannot at the moment overlook that fact." MacDonald to Dawes, in Dawes to Stimson, Sept. 24, 1929, *FR: 1929, I*, 253–6.

20. The Japanese navy minister publicly advocated the new ratio on Aug. 5. Ambassador Matsudaira soon afterward notified Dawes of Japan's desire for an increased ratio. Charles G. Dawes, *Journal as Ambassador*, p. 52 (diary entry for Aug. 12, 1929).

and Washington, the anticipated invitation for MacDonald to visit America did not arrive. In London negotiations became so friendly that it was "Mac" and "Charley," with no visible result. When reporters pressed Dawes for news, he angrily replied that "You newspapermen should mind your own business. Mac will get his invitation when I'm good and ready to give it to him and not before." [21] In Washington the British ambassador remembered the time when Edward VII wished to visit Pope Leo XIII and was afraid to ask for an invitation. In mid-September Sir Esme gave up hope and one day left for Bar Harbor, only to be stopped in New York City and told to return to Washington at once. Certain of an important development, he found another plaintive inquiry from MacDonald as to how best to obtain an invitation. The prime minister himself finally, upon President Hoover's "recommendation," asked to come.[22]

3

Cheering crowds on Broadway gave MacDonald a tumultuous reception when he arrived in the United States on October 4, 1929. Ticker tape swirled down as the prime minister's open car passed through the streets. At City Hall Mayor James J. Walker presented him the freedom of the city. Then the prime minister left for Pennsylvania Station and Washington, and more ceremony.

The train arrived in the late afternoon in the national capital, where welcoming officials and applauding citizens filled the Union Station. A band struck up a sprightly march as the pacifist prime minister strode smilingly through ranks of marines drawn up at attention. At the station's front entrance he heard the exciting boom of field pieces, marshalled on the Capitol plaza. Triumphantly the long procession of official cars moved down Pennsylvania Avenue, around the Treasury Building, past the White

21. Drew Pearson and Constantine Brown, *The American Diplomatic Game* (Garden City, N.Y., Doubleday, Doran, 1935), p. 80. This volume contains a considerable amount of misinformation, but also much "inside" information, on American diplomacy in the late 1920's and early 1930's.

22. Sir Esme Howard, *Theatre of Life* (2 vols. Boston, Little, Brown, 1935–36), 2, 538–40.

House where dwelt the Quaker president, and out to the British embassy where the prime minister spent the night.

After a round of official and social duties MacDonald two days later, on Sunday, October 6, found himself in the rolling hills of Virginia, at the president's camp on the banks of the Rapidan.

Here in the Blue Ridge Mountains, exactly a hundred miles from the White House, lay the Shangri-La of Herbert Hoover. The camp was in itself a little village, a series of log cabins planned by Mrs. Hoover to accommodate twelve to fifteen guests. There was even a town hall where the president met newspapermen and friends not staying at the cabins. In the heat of Washington summers Hoover found the Rapidan a great relief. On the bright Sunday morning in October 1929 when he entertained MacDonald, the two statesmen put on rough outdoor clothes and took a walk, following the headwaters of the Rapidan to what was known as the cascade, a series of little waterfalls about three-quarters of a mile from camp. En route the president showed the prime minister the small dams which guests had helped build. The dams formed sunning pools for mountain trout, and were named after the various builders. Hoover pointed out Newton Dam, Richey Dam, and Akerson Dam, named for his three secretaries. Then there was Stimson Dam; the prime minister chuckled when he heard of the hard work the secretary of state had bestowed on that structure.

It was a beautiful autumn Sunday morning, and the woods stood out brilliantly in a kaleidoscope of color. Hoover especially delighted in the crimson of the sumac. When the two statesmen, alone, reached the Rapidan's little cascade, they sat down on a log to enjoy the scenery. Years later, Hoover recalled that while sitting on the log he and MacDonald "threshed out" the remaining unsettled points on limitation of naval armaments. The Japanese government would go along on limitation, they felt, but they did not believe they could secure an agreement with the governments of France and Italy—which were carrying on an acrimonious politico-military rivalry in Europe.[23] The two statesmen, busily canvassing the prospects of naval disarmament, did not return to camp for mid-day dinner until nearly two o'clock.

23. *Memoirs of Herbert Hoover: The Cabinet and the Presidency*, p. 346.

As for the more official deliberations at the Rapidan Conference, these were summarized in formal memoranda prepared at the time by Stimson, Hoover, and MacDonald.[24] According to MacDonald's account, the conference had five principal topics for discussion: the naval question (i.e. the technical details of limitation of naval armaments); rights and immunities at sea in time of war; British naval stations in the Western Hemisphere; cooperative action for the reinforcement of world peace (amendment of the Kellogg-Briand Pact); and liquor smuggling from Canada into the United States in contravention of the Volstead Act. Liquor smuggling depended on the coöperation of Canada and the support of liquor-thirsty American citizens; neither was forthcoming. Not much was accomplished in respect to technical details of disarmament; these were adjourned for discussion by experts. As for rights and immunities of nations at sea in wartime, this was a grand question which had perplexed peoples, publicists, international lawyers, and their governments since the late Middle Ages; little progress was made at the Rapidan in 1929. The conferees did agree tentatively about British naval stations in the Western Hemisphere, MacDonald consenting to dismantle the fortification and harbor naval facilities of the stations; but this was no victory for Hoover because the stations were of insignificant military value, and after MacDonald returned to England the Admiralty induced him to take back his pledge. (In passing, one should remark that the State Department had itself contemplated dismantling some of the American Atlantic Coast naval yards, in return for British dismantling of bases at Halifax, Bermuda, Jamaica, and Barbados. The reasoning behind this suggestion was devious: if the American navy would dismantle some of the smaller yards, restricting activities to Boston, Newport, New York, and Hampton Roads, this would effect a needed reform in naval economy and, if incorporated in a treaty, might "lend the glamor of high moral principle to a desirable administrative measure.")[25]

The most interesting discussion concerned amending the Kel-

24. See *FR: 1929, 3,* 1–37; *Documents on British Foreign Policy,* 2d ser., *1,* 106–204.

25. Confidential memorandum by the division of Western European affairs, "Public Opinion and Naval Agrement," Oct. 3, 1929, 500.A15a3/250.

logg-Briand Pact. During the summer Stimson had pondered how to strengthen the pact, and had addressed a letter to an authority on the subject, Frank B. Kellogg. It was difficult, the secretary wrote to Kellogg, to put in writing so delicate a subject as the dispute over the Chinese Eastern Railway: experience, he said, had "brought home to me the absolute need of the existence of machinery for conciliation ready at hand." The winner of the Nobel Peace Prize answered without enthusiasm. Any amendment or change of the antiwar treaty, Kellogg opined, would not help.[26] Undeterred, Stimson wrote Hoover on October 1, giving his "first thought" as to a third substantive article to the Kellogg Pact. He had designedly made the suggested article weaker than a previous proposal by Hoover (of which there is no record), but "I think that if adopted it would prove to have very considerable potency for stopping a conflagration." His proposition stipulated investigation by an impartial commission of conciliation, similar to the proposal in July to China and Russia, and not dissimilar to William Jennings Bryan's conciliation or "cooling-off" treaties of 1913–14, never tested.[27]

At an early stage in the proceedings at the Rapidan, Hoover introduced a proposed amendment to the Kellogg Pact similar to Stimson's suggestion of the week before. "I expressed great interest in this proposal," MacDonald wrote privately afterward, "but pointed out that as it stood it would appear to conflict with the Covenant of the League. The matter was discussed at considerable length, but it became clear as the discussion proceeded that

26. Stimson to Kellogg, Aug. 21, 1929, 861.77 Chinese Eastern/333 1/4; Kellogg to Stimson, Aug. 23, 861.77 Chinese Eastern/333 1/2.

27. The text was as follows: "The High Contracting Parties further agree that if there should develop between any of them a controversy which is not satisfactorily settled by diplomacy it shall be investigated by an impartial commission of conciliation, to be selected by the parties to the controversy and upon which commission said parties may be represented, which shall have full power to examine all the facts concerning such controversy and to render to both parties and to make public their conclusions. To this end any of the High Contracting Parties not parties to such a controversy may suggest to them the propriety of the creation of such a commission of conciliation and such suggestion shall not be deemed an unfriendly act." "Proposed Article III for Kellogg-Briand Pact," enclosed in Stimson to Hoover, Oct. 1, 1929, Stimson MSS.

the President's advisers—and especially Mr. Cotton, the Under-Secretary of State—were far from convinced that the people of the United States would be prepared to enter into so far-reaching an engagement at the present time." [28] Nothing came of the idea. According to Stimson's memorandum of the Rapidan conversations,[29] amendment of the pact was decided to be superfluous because the League Council could impose conciliation on League members, and because the United States already had promised to resort to conciliation in the Bryan treaties. These conclusions, perhaps, should have been evident before Stimson broached his suggestion of a third article to the Kellogg Pact, pertaining to conciliation.

What, then, can one say of the deliberations at the Rapidan Conference of October 1929? Did the conference really accomplish anything? Were there any decisions of sufficient importance to justify the expense and trouble of an eight-day meeting between the heads of two great governments?

Certainly, on almost all the special subjects discussed at the Rapidan—a third article to the Kellogg Pact, liquor smuggling, dismantling of British naval stations in the Western Hemisphere, freedom of the seas, technical details of disarmament—there was no agreement between the British and Americans. President Hoover even injected into the conference an audacious proposal that the British sell Bermuda, British Honduras, and Trinidad. "I told him [MacDonald]," Hoover afterward recalled, "I thought we could give them a credit upon the war debt which would go a long way to settle that issue. . . . He did not rise to the idea at all." [30] The final communiqué produced by Hoover and MacDonald at the end of the conference was an obvious straddle of all special problems at issue, and devoted itself to praise of the Kellogg-Briand Pact. "Both our Governments," avowed the two leaders of the English-speaking world, "resolve to accept the Peace

28. Memorandum by MacDonald of conversations with Hoover at the Rapidan, Oct. 4–10, 1929, *Documents on British Foreign Policy,* 2d ser., *1,* 106–16.

29. *FR: 1929, 3,* 3–7.

30. "He even excluded British Honduras although, aside from officials, probably fewer than 1,000 Englishmen got a living out of it. I had a hunch he did not take the payment of the debt very seriously." *Memoirs of Herbert Hoover: The Cabinet and the Presidency,* pp. 345–6.

Pact not only as a declaration of good intentions but as a positive obligation to direct national policy in accordance with its pledge." [31] Secretary Stimson later announced in a public speech that this Hoover-MacDonald pledge at the Rapidan "marked an epoch." [32] The eminent international lawyer John Bassett Moore was rightly moved to inquire how a declaration of the parties to a pledge that they meant to keep it could be said to mark an epoch.[33]

That Anglo-American harmony at the Rapidan, as announced in the communiqué, did not go to any great lengths in practical naval matters became evident in an exchange between Stimson and the columnist David Lawrence shortly after the end of the conference. Lawrence seems to have taken the communiqué literally, when it announced that war between Britain and the United States was "unthinkable" and that "distrusts and suspicions arising from doubts and fears which may have been justified before the Peace Pact must now cease to influence national policy." From this statement and other similar pronouncements he deduced that Great Britain and the United States had in effect agreed to "pool" their navies to maintain the peace of the world. Stimson quickly set Lawrence straight on this matter. During the entire Rapidan conversations, he announced to the press, there was "not a syllable of such a suggestion. The tenor of the conversations was exactly the reverse." The understanding aimed at, during the Rapidan Conference, was a "moral understanding." The influence both nations sought to exert in world affairs was a "moral influence and not a military one." "Nothing could be further away from the truth" than Lawrence's assumption of pooling the two navies. No such idea, Stimson repeated, was broached or discussed.[34]

Even so, the Rapidan Conference, failing in its particulars, succeeded brilliantly in more general matters. One may doubt, in

31. For the communiqué, see *FR: 1929, 3*, 33–5.

32. "The Pact of Paris: Three Years of Development," special supplement to *Foreign Affairs, 11* (1932–33), vi.

33. John Bassett Moore, "An Appeal to Reason," *Foreign Affairs, 11* (1932–33), 550.

34. Press release by the Department of State, Oct. 11, 1929, *FR: 1929, 3*, 35–6.

fact, if the various discussions of technical problems between Hoover and MacDonald were ever really intended to amount to much, but were only accompaniments of a diplomatic visit. For it was the fact of MacDonald's presence in America, rather than any technical diplomatic pourparlers, that made the Rapidan Conference so memorable in the annals of Anglo-American relations. The prime minister addressed the Senate on October 7, 1929, and he brought the emotions of his listeners to a pitch of highest enthusiasm when at one point in his speech, referring to the feeling of Americans that there should be "parity" between their navy and that of Great Britain, he exclaimed: "There can be no war; nay, more: it is absolutely impossible, if you and we do our duty in making the peace pact effective, that any section of our army, whether land, or sea, or air, can ever again come into hostile conflict. Think upon that when we face many of our own problems—problems of jealousy, problems of fear, problems that the young and rising and successful generation put into the hearts of the old generation. They all disappear, and in virtue of the fact that they have disappeared we have met together and we have said 'What is all this bother about parity?' Parity? Take it, without reserve, heaped up and flowing over." [35]

MacDonald's trip left behind an atmosphere of friendliness for Englishmen such as Americans had not known for a long time. It was a diplomatic triumph. The visit of the prime minister eliminated much of the hard anti-British feeling in the United States that went back to the days before the Revolution when Americans were colonials. In a truly cooperative spirit the president of the United States and the prime minister of the Mother Country agreed in October 1929 that their two nations, taking cognizance of the opportunity for limitation of naval armaments that had arisen since the end of the War, would work together toward that great goal.[36]

In the warmth of the MacDonald visit the British government

35. New York *Times*, Oct. 8, 1929.

36. For a general review of relations between the two great English-speaking powers, from earliest times to the present, see the recently published volume by H. C. Allen, *Great Britain and the United States: A History of Anglo-American Relations, 1783–1952* (New York, 1955).

on October 7—the same day the prime minister was addressing the Senate—issued a formal invitation to the governments of Japan, France, and Italy to attend a five-power naval conference early the following year at London. Replies of the invited governments, quickly forthcoming, were favorable.

When MacDonald left New York City on October 12, 1929, for an official visit to Canada and then the voyage back to his own country, he wrote Hoover "a purely personal letter from guest to host to tell you and Mrs. Hoover how vastly well entertained were 'the visiting firemen.' I think and feel," he continued, "that with help of the local brigade—between us but not *entre nous*—we have done something to insure our citizens against conflagrations."

Hoover in reply wrote, in similar vein, that he supposed "the visiting fireman upon return to his engine house will find someone who will contend the job could be better done. You can if necessary," he added, "denounce him upon my authority." [37]

37. Letters of Oct. 12 and Oct. 26, 1929, Myers, *The Foreign Policies of Herbert Hoover,* pp. 65–6.

Chapter Six: THE LONDON NAVAL CONFERENCE

The delegation which Henry L. Stimson led to the London Naval Conference in January 1930 was the largest official mission to leave the United States since the Paris Peace Conference of 1919. The plenipotentiaries, with their large company of secretaries and clerks, left American shores aboard the liner *George Washington*—the same ship Woodrow Wilson had used for the Peace Conference eleven years before. During the voyage Secretary Stimson could hardly have avoided pondering the successes and failures of Wilson's diplomacy at Paris as he searched for analogies and contrasts to his own diplomatic negotiations a decade later. The conference of 1919 had opened with bright hopes; there had followed the quick appearance of European antagonisms, which made agreement between the wartime allies extremely difficult; as the conference went on and on, public attention in Europe and America turned to other problems; finally, in the United States, the Versailles Treaty met defeat by a politically minded Senate. Would a similar train of circumstance accompany the grand new conference on naval disarmament at London? Would European animosities, or the politics of the United States Senate, rise up to defeat Stimson's best efforts?

At least in one respect the secretary of state had profited from the experience of Woodrow Wilson. Stimson and Hoover had chosen a strong delegation, not open to any criticism of being "yes men" or "rubber stamps" of the administration. There were two well-known and respected senators—Joseph T. Robinson of Arkansas, a leading member of the Democratic party, once a supporter of Woodrow Wilson; and David A. Reed of Pennsylvania, an influential Republican senator. Among the other delegates was Dwight W. Morrow, American ambassador to Mexico; and Charles Francis Adams, secretary of the navy and a great-great-grandson of President John Adams. Ambassadors Gibson and Dawes also were delegates. The American delegation to the London Conference was as distinguished a group of men as the United States had sent abroad since the Conference of Ghent in 1815.

The *George Washington* made fairly good time on the crossing, although the voyage was cold and rough, and many of Stimson's party became seasick.[1] The ship dropped anchor at Plymouth on January 17, 1930. From there the official party departed for London aboard a special train.

The naval conference was scheduled to begin four days later, and upon arrival in the British capital Stimson busied himself in settling into a rented estate, Warren House, at Stanmore near London. In the British capital the American delegation took over the fifth and sixth floors of the Ritz and the fourth floor of the Mayfair. There was barely time to get organized when the opening of the conference was at hand.

1

The London Naval Conference held its beginning session on the morning of January 21, 1930, in the brilliantly lighted Royal Gallery of the House of Lords.[2] The Gallery is a magnificent place, one hundred and ten feet long, decorated with statues of English monarchs and murals of such events as the death of Nelson and the meeting of Wellington and Bluecher after Waterloo. No better hall could have been chosen to lend formality to an international conference. There was an increasing buzz of conversation as the distinguished representatives of Great Britain, the United States, Japan, France, and Italy came together.[3] Then, at precisely the appointed hour of eleven o'clock, a sudden silence fell. At the end

1. Stimson to Hoover, Jan. 24, 1930, 500.A15a3/708 1/2.

2. The following account is based on the colorful dispatch by Edwin L. James, London, Jan. 21, 1930, in the New York *Times*, Jan. 22.

3. For a list of the delegates and delegations, see *Proceedings of the London Naval Conference of 1930* (Washington, 1931), pp. 9–18.

of the hall a door opened and through it walked King George V, escorted by his prime minister.

Dressed in a sober frock coat, the monarch looked well, although this was his first public appearance since a long illness. The King's beard was perhaps a little grayer. A bright diamond flashed from the circlet which held his tie. He moved with measured step onto the dais at the end of the gallery, and halted in front of a gilded throne at one end of the delegates' table. Taking from his pocket a crimson-colored spectacle case, slowly placing his glasses on his nose, he received from an attendant the enscrolled copy of his speech, and read it in a strong, well-modulated voice.[4] When the King had finished, he sat on the throne somewhat nervously until the address was translated. Then, bowing in response to bows of greeting, he left the hall, with the same slow measured tread with which he had entered. Three strong men carried the throne from the dais.

Prime Minister MacDonald took the place the King had vacated. Secretary Stimson moved the election of the British prime minister as permanent chairman of the conference. There followed short speeches by the several chief delegates, and adjournment until the following day.[5]

Succeeding plenary meetings took place in St. James' Palace, where once again the delegates of the conference were ringed about by history, with gilded portraits of English nobility looking down upon their deliberations. The departed noble lords might well have wondered what was going on amidst the conference's general

4. The King stood before a silver and gold microphone, which carried his voice into far lands. In America, President Hoover listened from the basement of the White House. Clad in gymnasium clothes, he had called an early meeting of the Medicine Ball Cabinet.

5. At the Washington Conference, Secretary Hughes had startled the delegates by making his proposals during his first speech. This procedure was not followed at London, and by consent of the delegates the opening speeches were perfunctory. Ambassador Dawes feared until the last moment that at least one of the foreign delegates at London would attempt to imitate Hughes' Washington démarche. As he told Stimson, it was impossible to control the delegates, and accidents might therefore happen, since "the reason for the ass's bray, is that the ass is built that way." Dawes diary, Dec. 4, 1929.

confusion and commotion—the throb of the Morse code, the click of typewriters, the amplified voices of the conferees.[6]

The conference appointed committees and subcommittees to consider special technical aspects of naval limitation. Newspapers in Tokyo, Washington, Paris, Berlin, Rome, and lesser capitals announced this heartening news to their readers, many of whom expected great results from the international meeting at London.[7] Popular confidence continued to rise when, early in February, the powers made tentative proposals of naval limitation—the United States on February 6, Britain on February 7, France on the ninth, Japan the thirteenth, Italy the nineteenth.

Meanwhile the various expert subcommittees had set to work on the technical details.

2

Experts and lawyers, Ramsay MacDonald once remarked, made nearly all the reefs in the seas of life upon which men and states foundered.[8] The experts at the London Naval Conference were no exception to MacDonald's rule, and it may be said with something approaching certainty that if the statesmen at the conference had listened closely to and followed without question the advice of the experts, the conference would never have reached any kind of agreement whatsoever. The experts lived on technical controversy, and cared little for political consequences. They were not inclined, most of them, to see merit in the proposals of nations other than their own, and usually united with their foreign confreres on only two points, namely, that there should be neither reduction nor limitation of naval arms.

The invocation of numerical ratios by an anonymous newspaperman at the Washington Conference had been a simple device, seeming to provide a common-sense headline description

6. Harold Nicolson, *Dwight Morrow* (New York, 1935), pp. 361–2.

7. Western Union reported that it had sent 120,000 words from London in press messages, as of Jan. 25, 1930. This excluded messages sent over cables not owned by Western Union, or via wireless. New York *Times*, Jan. 26, 1930.

8. MacDonald to Dawes, Aug. 22, 1929, in Dawes, *Journal as Ambassador to Great Britain*, p. 58.

for proposed fleet strengths while experts translated the ratios into concrete details of ship construction. But at London in 1930, when the Washington ratios were to be extended to all categories of naval vessels, not merely battleships, the experts soon managed to refine the ratios almost out of existence. The problem was as follows: (1) it proved impossible to obtain agreement among experts on the optimum proportions, in naval construction, of such technical naval factors as speed, armor, and guns; (2) without such agreement it would be impossible to measure the relative fighting value of ships; (3) without a technical "yardstick" the ratios were of no value. The matter of a yardstick admittedly was complicated. Many special qualities determined the fighting value of a vessel. For example, guns of a specified caliber if placed in a ship equipped with "bulges"—compartments which could be flooded to increase gun elevation—would shoot as far as guns of a larger caliber. Range thus increased had to be equated with reduced armor-piercing ability of shells from bulged guns. Such calculations kept the experts moderately busy. Then there was infinite debate over the proper measuring of tonnage. And tonnage was an insufficient measure for comparison of vessels, if only because there had also to be considered a ship's age (and should age be computed from the date the keel was laid, or from the date the vessel was completed?). In addition to age, tonnage, and bulges, naval experts could argue heatedly about engines, fuel, torpedo tubes, and batteries. In the larger argument as to which fleet, British or American, was the stronger, debate sometimes rose to such heights that it was suggested that there should be a simple exchange of navies. Unfortunately, the crux of the problem of measuring Anglo-American naval parity, and of measuring or modifying the ratios established at the Washington Conference for the lesser naval powers, was the large element of theory and opinion in comparisons of vessels. The merits of any given type of ship could only be settled by a naval battle, which was (as a member of the American delegation wrote home) "just what we are trying not to have." [9] Even in such a test (which Heaven might forbid), much would depend on the quality of the crews.

9. Memorandum by Pierre Boal to Cotton, Feb. 21, 1930, 500.A15a3/742 1/2.

Nowhere did the theoretical nature of expert discussion appear more clearly than in the controversy, chiefly between British and American experts, over the merits of the 10,000-ton cruiser equipped with 8-inch guns. The Washington Conference had set 10,000 tons as an upper limit on cruiser tonnage, to prevent evasion of the battleship agreement, and also to accommodate the British Admiralty which had in commission several cruisers of the *Hawkins* class displacing about 9,850 tons and carrying 7.5-inch guns. But to the experts of the American navy, this theoretical maximum of 10,000 tons for a cruiser became—by the easy logic that 10,000 tons was the largest possible size—the ideal displacement for all American cruisers. After the close of the Washington Conference, naval architects in the United States began drawing 10,000-ton cruisers, and the first of these, the *Salt Lake City,* went down the ways at Camden in early 1929. At the London Naval Conference, Anglo-American negotiators then had to deal with the impossible problem of ascertaining the number of small British cruisers necessary to equal the twenty-one large cruisers demanded by the United States. It became apparent that because of American preference for large cruisers, the small British cruisers would have to be "discounted," and that this was going to mean a larger total cruiser tonnage for Britain than for the United States, parity being in classes rather than tonnage. The discount arrived at was that a 10,000-ton large cruiser equalled 15,166 tons of small cruisers; the United States could build 30,000 more tons of large cruisers than could Britain, and 50,000 less tons of small cruisers. In calculating this arbitrary discount, and in making further compromises, the American experts fell into sharp disagreement among themselves, and one of the most distinguished of their number, Rear Admiral Hilary Jones, suffered an acute attack of stomach ulcers and had to leave the conference. The chief of naval operations, Admiral William V. Pratt, was willing to settle finally for eighteen large cruisers together with four or five small cruisers, rather than the twenty-one large cruisers originally asked for. Admiral Jones contended that only twenty-one 10,000-ton vessels—no more, no less—would ensure

American parity with Great Britain. He later so testified before the Senate Committee on Foreign Relations.

In the cruiser controversy Admiral Pratt eventually received a measure of vindication. The first four 10,000-ton cruisers launched by the American navy were full of mechanical flaws, each ship cracking its steering gear on the shakedown cruise. It might be recalled here that large cruisers showed poorly in the first notable naval encounter of the second World War. When the *Graf Spee* was assaulted off Montevideo in 1939, it met three British cruisers, one of which was an 8-inch large cruiser. The *Spee* carried 11-inch guns (in a total displacement of 10,000 tons), and during the first few minutes of the fight it put the large British cruiser out of action. The two other cruisers, both 6-inchers, continued the attack and drove the heavier *Spee* into Montevideo Harbor.

In addition to the cruiser controversy at London there were, as mentioned, other equally technical issues, though none so sheerly technical. Most of the experts at London, as we have seen, were quite uninterested in either naval reduction or limitation, and their discussions in committee usually bogged down in technicalities and detail. The experts who met at London in 1930 were, most of them, "old sea dogs," who had watched with enormous pride the fairly recent development of their own national navies. Some of the experts had served on active duty during the entire naval revolution of 1880–1930, and had watched navies change from sail to steam to oil, an epochal transition in the annals of naval warfare. To see the creations of their professional careers destroyed, or a limit placed on further innovation, was more than the old sea dogs could bear. It is understandable that in their professional discussions they resorted to obscurantism. The political leaders of the London Conference were quite right in believing that the path to limitation of armaments did not lie through the expert committees. The political leaders did not understand the finer points of the technical controversies, but on all scores it was easier to turn to "high-level" political discussions. After a few weeks of organization and futile technical exploration, the London Naval Conference did just that.

3

Secretary Stimson realized, soon after the conference opened, that private discussion would prove the most important means of reaching decisions, and during an early formal meeting he hastily scribbled a note to the French premier, André Tardieu:

> My Dear Tardieu
>
> The whole purpose of the appointment of committees is to gain time so that the *real issues* may be settled by *informal* discussion *outside*. I just said the same to Briand.[10]

Because of the work of setting the conference in motion—establishing the committees, getting acquainted with members of the other delegations, attending the first round of ceremonial receptions and dinners—the secretary did not immediately get down to the real business of negotiation, and so it was early February before informal political discussions really got under way. Stimson on February 6 held an interview with Tardieu. The premier during this informal meeting raised the subject of a security pact.

It had been patent to all informed observers as early as October 1929, when the naval conference was first announced, that the statesmen at London would have to face the problem of French security in Europe vis-à-vis Germany. Any disarmament conference, even a meeting called for the purpose of limitation of naval armaments, could not ignore this problem, the central political fact of Europe after the first World War. Ever since its end, French diplomatists had been declaring at international gatherings that for the French nation in the post-Armistice world, disarmament held a special difficulty. Limitation of French armaments on land or sea was possible, they said, only if there were a simultaneous increase of French security, by which they meant conclusion of treaties of political guarantee. Examples of acceptable treaties were the ill-fated Franco-American and Franco-British alliances concluded during the Paris Peace Conference, and the network of French alliance treaties constructed during the early 1920's with Belgium, Poland, and the nations of the Little Entente. Other

10. Note of Jan. 27, 1930, Stimson MSS.

and perhaps less acceptable treaties, security pacts of a more political nature, were the Geneva Protocol of 1924 and the Locarno pacts of 1925. Premier Tardieu at the London Naval Conference, during his first informal political discussion with Secretary Stimson, broached therefore the proposition of a new security arrangement for France. Without such an agreement, as Stimson would discover in subsequent meetings, the French at London would refuse to adhere to any scheme of naval limitation. French abstention would mean Italian abstention (because of the two nations' rivalry over Nice, Corsica, and Tunis the Italians would sign no agreement on naval limitation unless the French signed). The outcome would be a three-power rather than five-power naval treaty.

What sort of security arrangement did the French have in mind? Tardieu remarked to Stimson at the meeting of February 6, 1930, that France as a member of the League of Nations was already under even greater guarantees than the Four-Power Treaty of Washington of 1922—Article 2 of which stipulated for consultation in event of aggression.[11] Tardieu was not interested in another such declaration. The Four-Power Treaty might be very well for the Pacific region, he said, but not for Europe and especially the Mediterranean. "To be effective something more should be granted." The premier was not specific.[12] When Stimson a few days later spoke with Briand, the latter proposed an amendment to the Pact of Paris; Briand claimed to see great possibilities in the antiwar treaty which already had proved so useful in the hostilities between Russia and China. He had been thinking, he said, of a possible amplification of the Kellogg Pact in a form "wholly acceptable to America," but he would discuss his thoughts later.[13] Such were the initial French inquiries to the American delegation.

11. "If the said rights are threatened by the aggressive action of any other Power, the High Contracting Parties shall communicate with one another fully and frankly in order to arrive at an understanding as to the most efficient measures to be taken, jointly or separately, to meet the exigencies of the particular situation."

12. Stimson diary, Feb. 6, 1930.

13. Stimson diary, Feb. 9, and memorandum by Dwight W. Morrow of a conversation between Stimson and Briand, Feb. 10. There are copies of Morrow's numerous contemporary memoranda in the Stimson diary.

From the British, the French received no encouragement when they made similar proposals. When René Massigli of the French delegation at about the same time raised the question of a Mediterranean pact with Robert L. Craigie of the Foreign Office, Craigie unsympathetically recommended that the French diplomatist study the Four-Power Pacific Treaty. "Quite frankly," Craigie said, "the British Government were not anxious to conclude any agreement of this kind." [14] At a meeting on February 13 between the British, French, and American delegations, Tardieu during long discussions of naval figures remarked occasionally that the Kellogg Pact and the Covenant had not yet been brought together, that this would take time, and that France meanwhile possessed no real guarantees. To these suggestions the British foreign secretary, Arthur Henderson, blandly responded that France enjoyed the protection of the Covenant, "even before it was strengthened by the inclusion of the Briand-Kellogg Pact." [15]

In such manner the British, French, and American delegations debated the naval conference's prime political problem: additional security for France. A musically inclined observer might have compared the French security negotiations at London in 1930 to a stately 17th-century passacaglia: there was constant iteration of a ground bass of security, to the accompaniment of a vast and intricate polyphonic superstructure of formulas proposed by the French to make a security pact acceptable to the American and British governments. There were introductory descants—a Mediterranean pact, elaboration of Article 2 of the Four-Power Treaty of Washington, a third article to the Kellogg Pact. There were new and ingenious harmonies, directed at Great Britain: (1) amendment of the Covenant of the League of Nations, so as to bring Article 12 (consultation) into Article 16 (sanctions); [16] (2) a guar-

14. Note by Craigie of a conversation with Massigli, Feb. 13, 1930, *Documents on British Foreign Policy*, 2d ser., *1*, 209–11.

15. Notes by Sir Maurice Hankey of a meeting of the delegations of the United States, France, and Britain, Feb. 13, 1930, *Documents on British Foreign Policy*, 2d ser., *1*, 211–18. Dwight Morrow of the American delegation next day told Massigli that a security pact was no concern of the United States. Memorandum by Morrow of Feb. 14, in Stimson diary.

16. The real purpose of the French in this regard was to conclude bilateral

antee somewhat different from Annex "F" of the five-power Locarno treaty; [17] (3) a declaration for consultation to be written into the preamble of the eventual naval treaty. Aristide Briand, veteran of dozens of international conferences, artfully wove the theme of security into his innumerable private discussions. In pourparlers apropos French security, Briand usually was in good humor, occasionally serious, sometimes whimsical. He seldom tired in his expositions. Once or twice he flew into a rage, for some reason or other, and on one occasion he momentarily went back to Paris in a huff. When the foreign minister gave evidence of becoming difficult, Stimson, MacDonald, or perhaps Dwight Morrow would hurry to the Carlton and humor him.

The American secretary of state began to wish that he were home and away from all this European diplomacy, as the unending theme of French security throbbed through all the political negotiations of the conference. The absorbing interest of his first year and more at the State Department had been naval limitation,[18] and when the climax arrived and the London Conference opened,

---

and multilateral treaties which would remove discussion of sanctions from the League of Nations and make sanctions a matter to be determined among France's wartime allies and associates. This would allow bypassing the stipulations of Article 15, which called for an elaborate and time-consuming inquiry before resort to sanctions under Article 16.

17. The League of Nations Assembly in 1921 had adopted a resolution that in event of international aggression each League member should judge for itself whether the Covenant had been violated and whether it should impose an economic boycott as stipulated in Article 16. Nonetheless, to give additional satisfaction to Germany after conclusion of the Locarno treaties, and in prospect of German entrance into the League, the Locarno powers declared in Annex "F" of the five-power Locarno treaty that although they were not in a position to speak for the League they had no hesitation in stating for themselves that they regarded each League member as "bound to cooperate loyally and effectively in support of the Covenant and in resistance to any act of aggression to an extent which is compatible with its military situation and takes its geographical position into account." Such an interpretation, weakening Article 16, was now, at the London Conference, to be "clarified" by the British government, i.e. the British were to renounce Annex "F". See the lucid discussion in William T. Stone, "The London Naval Conference," *Foreign Policy Reports, 6* (1930–31), 105.

18. *On Active Service,* p. 162.

only to flounder in endless political negotiation, he was ready to call it quits. To his former law partner in New York he wrote that "When I think of the speed with which I galloped through my problems in Nicaragua and the Philippines, I writhe over this situation every day." [19]

Perhaps one of the reasons for the tedious pace of the conference lay not so much in the incessant demands for French security as in the domestic political troubles of MacDonald and Tardieu. Both statesmen headed minority governments, and spent most of their time thinking how they could stay in office. "The result is that MacDonald can see me only at odd intervals during the day, and Tardieu comes over [to England] only on Sundays—a day which unfortunately corresponds to the British institutional week-end. Italy does nothing helpful and Japan is on the other side of the world." [20]

Part of Stimson's despair stemmed also from the rigors of the London social round. The secretary and Mrs. Stimson attended innumerable receptions, dinners, luncheons, at homes, teas, theaters. They "regretted" dozens more. All this social activity piled upon the worry of keeping a large delegation and staff busy and in line, and the daily encounters with correspondents looking for news when there was no news, and the continuingly delicate personal task of keeping in touch, across the Atlantic, with President Hoover.

Still the most difficult problem of the naval conference consisted of meeting, somehow, the security demands of the French. On this vital point it was unfortunate that Stimson during most of the conference was so poorly prepared, and even confused. Years later he would recall that at London he had favored a security pact with France, but knew that the Senate would not consent and that hence it was foolish to talk about it.[21] Actually he did talk about it at London. He did not know what to do about it. Having

19. "Don't worry about what you see in the press. Our conferences are necessarily in secret and the reports in the press are mostly fables." Stimson to George Roberts, Mar. 19, 1930, Stimson MSS.

20. Stimson to George Roberts, Mar. 19, 1930, Stimson MSS.

21. *On Active Service,* p. 170.

listened to French arguments for a month, occasionally warming to them, he told Briand on March 8 that he was not against consultative pacts as such but was against their connection with the naval conference.[22] After Briand on March 20 left for Paris in disgust, announcing the interment of the conference, Stimson said to MacDonald on March 24 that the United States might be willing to agree to consultation if Britain could meet France's security demands. This move, Stimson afterward believed, saved the conference.[23] But while Arthur Henderson was making arrangements to get Briand back to London, the American secretary of state found himself so embarrassed by sensational accounts in French newspapers of an American diplomatic "surrender" that he issued a statement at 1:00 A.M. on March 26 affirming once again that he would sign no consultative pact if it were coupled with naval limitation. Briand returned to London to find nothing in the way of American concessions.[24]

The end to French security negotiations at London came when Ramsay MacDonald, after allowing Henderson to engage in discussions with the French looking toward a bilateral declaration strengthening Article 16 of the Covenant, grew cold to the effort and backed out. As he told Stimson, the cabinet had scaled down Henderson's tentative proposition, and the leaders of the Conservative and Liberal parties would not support any extension of security.[25] In the delicate proposals which passed between the French

22. Stimson diary, Mar. 8. The secretary made a public statement on the eleventh.

23. Stimson to Major General William Lassiter, May 1, 1930, Stimson MSS.

24. Hoover in his memoirs has said that although Stimson urged to the contrary, he instructed his secretary of state to abandon consultation. *Memoirs of Herbert Hoover: The Cabinet and the Presidency*, pp. 348–9. Hoover's views did not at the time seem quite so strong. In a speech before the DAR on Apr. 14, 1930 he said that there was "clear need" for strengthening the Kellogg Pact. Cooper, *American Consultation in World Affairs*, p. 54.

25. Stimson diary, ca. Mar. 26, 1930. Conyers Read, "More Light on the London Naval Treaty of 1930," *Proceedings of the American Philosophical Society, 93* (1949), 290–308, contends that the British prime minister was oscillating between the idealistic pull of Henderson—the old MacDonald of the Geneva Protocol—and the pull of political realities; and that there was emerging in the spring of 1930 the new MacDonald, the MacDonald with an eye to

and British during the London Conference (press reports had it that there were twenty-two different formulas dealing with Article 16 alone), the British were inclined to read a new entente cordiale —and having had one experience where friendship had changed into something approaching a most positive obligation, they did not desire another.[26] A further difficulty to security negotiations with France in 1930 was that MacDonald in his electoral campaign of the previous year had stressed the subservience of the Conservatives to the French. It was with something approaching relief that by the end of March 1930 the prime minister found the Americans willing to abandon entirely the search for a security pact; willing to let Franco-German rivalries take care of themselves; willing to forego all hope of a five-power naval agreement including France and Italy, and to settle instead for the more limited goal of a three-power naval agreement, between Britain, the United States, and Japan.

4

Several months before the opening of the London Naval Conference the Japanese had asked for a ratio of auxiliary ships higher than Japan's Washington battleship ratio. On this matter of 10-10-7, rather than 10-10-6, Japan's representatives at London re-

---

the main chance, already making friends of the Mammon of unrighteousness, the MacDonald who a little over a year later would break with Henderson and his old Labor friends and virtually go over to the Conservatives. This is an interesting thesis, but despite its plausibility it is not quite fair. MacDonald, to be sure, was no great figure during the years of his political decline, which set in quickly after formation of the National Government in August 1931. But he could not have made an arrangement with France at the London Conference even had he wished to, for press and parliamentary opposition plagued his every move.

26. The British attitude toward a security pact with France reflected accurately the soul-searching and voluminous investigation which went on in Britain during the 1920's concerning the catastrophe of 1914. Everyone recalled the obtuse honesty of Sir Edward Grey, and the hopeless anguish of such liberals as Viscount Morley who when their country became caught in the web of military conversation and naval arrangement which followed secretly upon the Anglo-French entente of 1904, could do nothing except resign from the cabinet. No Britisher in the 1920's could forget the entente cordiale.

fused to make any compromise. Tenacity had its reward. The Japanese ambassador at London, Tsuneo Matsudaira, who was a member of the Japanese delegation, met for a long series of conferences with Senator Reed, and the outcome was the so-called Reed-Matsudaira compromise in regard to heavy cruisers, in which Britain and the United States preserved the principle of 10-10-6 in that category of vessel and allowed to Japan the practice of 10-10-7. The United States agreed not to build up to its London-allotted strength of eighteen large cruisers until after 1936. Under the agreed schedule of construction the American navy would possess only fifteen large cruisers on December 31, 1936, with the remaining three under construction. Meanwhile the Japanese, under the agreed schedule, could build up to a total of twelve large cruisers. As of December 1936, Japan would actually have a 72 per cent ratio in heavy cruisers.[27] The Japanese at the London Conference also received outright a 70 per cent ratio in small cruisers and destroyers, and parity in submarines.

One should note in passing that, while the Japanese government accepted without delay the Reed-Matsudaira compromise, conflict within the London delegation and naval circles in Tokyo was much more serious than appeared at the time. The principal Japanese naval representative at London, Admiral Takarabe, agreed to the large-cruiser compromise over the strenuous objection of his technical staff. Upon Takarabe's return to Japan a nationalist fanatic formally presented him with a hara-kiri dagger. In Tokyo at the Navy Ministry and Naval Board argument rose to such a pitch that the chief of the naval general staff, Admiral Kanji Kato, resigned. In the autumn of 1930 a crazed youth assassinated Premier Yuko Hamaguchi because of the premier's role in forcing the reactionary privy council to agree to the London Treaty. The quiescence if not acquiescence of the Japanese navy a year later in

27. If the Japanese-American ratio of heavy cruisers had been calculated cruiser for cruiser—12 Japanese to 15 American—the ratio would have been 80 per cent. The figure of 72 per cent was computed on the basis of tonnage. All the American large cruisers were of 10,000 tons displacement, whereas the Japanese possessed four cruisers of the *Furutaka* class, armed with 8-inch guns but only of 7,100 tons.

the Mukden Incident,[28] despite the fact that the navy generally was a more level-headed service than the Japanese army, occurred partly because of navy pique at the "humiliation" of the London Conference. It is possible to argue that any benefits the Western powers derived from the London Conference were more than balanced by the naval treaty's adverse reception in extremist quarters in Japan.[29]

At the moment, in the early springtime of 1930, all seemed well. The conference met in plenary session on April 14, 1930, to approve formally the agreement reached in the private discussions of the statesmen. This was the first plenary session since February 11. A group of jurists then commenced work on the conference's final instrument, and labored for an entire week, through Good Friday, Saturday, Easter Sunday, and the Bank Holiday. MacDonald went off to Scotland for a small vacation. When Stimson called him up and said he had to be back on Tuesday to sign the treaty, the Scotch statesman irritatedly answered, "The Devil." [30] But he was back in time to sign the London Treaty—the first complete treaty of naval limitation, in all categories of vessels, in the history of the modern world,[31] the (as Arnold Toynbee put it) "great outstanding international success of the year 1930." [32]

The main provisions of the London Naval Treaty were as follows: (1) extension of the capital ship "holiday," established at Washington, until 1936; (2) limitation of tonnage levels for cruisers, destroyers, and submarines, until 1936; (3) an "escalator

28. See below, Ch. 8.

29. The question was one of civil versus military control of the Japanese government, but it "was wrapped shrewdly in a highly emotional patriotic bunting involving the power of the Emperor . . . Since the military high command was directly responsible to the Emperor, it was charged that the politicians had forced a barrier between the Emperor and the high command, taking into their hands powers that did not belong to them." Royal Wald, "The Young Officers Movement in Japan, ca. 1925–1937: Ideology and Actions," doctoral thesis (1949) at the University of California, p. 54.

30. Memorandum of Stimson's press conference, Wed., Apr. 30, 1930, 500.A15a3/790 1/2. MacDonald's answer was off the record.

31. Walter Lippmann, "The London Naval Conference: An American View," *Foreign Affairs, 8* (1929–30), 518.

32. Toynbee, *Survey of International Affairs: 1930,* p. vi.

clause" by which each power received the right to exceed established tonnage levels if in its opinion new construction by other powers affected the requirements of national security (the clause was directed at the intransigent French); (4) a series of regulatory agreements under which the five powers established rules for replacement, scrapping, and conversion of war vessels, and definition of what constituted special and exempt vessels. The treaty allotments were: United States 1,123,000 tons; Britain 1,151,000; Japan 714,000. This amounted in tonnage to 100 for the United States, 102.4 for Britain, and 63.6 for Japan; departures from the scale 10-10-6 indicated variations within categories (Britain, for example, receiving additional tonnage because of her large number of small cruisers). As a gesture to France and Italy, the three great powers in agreement at London drafted the naval treaty so that representatives of the two Continental powers could sign all of the treaty except Part III, which part contained the agreed naval ratios of the United States, Britain, and Japan.[33]

Compared to the pomp of the conference's beginning, the end was a modest occasion. The twenty-second day of April 1930 turned out to be a fine spring day. Brilliant sunshine streamed through the windows of Queen Anne's drawing room in St. James' Palace, playing upon the room's *décor* of crimson and gold, and it seemed a fitting close to the conference's deliberations. The delegates sat around a red-covered horseshoe table. In the center of the table were the interpreters and secretaries, and technical experts at each end. One side of the crowded room contained seats for a hundred newspaper correspondents. Before signing the treaty, the several chief delegates made speeches. Secretary Stimson in his speech restated the American outlook toward disarmament: "we believe

33. Following the conference the French and Italians continued to negotiate, with the British and Americans as interested mediators. Negotiations dragged on for nearly two years, only to fail in January 1932. They marked the fall of Grandi's star at the Foreign Office. Grandi, knowing that the admirals and navy party were systematically blocking his negotiations by insisting on parity with France, did not know that Mussolini himself had turned against him and indeed was beginning to undermine the whole basis of European peace. H. Stuart Hughes, in Gordon Craig and Felix Gilbert, eds., *The Diplomats: 1919–39* (Princeton, 1953), p. 231.

naval limitation of itself increases security, so we look forward in the future to periodically recurring conferences, confident that we shall obtain ever-increasing security with ever-decreasing armament." [34]

The secretary of state signed first, using a special golden pen. The other delegates followed. Thirty-one signatures required fourteen minutes. Briand made a little speech and presented the pen to MacDonald, wittily remarking that although the pen had been collective property, the conference desired MacDonald to make the pen his own private property. In reply the socialist prime minister joked with Briand, saying that he had thought that the foreign minister, once also a socialist, had had the same ideas about property as he. After presentation of the pen, Ambassador Bordonaro of Italy thanked the conference's secretary, Sir Maurice Hankey, for the hospitality at London, and the conference closed.

Ratifying the treaty required several months. In the United States the Senate Foreign Relations Committee held open hearings and engaged in a petty controversy with Hoover and Stimson, requesting all documents bearing on the conference and the treaty, including all confidential correspondence. Hoover refused. The Senate adjourned. The president summoned a special session for July 7. Two weeks thereafter, on July 21, impelled by a combination of conviction and the hot Washington summer, the Senate consented to the treaty, 58 yeas, 9 nays, with a reservation that there were no secret agreements modifying the treaty's provisions. Hoover on July 22, 1930, signed the instrument of ratification. Upon ratification by Japan, Great Britain, and the Dominions and India, the treaty came into force on January 1, 1931.

Stimson's great work during his first year as secretary of state at last was done. What, then, was the significance of the London Conference? What was its contribution to international peace and security in the year 1930 and afterward?

When all was done there seems to have resulted little except a publicizing of the previous agreement for naval parity arrived at by Britain and the United States during the Rapidan Conference. Japan, it is true, accepted in principle a large-cruiser ratio of

34. New York *Times,* Apr. 23, 1930.

10-10-6, but in fact achieved the 10-10-7 ratio which was her announced goal long before the Japanese delegates reached London. This paper victory for Britain and the United States came at the grave cost of an internal crisis in Japan. As for France and Italy, the conference probably worsened their mutual relations, for it emphasized the disparity of their views on political matters. One could conclude that the London meeting was a failure so far as concerned anything really new, and a very pronounced failure in that it aggravated old issues. It gave Japan respite from Anglo-American competition and a head start in the naval race which began in 1935 when the Japanese denounced the treaty and refused compromise at another London Conference. Perhaps the conference of 1930 had a certain moral value, being an affirmation of faith in the limiting of armaments. Such affirmation was of more than doubtful utility at the beginning of so hectic a decade as the 1930's.

Chapter Seven: THE HOOVER MORATORIUM

With the end of the London Naval Conference the foreign relations of the United States returned for a time to a more leisurely pace. For a number of months no large international events took the attention of American statesmen. American diplomatists abroad busied themselves in conversations at foreign offices and in sending messages to Washington. In the Capital the State Department continued industriously at work, receiving cables and sending answers. All this routine was of no special diplomatic importance. The nations during this period were, in truth, too concerned with domestic economic difficulties to bother with foreign affairs. In the United States the full effect of the stock-market crash was making itself known. The Great Depression rapidly settled over the land. Individuals everywhere, not merely in the United States, found themselves without jobs and savings as a result of the mysterious but omnipresent economic blight that was fastening itself upon the production and commerce of the world.

In these increasingly dismal months after the close of the London Conference it became evident that the Great Depression was no temporary phenomenon of American and European and world history, no ordinary adjustment in what economists were wont to describe as the price mechanism. The price mechanism was not functioning properly at all. Professional economists did not know what was ailing the world's economy. They did not, of course, admit their ignorance, and talked learnedly of disequilibriums and marginal productivity and capital accumulation and disaccumulation; but to anyone who collated the various pronouncements by the men of scholarship in economics it became clear that they simply did not know what they were talking about. Even the usual blind reliance which Americans put in the functioning of their specially endowed economy, the trust that somehow the very richness of the United States would carry it through all earthly difficulties, proved misplaced. The American economy was not responding, not rousing itself from what, by the spring of 1931, had been a year and a half of altogether unaccustomed torpor. The Depression was proving to be an economic cataclysm—no mere "disturbance" such as statesmen and economists and businessmen had announced at its outset.

The first reaction of people everywhere to the unprecedented rigor of the Depression was a stunned feeling, a sense of dumb confusion, and it is altogether understandable why the usual business of international diplomacy ground to a halt in the midst of this vast economic disaster. After a while, nevertheless, it appeared that despite the general diplomatic détente one special problem of international relations would have to be taken under serious consideration, for this problem was being aggravated to an alarming degree by the Depression. After the stock-market crash war debts had become a major international issue, partly because the various debtor nations began to default their already refunded obligations, partly because the American taxpayer, seeking relief from the levies of his own government, looked abroad to America's debtors, who by paying their recently reduced schedule of installments promptly would decrease the cost of the Government of the United States. It is easy to see now that the "war debts"—they were also largely peace debts, borrowed after the Armistice of November 11, 1918—rested upon precarious conditions of international trade, and that default would likely follow the first large economic upset; but such an observation was difficult at the time, especially when a wish usually was father to the thought: the American people hoped that these greatly curtailed debts could be paid. No politician could remain in office in the United States if he took the opposite side of this question and advocated cancellation of the debts. In a previous chapter we have seen how Secretary of State Stimson wished the war debts written off, and told

President Hoover as much. We have seen that Hoover adamantly refused to adopt any policy toward the debts that looked even obliquely in the direction of cancellation. Hoover knew the temper of the American people in this regard, for he was an elected official of the United States; Secretary Stimson, having received his own office by appointment, could be less sensitive.

Hoover and the American people opposed cancellation. None-theless, by the spring of 1931 a special situation had arisen wherein Hoover could find it possible to advocate a moratorium on war debts, a one-year postponement of the semi-annual payments by the several European debtor nations. Hoover had to choose in the spring of 1931 between a moratorium and a default of the large private loans which American bankers had made to Germany and Austria. Default would force bank liquidations within the United States. It was a choice between evils, and the president reluctantly chose a moratorium.

1

By the spring of 1931 Germany, on the verge of financial in-solvency, had borrowed from foreign sources—in large part American—between two and one-half and three times as much money as she actually had paid out in reparations to the Allies after the beginning of the Dawes Plan of 1924. The reparations, as all informed individuals knew, were in part sent on to the United States as war debt payments, by Britain, France, and other nations. American bankers unfortunately had used the money of their fellow citizens (who, one should add, lent the money willingly enough because of the high German interest rate) to finance both the circular payments, Germany to the Allies to the United States to Germany etc., and much additional German borrowing. When the Germans began to act as if they might default these private loans, the bankers had in their possession a great mass of paper which they could not easily convert into cash to pay depositors when the word got around, and runs began on their cash holdings. The American people had financed an enormous increase in the German standard of living. Germany in the years after the begin-ning of the Dawes Plan was able to carry through a program of re-equipment which enormously raised her industrial productivity, and included an entire remodeling of her iron and steel industry, which had been cut in two by detachment in 1919 of Alsace-Lorraine; by 1929 Germany had attained an output of raw steel only slightly short of the level of 1913.[1]

At least part of the financial jugglery by which this achievement was accomplished, one should add, came at the expense of the Germans themselves in the inflation of the war and immediate postwar years. The cause of the inflation was not, as many people supposed, the Versailles Treaty. Its roots lay in the war years when the German government solved its financial problems the easy way, by bond issues, rather than outright and straight taxation.[2] The inflation, aggravated by the postwar difficulties, sank the mark out of sight by 1923, and conveniently liquidated all the indebtedness of German industry. It is a fine question whether certain interested industrialists in the Ruhr and Rhineland did not encourage the early postwar German governments to inflationary policies. This calculation, if such it was, eventually proved a boomerang when the petty bourgeoisie and rentiers—the classes which had lost their savings in the inflation—turned to Hitler for assistance. But by inflation, and reckless borrowing from foreign sources, German industry during the 1920's waxed strong. And when the Depression arrived, the Germans were ready to default their foreign loans—doubtless no more dishonest an act than inflating domestically-held bonds. It was at first necessary however to move cautiously with the powerful bankers of London, Paris, and New York, and their respective governments.

It would be inaccurate to say that calculation lay behind the acts of leaders of the German government in the early Depression years. The German chancellor, Heinrich Bruening, was an honest man, and so beyond doubt were many if not most of his lieutenants, though there must be some question about Dr. Hjalmar Schacht, who assisted Bruening at many international financial

1. C. R. S. Harris, *Germany's Foreign Indebtedness* (London, 1935), p. 11.

2. Inflation, let it be added, hurt not merely the German middle classes, which invested in bonds during the war, but also nationals of the victorious Allies who held large blocs of German obligations purchased prior to the war.

sessions. Yet behind the honesty of the government as then constituted lay the passions of the first World War, the belief that the Allies had burdened Germany with impossible reparations, and that the motto of all the Allies was the slogan often attributed to the French, *"le Boche payera tout."* Inside the defeated Reich there was a feeling, indeed an adamantine belief, that Germany had paid enough; and it was not difficult to twist such a sentiment into support for repudiation of all international financial obligations, even those freely negotiated, such as the American-held bonds and short-term credits. At the outset of German financial stringency in 1930 it was not necessary, either in government circles or the coteries of the large industrialists, to speak openly of repudiation. Germany had only to present her case to the nations, and it was impossible for a country such as the United States, with a weak banking structure, to ignore German pleas. The United States Government perforce had to assist American bankers so that they would not lose their German collateral.

Further details of the German financial situation need not detain us here. The technical arrangements of the Dawes (1924) and Young (1929) Plans, for example, are not of sufficient pertinence to warrant their explanation. Suffice to say that it was from more than mere politesse that the two schemes to adjust payment of German reparations took the names of American financiers; the United States was vitally interested in Germany's capacity to pay. In accord with a policy established at the close of the war the American government always refused to admit a connection between reparations and war debts, for that would have openly involved Americans in the politics of Continental Europe. The connection was well understood by American bankers and high government officials. There later was much criticism of the United States' refusal to participate officially in the reparations adjustments (Dawes and Young were both without official connection with the government). This seemed a pettifogging and obscurantist approach to international relations. Yet in view of the complexity of the entire reparations question—involving, as it did, so much ill feeling in Europe—it was the better part of prudence for the

American government to keep out, even if this involved some dubious circumlocution.

By early 1931 the German financial situation was precarious in the extreme, and American bankers had deeply committed themselves. Even after the initial shocks of the Depression, some banks —notably the Chase National, and Lee, Higginson and Company —had pumped additional money across the Atlantic chiefly in the form of short-term credits, which though actually the funds of their depositors, did not have to be sold as bonds to an investment-soured public. In the first four months of 1931 there were some signs of improvement in American business, and the prices of industrial common stocks, indicated by the Dow-Jones averages, rose from 181 on December 5, 1930, to 191 on February 21, 1931, but beginning with April the economic and financial position of almost all countries deteriorated rapidly. Simultaneous with an agreement for a customs union between Germany and Austria, announced on March 21, a financial crisis occurred in Vienna. The French government promised help if Austria would abandon the customs union. Presumably because of French pressure, though certainly also because of its own unsound condition, the oldest and largest bank in Austria, the Creditanstalt, came to the verge of collapse on May 11. This bank did about 70 per cent of the country's banking business and controlled more than half the country's industry. There followed in Germany a precipitate flight from the mark, threatening the Reichsbank's reserves of gold and foreign currency. President Hoover for the first time realized the seriousness of this situation when early in May 1931 he conversed with Ambassador Frederic M. Sackett, home on leave from Berlin.[3]

2

Hoover waited until the trend of events in Europe was utterly clear. Almost a month elapsed after the dinner conversation with Ambassador Sackett before he made a definite move. Then early in June he called together Secretaries Stimson and Mellon and

3. *Memoirs of Herbert Hoover: The Great Depression*, pp. 64–5.

Undersecretary of the Treasury Ogden L. Mills, and broached a possible one-year moratorium on all intergovernmental payments, both debts and reparations. Such a moratorium would have the effect of lasting a year and a half, as debt installments already had been paid on June 1.

It was a serious political move, to interfere with payments by the numerous debtor countries to the United States Treasury. Hoover told his press secretary that "This is perhaps the most daring statement I ever thought of issuing." [4] Something, however, had to be done quickly, for the German government on June 3 promulgated a decree over the signature of President von Hindenburg cutting government expenditures, and on June 6 Bruening issued a manifesto to the German people containing such alarming phrases as "the German nation is in a decisive struggle for its future"—phrases which, while meant to stir emotions, were read with alarm outside Germany, increasing the demands of foreign creditors for quick payment.

Hoover undertook to sound congressional opinion on a moratorium. During the long progress of a journey to Springfield, Illinois, and a dedication on return of the Harding memorial at Marion, Ohio, the president met or conversed over the telephone with numerous members of the House and Senate. At Marion he learned that in two weeks (June 1–15) the Reichsbank had lost $150,000,000 in gold out of a total reserve of $600,000,000. From June 10 through June 18 the New York Federal Reserve Bank paid out for account of the Reichsbank more than $82,000,000.[5] In Washington the president's advisers were uncertain of what to do. Ogden Mills wanted to remit all debt payments for two years.[6] Stimson argued vehemently that the moratorium should not be long delayed, that Germany could crack within twenty-four hours.[7]

4. Joslin, *Hoover Off the Record*, p. 91.

5. Mark Sullivan, "President Hoover and the World Depression: The Story of the Moratorium from Official Records," *Saturday Evening Post*, 205 (Mar. 11, 1933), 28.

6. Castle diary, June 12, 1931.

7. Joslin, *Hoover Off the Record*, p. 93. Stimson on the afternoon of June 12 came into his office at the Department for a few minutes and asked Under-

Mellon and Undersecretary of State Castle thought that before the United States took any stand, France should be consulted.[8] Hoover waited, preferring caution and the approval of congressional leaders; and the Bank of England came temporarily to the rescue of Austrian finances, after the French had offered political conditions to the Austrian chancellor in a three-hour ultimatum.[9]

Bringing Congress into the problem invited a premature disclosure of the president's plans; and after an indiscretion by Senator King of Utah the president released his project to the press.[10] There was a preliminary announcement on June 20 and a complete statement the following day. Hoover's announcement, promising an end to the deteriorating international financial situation, was probably the high moment of his presidency. Millions of Americans received the news with acclaim. They felt that Hoover had at last taken the inevitably necessary action. The moratorium was beyond doubt an act of real statesmanship. One of its principal attractions was its simplicity.

The French, not consulted in advance by Hoover and standing to lose the principle of *le Boche payera tout,* were most displeased. The moratorium had been announced on a Saturday, which gave the Paris press time to prepare its Monday editions; on the following Monday it indulged in a field day against the United States. It took more than two weeks to placate France, a fortnight of the

---

secretary Castle if there was anything urgent for him to sign. Castle said there were two or three things, to which the secretary responded, "Then go ahead and sign them. I cannot be disturbed when I am trying to prevent Europe from going bankrupt tomorrow." Castle diary, June 12, 1931.

8. Castle diary, June 19.

9. The French wished the Austrian government to put its finances under trusteeship of the League of Nations, and to give up the proposed Austro-German customs union. Castle diary, June 19, 1931.

10. *Memoirs of Herbert Hoover: The Great Depression,* p. 70. Hoover's press secretary thought that with certain members of Congress the president stood no better chance of having a confidence kept, even if the fate of the nation should depend upon it, than would the pastor of a country church if he told the women's sewing circle that he was about to elope with the blonde choir singer, but did not want them to say anything about it until after the marriage had taken place. Joslin, *Hoover Off the Record,* p. 138.

most delicate negotiation in Paris and hectic discussion in Washington. The expensive transatlantic telephone was employed several times a day—incidentally, the first true diplomatic use of this instrument. Secretary Mellon, having gone to Europe on what he had thought would be a holiday, assisted Ambassador Walter E. Edge in Paris. Because the French telephone system was being revamped, there were only two telephones in service in the embassy, one in Mrs. Edge's bedroom, the other in the concierge's room in the basement; and to these places the seventy-seven-year-old Mellon often went for lengthy conversations. The discussions in Washington were between Hoover, Castle, and Mills—Stimson meanwhile having left on what he, too, thought would be a holiday in Europe. White House conferences were almost continuous. It was said that Ogden Mills threw himself back and forth between the Treasury and the White House, via the underground passage, like an animated shuttle.[11] Castle as acting secretary of state was on the job daily from 9:00 A.M. to 10:00 or 11:00 P.M.[12] Hoover was soon irritated at everyone—Stimson for going off to Europe, Edge and Mellon for taking the French viewpoint, Castle and Mills for occasionally disagreeing with him. Dwight Morrow was at the White House much of the time, attempting to mediate between Hoover and his assistants.

As the Germans sat supinely and the French dawdled, a first-class run began on German banks. The French seemingly were hoping that the German economic situation might deteriorate to such an extent that France could intervene in Germany, as she had sought unsuccessfully to do in Austria, with an offer of assistance conditional upon political concessions. In Paris each point settled between the Americans and the French seemed to shed a pollen which instantly became several more points.[13]

11. Drew Pearson and Robert S. Allen, *More Merry-Go-Round* (New York, 1932), p. 136.

12. Diary, July 1, 1931.

13. Sullivan, "President Hoover and the World Depression: The Story of the Moratorium from Official Records," p. 31. See also Walter E. Edge, *A Jerseyman's Journal: Fifty Years of American Business and Politics* (Princeton, 1948), pp. 191–200.

The crisis came on Sunday, July 5. Hoover had to dash back to the capital in a one-hundred-mile motor trip from his camp at the Rapidan. Tempers flared. Ogden Mills was mad, and sat in Castle's office shouting about Hoover's and Castle's iniquity—that by advising acceptance of French reservations to the moratorium they were ready to throw the world over for a bit of political prestige. Castle worked as well as he could, "shouting back a few insults when Ogden became utterly impossible." The French ambassador, Paul Claudel, came in and listened to a finished memorandum, on the basis of which it was hoped the French might give in. Claudel believed it likely to succeed, and this enraged Mills, who intimated that Claudel did not understand the French mentality. Next day the French replied. Mellon telephoned from Paris at 3:30 P.M., and when he said the French reply "seemed to him satisfactory we thought he had probably gone crazy. But as he read it we saw that it was all right, really a paraphrase of our memorandum of the night before. We almost hugged each other and all—I had sent for Dave Reed—congratulated the President. I telephoned Sackett—got him in five minutes —and he shouted with joy. Then we helped in the preparation of a statement to the press for the President himself to give out. So it was finished and we were a very cheerful and surprised crowd." [14]

Thus on the seventeenth day of negotiation, on July 6, 1931, the French signed in Paris with Ambassador Edge a 35-line agreement.

It was too late to restore confidence. On July 13 the second largest German private bank, the Darmstaedter-und-Nationalbank, closed its doors. Within a few days the whole German banking system was ready to collapse, and only German government intervention and a banking moratorium saved it from complete ruin. When the German banks reopened, and in spite of a joint international credit to the Reichsbank of $100,000,000,[15] it was obvious that huge volumes of foreign short-term credits were practically

14. Castle diary, July 7, 1931. Ogden Mills wrote to a friend this same day that he hoped the United States had now made the world safe for the Germans. Letter to Robert McKay, Mills MSS in the Library of Congress.

15. From the Bank of England, the Bank of France, the Federal Reserve, and the Bank of International Settlements.

frozen—one of the exigencies which the Hoover Moratorium had been expressly designed to avoid. Only stringent exchange control prevented a collapse of the German currency.

3

After the Hoover Moratorium there came two developments, in regard to German private debts and the Allied war debts, which remain to be mentioned. A "standstill" agreement on certain privately held German short-term credits was negotiated in principle at London July 20–22, 1931, and arranged in detail during the following month.[16] A year later in a conference at Lausanne the several debtor nations of the United States put to rest the entire debt-reparation problem.

The standstill conference of July 1931 met at the request of Hoover, who at the outset of the additional German difficulties after the moratorium had felt that German financial distress was a European problem. He soon discovered, to his dismay, that American bank holdings in Central Europe probably exceeded 1.7 billion dollars, and that many of these holdings were in flimsy "bank acceptances," sixty- and ninety-day paper without any collateral. Although the ordinary necessities of international trade—the need, in trade, for short-date loans to finance the movement of goods in and out of a country—justified some of these acceptances, many were simply "kited" bills. The kiting was on a gigantic scale. It was part of the shaky "financing" of German prosperity in the latter 1920's. Hoover upon discovering the size of this operation was appalled. As he afterward described his feelings, "I don't know that I have ever received a worse shock." The new bank runs in Germany threatened the security of all banks in the United States holding these German bank acceptances. The new German

16. As subsequent pages will explain, the six-month standstill agreement commencing Sept. 1, 1931, applied to bank acceptances and cash advances. These credits were only a part of the foreign short-term credits invested in Germany. It was to prevent withdrawal of other short-term credits—investments in real property, mortgages, securities of joint-stock companies—that the German government established exchange control in the summer of 1931.

financial distress became not merely a European but also an American problem.[17]

Secretary Stimson, assisted by Secretary Mellon, led the London Conference on these German short-term credits.[18] The head of the Reichsbank, Dr. Hans Luther, began the meetings at London with an audacious proposal of a $1,000,000,000 loan—a strange request after the Allies through the moratorium had just relieved Germany of a $400,000,000 reparation payment! The French at London, knowing that neither the British nor the Americans wished to make further loans to Germany, and knowing further that the United States Government could not make a Treasury loan without consent of Congress (which would not be forthcoming), proposed an international loan of $500,000,000. Nonetheless, the principle of a standstill on bank acceptances was agreed upon after only three days of discussion. The conference appointed a committee of experts to investigate the immediate credit needs of Germany, and this conference, presided over by Albert H. Wiggin of New York, reported in August. Meanwhile a committee of bankers met in Berlin on recommendation of the conference and hastily improvised the details of a standstill agreement. The

17. *Memoirs of Herbert Hoover: The Great Depression,* pp. 73–8. See also Sullivan, "President Hoover and the World Depression: From the German Moratorium to the Fall of the British Pound," *Saturday Evening Post, 205* (Mar. 18, 1933), 79. At the end of July 1931 German debtors owed United States citizens a total of $2,369,750,000. This was 41 per cent of the total German foreign debt. The remainder was distributed roughly as follows: Great Britain, 15 per cent; Netherlands, 14; Switzerland, 12.5. Curiously, although France received the lion's share of reparation payments, Frenchmen held only 4.8 per cent of Germany's foreign debt. Mildred S. Wertheimer, "The Financial Crisis in Germany," *Foreign Policy Reports,* 7 (1931–32), 458, 464.

18. The secretary of state began his negotiations with a minor diplomatic confusion, asserting that the idea of a standstill was an Anglo-American notion, hoping thereby to make it more acceptable to the French who, still angry about the moratorium, might have balked at a new American proposal. Undersecretary Castle in Washington, seeking to give Hoover the credit for the new idea, had meanwhile announced that the standstill was an American proposal. Stimson found himself for a moment in a position of denying that this was so, until authorship of the standstill was cleared up. Castle diary, July 24, 1931.

bankers' committee optimistically negotiated the standstill for a six-month period commencing September 1, 1931. A second standstill, negotiated at the beginning of 1932, extended the agreement until March 1, 1933.[19]

Undoubtedly the moratorium on war debts and reparations and the standstill on private short-term credits in the form of bank acceptances, proved advantageous to the world financial community, even if the scaled-down German obligations eventually went into default despite Hoover's heroic efforts. For the moment the American president had halted a disastrous liquidation. His moves were acts of political courage. Negotiations leading to eventual acceptance of his proposals by the French had been tortuous and nerve-wracking, and the American participants in Paris and Washington showed much skill and persistence. There were nonetheless certain unfortunate special effects of the moratorium which, although not anticipated by the Hoover Administration and in no sense the responsibility of Hoover and his assistants, detracted from the initial achievement. When it became known that not only reparations were frozen but also a large proportion of Germany's private debt, a run began on the Bank of England which by mid-September 1931 led Britain to abandon the gold standard.[20] In the last two weeks of July the Bank of England lost over $150,000,000 in gold. After devaluation of the pound there began a run on the dollar. Japan went off gold in December 1931. A conference for discussing German reparations after expiration of the Hoover Moratorium, called by Britain to meet in Lausanne in January 1932, postponed from month to month, at last met in June 1932. The European powers at Lausanne, after scaling reparations to an insignificant figure, made the adjustment contingent upon similar American reduction of the war debts. The effect of this agreement was to end the debt-reparation complex by a mutual, though not immediate, cancellation of debts and reparations by the European nations. The debtors had combined success-

19. A third standstill came at the beginning of 1933, and opened the way to adjustment of these German debts through an ingenious system of indirect exchange depreciation. See Harris, *Germany's Foreign Indebtedness,* pp. 32 ff.

20. See below, pp. 121–2, 131.

fully against their creditor, as is usually the case. After the November 1932 elections in the United States there came a crucial period prior to the date for resumption of postponed debt payments, December 15, 1932. Seeking to maintain a united front between the outgoing and incoming administrations, Hoover inadvertently engaged the ill will of the inexperienced president-elect, which had fateful consequences during the domestic financial crisis which set in just before the defeated president left office.[21]

One may say that of all the European political issues of the 1920's and early 1930's debts and reparations proved nearly the most fruitless—to the United States especially, but also to all the nations concerned. Clemenceau once described the war debts as a "tradesman's account," [22] and so they were; and so also were reparations, although Clemenceau would never have admitted that. Debts and reparations, like disarmament, were one of the great disturbing factors of European politics of the interwar period, keeping nations at loggerheads when they should have been thinking of how to preserve and ensure peace. Yet if one could have removed the whole controversy from world history by some curious *ex post facto* unhistorical operation, it is probable that the tragic course of European international relations after 1918 would have been much the same.

21. Below, pp. 234–7.

22. Georges Clemenceau, *Grandeur and Misery of Victory* (New York, Harcourt, Brace, 1930), p. 25.

Chapter Eight: THE MUKDEN INCIDENT

Henry L. Stimson in early September 1931 was enjoying his leisure amidst the quiet ease of his Washington mansion, Woodley. He delighted in that historic house with its green-shuttered windows and stately white portico, surrounded by broad lawns and shady trees. By now the house and grounds were ringed about, indeed they were almost enveloped, by the garish ostentation of Washington Northwest in the 20th century. Connecticut Avenue had pushed out from downtown, lined with hulking apartment buildings and modish shops, and stretching westward past Woodley, out to and beyond the slowly rising Washington Cathedral, were the countless rows of little stuccoed chateaux, miniature villas, Tudor "copies," and other indeterminate structures built during and after the War. Woodley stood back alone in the architectural hodgepodge. Stimson on his island could maintain a quiet detachment.

Only one physical discomfort marred the pleasantness of life at Woodley in September 1931. The weather was unduly warm—humid in a way familiar only to persons who have lived in the nation's capital. The secretary could remember no more disagreeable weather since he took office. No longer a young man (Stimson now was nearly sixty-four years of age) he could not stand the heat the way he had twenty years earlier when secretary of war. It seemed as if summer would never end. The humidity lasted for days and weeks into autumn. The thermometer hovered between 94° and 95°, and there was no air conditioning then. Evenings the secretary exhaustedly sat out under the trees, fanning himself, taking comfort only in the knowledge that if Woodley was hot, the rest of the city was hotter.

In such unpleasant weather it was sheer effort to spend time at the Department. The secretary of state did have a long talk with President Hoover on September 8, in the nature of a get-together after Stimson's return in early September from the summer trip to Europe. Discussion centered on domestic economic questions, and international disarmament. While in Europe the secretary had visited the important diplomatic capitals and talked with leading statesmen. A grand World Disarmament Conference would meet in Geneva the next year and preparation was already demanding attention. The Assembly of the League of Nations in early September was considering a "truce" in armaments prior to the convening of the conference—no nation would increase its arms beyond their present level. An invitation would go out to the American government on September 19.

But the most important problem for the United States in early September 1931 was, beyond all doubt, the Great Depression. In August, 158 banks had closed. In September the number was doubling. October would set a record of 522 closings. Stimson on return from Europe had found his New York law partners in deepest gloom. He was himself safe financially, but many of his closest friends were beginning to feel the pinch, and on all sides he found pessimism and worry. People feared for their funds and began to hoard; industrial unemployment increased: estimates of the number of unemployed were beginning to run to between six and ten millions. After a cabinet meeting on September 16, when he saw his chief President Hoover for a few minutes, he found the president "very blue and pessimistic." [1]

The Great Depression by this time had spread to all the countries of Europe and Asia. International trade had fallen off drastically and international balances of payments were shifting in new and strange directions. In early September 1931 there was in full course in Great Britain the extremely serious "flight from the pound" which soon would force the Bank of England off the gold standard. The financial situation in America, already serious, would become worse when the British went off gold, for along with Britain would go other nations with large sterling holdings,

1. Stimson diary, Sept. 16, 1931.

throwing world trade into confusion. Stimson on the evening of September 18, 1931, dined at the White House with the president, Secretary of Commerce Robert P. Lamont, and Secretary of the Treasury Mellon. The subject was the British financial situation. After dinner the company sat around discussing the problem, and decided that nothing could be done. The New York Federal Reserve Bank was completely loaned out; no money stood available through private means; the American government itself could not lend without consent of Congress; Congress was not in session; and if Congress could have been called in time, to suggest lending more money abroad would have opened the door to a flood of domestic relief legislation. Late that night Stimson saw one of the representatives of the British embassy and told him, as considerately as possible, the result of the discussion.[2]

It was at this most inopportune occasion, while Stimson, Hoover, Lamont, and Mellon disconsolately canvassed British and American economic problems in sultry Washington, that across the Pacific a new international conflict arose in Manchuria—this time not between China and Russia, but between China and Japan.

The Mukden Incident, as the Japanese later described the initial outbreak of hostilities, was the most important international event during Stimson's tenure of the State Department. It set in motion a train of difficulties which continued, almost without let-up, until the Hoover Administration departed from office in March 1933. Yet at the outset the incident did not seem of momentous importance. When the news became known in Western capitals that Japanese and Chinese troops had clashed along the line of the South Manchuria Railway a few miles north of Mukden, there was considerable initial worry and concern but no alarm. The affair bore the marks of a typical Oriental dispute: the issues were confused, the disputants irritable, the resort to arms accidental, hasty, ill-considered. It was only after weeks had passed, during which the Japanese army in Manchuria had occupied territory all along the line of the S.M.R. and spread out into Chinese areas far beyond the borders of the railway zone—all the while receiving firm diplomatic support from the Japanese government

2. Ibid., Sept. 18, 1931.

in Tokyo—that Western statesmen finally sensed the existence of not another Oriental incident but the Far Eastern Crisis.

1

It has long been a subject for speculation as to who on the night of September 18, 1931, destroyed a small section of the track on the South Manchuria Railway's main line a few miles north of Mukden.[3] According to contemporary Japanese accounts, Chinese soldiers exploded a bomb, requiring defensive military action by nearby Japanese troops. According to the Chinese, the Japanese merely concocted an incident for the purpose of taking Manchuria. Whatever explosion actually occurred (if one did) it caused slight damage; the Japanese themselves admitted that a short time afterward a southbound express train passed over the rails without difficulty. They never explained how a modern train, running at full speed, could jump what was asserted to be a thirty-one-inch gap in the tracks. As if to confuse things further, the first Japanese proclamation concerning hostilities with the Chinese, as also several other Japanese reports, placed the hour of explosion at 10:30 P.M., when the southbound express had already arrived in Mukden station.[4] Although the alleged explosion occurred on the night of September 18, it was not until the twenty-third that the Japanese would guide foreigners to the spot.[5] The

3. For a map of Manchuria and its railway system, see above, p. 48.

4. Ben Dorfman, "The Manchurian 'Incident' of 1931," *Harper's, 169* (1934), 459. The first official report from Consul General Kyujiro Hayashi to Shidehara, Sept. 19, 1931, placed the time of explosion at 10:30 on the night of Sept. 18. Translation by Yukiko Hollie of microfilmed Japanese Foreign Office archives in the Library of Congress, UD75, reels UD48–UD49, p. 3.

5. Outside the Mukden office of Lieutenant General Shigeru Honjo, commander of the Kwantung Army, the Japanese placed a pile of wreckage—iron plates, bent spikes, sections of shattered cross ties. This was known to foreign correspondents as the "chamber of horrors."

Leon Hubbard Ellis, at the time of the Mukden Incident the second secretary of the American legation in Peking, upon reading a draft of this present chapter commented: "Shortly following the Mukden Incident, several of the assistant military and language attaches at the American legation in Peking were sent to Mukden to investigate the matter of the blowing up of the rail-

Lytton Commission, sent by the League of Nations, investigated the incident in 1932 and could only repeat the Japanese story of a broken rail and fleeing Chinese soldiers—several of whom were shot and killed by the nearby Japanese patrol. The commission referred delicately in its report to "the events" of the night of September 18, and "the so-called incident." It concluded that the subsequent Japanese military operations could not be regarded as legitimate self-defense, though officers on the spot may have thought they acted in self-defense.[6] Writing about the Mukden Incident in the mid-1930's, Henry L. Stimson believed that in the light of what the Japanese did afterward the incident itself so dwindled in importance as to suggest the probability that it never occurred in the first place.[7] The incident's historicity rested uncertainly until after the second World War and the Tokyo war crimes trial, when there emerged for the first time a long and devious story about the internal workings of Japan's domestic and international affairs.

---

way track. Upon their return to Peking they submitted a report to the Legation which stated that the Japanese showed them pieces of rail which they claimed had been blasted from the railway line. These fragments failed to bear the impressed name of the Carnegie Steel works which appeared on all rails still in place at the point of the explosion. The attaches were definitely of the impression that the Japanese had blown up the railway and had produced false evidence for the inspection of the foreign attaches."

6. League of Nations, *Appeal by the Chinese Government: Report of the Commission of Enquiry* (Geneva, 1932), pp. 67–71. See also C. Walter Young, "Legal Aspects of the Lytton Report," *Essays in Political Science in Honor of Westel Woodbury Willoughby* (Baltimore, 1937), pp. 306–38. Lord Lytton believed that the Japanese themselves produced the incident, whereas the French representative on the commission, General Henri Claudel, disagreed. The American minister in The Hague, Laurits S. Swenson, to Stimson, Jan. 20, 1933, 793.94/5851. The American representative on the Lytton Commission, Major General Frank R. McCoy, later told Ambassador Joseph C. Grew in Tokyo: "We are convinced that the Japanese Army planned the whole thing. First they tried the Nakamura case [wherein a Japanese army officer named Nakamura had been murdered by the Chinese], but that did not work as a pretext. So they blew up the railway." Memorandum of a conversation between Grew and McCoy, July 14, 1932, 793.94 Commission/310. See also Grew to Stimson, July 16, 1932, *FR: Japan 1931–41, I,* 93–4.

7. *Far Eastern Crisis,* p. 32.

In the following pages it is impossible to do more than summarize the political and military circumstances in Japan which led to outbreak of the Mukden Incident in September 1931.[8] A patriotic and pseudoscholarly Japanese, Dr. Shumei Okawa, who held a sinecure in the South Manchuria Railway Company, had brought together in the spring of 1931 certain army officers in the War Ministry and general staff in Tokyo and with them elaborated a plot against the Japanese civil government. The hope of Okawa was to overthrow what he deemed a government of politicians, and to replace it with a government of patriots. These patriots in turn would produce a Showa Restoration; just as the Meiji Restoration had given back to the Emperor his rightful political prerogatives, so a Showa Restoration would restore the nation's morals, which had been debauched by the politicians. Okawa's scheme of the spring of 1931 failed. The minister of war, General Kazushige Ugaki, after some hesitation vetoed it. Okawa did not cease to agitate and conspire, and by autumn was busily hatching another plot. One day in August he drank too much sake and told a friend that together with three army colonels he was going to bring about an incident in Mukden. Even so, his was not the mind behind the Mukden Incident, for that affair seems to have been the singular achievement of Colonel Seishiro Itagaki of the headquarters staff of the Kwantung Army, assisted by several fellow officers.[9]

Itagaki, before his final humiliating end in 1948 in Sugamo prison, where the Allies executed him for war crimes, enjoyed a

8. The reader who desires to pursue the matter further may wish to consult my historical note, "The Mukden Incident," *Journal of Modern History*, 27 (1955), 66–72.

9. It seems probable that the incident occurred without direct participation of Okawa, though the latter claimed afterward to have taken part. In 1932 he told Major General Ryukichi Tanaka, an invaluable prosecution witness at the Tokyo trial, that Itagaki and Lieutenant Colonel Kanji Ishihara were the central figures in the Kwantung Army, and that in Japan the leaders were himself, Lieutenant Colonel Kingoro Hashimoto, and Captain Isamu Cho. International Military Tribunal for the Far East, *Proceedings*, p. 1981. The tribunal's proceedings, issued in mimeograph form, are available in a number of large libraries throughout the United States.

brilliant career in the Japanese army. He was war minister in the first Konoye cabinet of 1937, and afterward held posts at Singapore and other places. He typified the caste of military men which ran the affairs of Japan in the 1930's and during the second World War. In 1931 he seems to have had as his goal the introduction to Manchuria of peace, tranquillity, and happiness, through *Kodo,* the Imperial Way, which would lead also to the Showa Restoration in Japan. Itagaki knew in 1931 that if he led Japanese troops in Manchuria on a campaign against the Chinese, he would have immediate support from Tokyo army headquarters, and that if he successfully introduced *Kodo* into Manchuria, he would obtain the praise and approbation of almost all Japanese citizens.

Had he merely desired harmonious relations between his country and China, a more prosaic wish than *Kodo,* he could have ceased his plotting. In early September 1931 a peaceful solution to some of the more troublesome aspects of Sino-Japanese relations in Manchuria lay at hand. For decades, and especially since the advent of the Kuomintang nationalists to power throughout China in 1927–28, there had been friction between Japan and China in Manchuria. Especially in the latter 1920's there had been difficulty, when the Chinese by ingenious financing, much of it at Japanese expense, had tried to establish in Manchuria a system of new railroads, with a projected port at Hulutao, with the purpose of taking business away from and perhaps bankrupting the South Manchuria Railway. This scheme had raised grave trouble between the Chinese and Japanese in Manchuria.[10] But in early September 1931 the Chinese were attempting a settlement. The Japanese minister to China, Mamoru Shigemitsu, and the Chinese finance minister, T. V. Soong, were both planning to leave for Mukden on September 20, 1931 to confer with the warlord (nominally the Kuomintang governor) of Manchuria, the Young Marshal Chang Hsueh-liang. On the afternoon of September 18 preliminary negotiations were in progress in Mukden over the so-called "Nakamura butchery case," one of the current irritants

10. Harry L. Kingman, *Effects of Chinese Nationalism upon Manchurian Railway Developments: 1925–31,* Berkeley, Calif., 1932.

of Sino-Japanese relations.[11] The brightening hopes for a Chinese-Japanese détente in Manchuria came to a sudden end when Colonel Itagaki, in his strategic position as a staff officer of the Kwantung Army, engineered the Mukden Incident that very evening, making possible at once the conquest of Manchuria by the Japanese.

Itagaki's incident went off like clockwork. The competent manner in which Japanese troops moved against the Chinese in 1931 afterward astonished and immensely impressed foreign observers. As the Lytton Report later put it, in a much-quoted phrase, the Kwantung Army attacked the Chinese "with swiftness and precision," despite the fact that Marshal Chang Hsueh-liang's troops enormously outnumbered the Japanese. Chang himself apparently did not know how many troops he possessed, it being customary in Chinese armies to pad the muster rolls so that surplus payroll could go to the officers, but he seems to have had an army of well over 200,000. The Kwantung Army mustered 10,400. Difference in size of the armies was more than compensated by Japanese military efficiency. Illustrations of Chinese military ineptitude in September 1931 were so numerous that it is impossible to describe them all. Typical was the ease with which the Kwantung Army acquired the Chinese code, captured in the barracks at Mukden on the night of September 18–19. Chang Hsueh-liang did not bother to change his cipher, despite the probability of its capture, and for weeks afterward the Japanese read his messages to his followers throughout Manchuria.[12]

Effective leadership of the Chinese troops in Manchuria was from the beginning almost nonexistent. On the night that the Japanese moved upon his Manchurian satrapy, Chang Hsueh-liang was attending the theater in Peking. He had had some warnings of the impending Japanese attack. His close adviser, the Australian

11. Shintaro Nakamura was a Japanese army captain shot by the Chinese in the summer of 1931 while engaged in unauthorized plainclothes reconnaissance of a remote area of Manchuria.

12. Testimony of a staff officer of the Kwantung Army, Tadashi Katakura, IMTFE, *Proceedings*, p. 18947

adventurer and Old China Hand, W. H. Donald, had told him that if the Japanese attacked in Manchuria he would have to be like the bamboo and bend with the wind, since resistance would be impossible. Chang on September 6 had consented to instructions to his commanders to avoid any clash with the Japanese. When during the performance at the theater on the night of September 18 he received an urgent telephone call from Mukden, there was little to do but maintain contact until early the following morning when the operator was heard to say, "I can talk no more. The Japanese have entered my office." [13]

The Young Marshal, watching from Peking the dismal collapse of his armies, may have hoped for help from Chiang Kai-shek's Nationalist troops. Certainly none was forthcoming. Chiang was so hedged about by contumacious provincial generals, not to mention the serious Communist threat in large areas of Central China, that he could not have thought of dispatching Nationalist troops to Manchuria. His principal concern in 1931–33, the years of the Far Eastern Crisis, was not the loss of his nominal Manchurian provinces but the effect it might have on his personal political fortunes. The Nanking Nationalist government, although more stable than any Chinese government since the time of Yuan Shih-kai, constantly teetered on the brink of dissolution, and since reaching Nanking, Chiang had been buying off one rebellious warlord after another. During a few months in later 1930 and early 1931 Nanking seemed to have conquered or purchased all, but by summer Canton was parting company and trouble brewed elsewhere. In the autumn and early winter of 1931 domestic politics filled all the Kuomintang leader's waking hours In his official biography, *Chiang Kai-shek: Soldier and Statesman,*[14] a chapter on this period of his life required the following heads: Rebellion Again Brewing at Canton—Chiang's Resignation Demanded—Canton's Overtures to Japan—Japanese Invasion of Manchuria—China Appeals to League of Nations—Chiang Pleads for National Unity—"Peace Conference" in Shanghai—Southerner

13. Earl Albert Selle, *Donald of China* (New York, Harper, 1948), pp. 267–8

14. Hollington K. Tong, *Chiang Kai-shek: Soldier and Statesman,* 2 vols London, 1938.

Intransigent—Revival of Student Movement—Student Excesses at Nanking—Chiang Suddenly Resigns—Impotence of New Government—Clamor for Generalissimo's Return—Cordial Relations Established with Wang Ching-wei. To the principal figure in this altogether unstable domestic situation the Mukden Incident was a bothersome interruption.

For a short time in mid-September 1931 there developed within the Japanese government some opposition to the Kwantung Army's manufactured incident in Manchuria. The responsible civilian ministers in Tokyo had received almost no warnings of trouble in Manchuria prior to the incident, but afterward they quickly discovered what was going on across the Japan Sea. The consul general in Mukden wired Foreign Minister Shidehara on September 19, 1931 that "the recent incident was wholly an action planned by the army." [15] Shidehara protested to the then war minister, Lieutenant General Jiro Minami, who promised to stop the incident. The civilian members of the cabinet each day inquired of the war minister as to the progress of his efforts. The prime minister, Reijiro Wakatsuki, recalled years later at the war crimes trial that each day in cabinet meeting General Minami promised to restrain his troops. But each day the area of Japanese occupation in Manchuria continued to widen from its starting point at Mukden.

There was an extremely difficult situation existing between the civil and military authorities in Japan in 1931. The civil authorities, as we see in retrospect, should have stood up to their military colleagues in the government. For many reasons they failed to do so: the Great Depression, the ability of military leaders to give their actions the color of patriotism, the corruption and factionalism of Japanese political parties, the antidemocratic nature of Japanese feudal traditions.[16] The civil leaders in Japan, after

15. Consul General Hayashi to Shidehara, urgent top-secret telegram, Sept. 19, 1931, IMTFE, *Proceedings,* pp. 2178–9.

16. See Wald, "The Young Officers Movement in Japan"; Robert A. Scalapino, *Democracy and the Party Movement in Prewar Japan,* Berkeley, Calif., 1953; and especially the able volume by Delmer M. Brown, *Nationalism in Japan,* Berkeley, 1955.

some expostulation, gave in almost completely to the military. Two contemporary diaries of highly placed Japanese political leaders now available to Western students, the diaries of Baron Koichi Kido and Prince Kimmochi Saionji, indicate the feebleness and lack of spirit with which the civil leaders faced their military opponents. Individuals such as Colonel Itagaki easily carried the day.[17]

2

As history unfolded in the Far East it was complex and confusing even to the "insiders"—the principals—not to mention outsiders. Quite naturally, the events of September 18–19 did not at first make much sense to Secretary Stimson in Washington. His mind had been fixed on domestic economic matters and the British financial crisis, and he had meditated a little about the forthcoming World Disarmament Conference scheduled to meet in Geneva early in 1932. The Far East was completely out of his thinking. When he first learned of the Mukden Incident he was annoyed but not worried. "Trouble has flared up again in Manchuria," he dictated to his diary.[18] He decided to tell his press conference that this was a local incident. At the persuasion of his Far Eastern adviser, Hornbeck, he changed his mind. Confronted by the clamor of Department correspondents he changed it again and said he thought it *was* a local incident. He had little information, he added, but unless the Japanese government itself were implicated, the Kellogg-Briand Pact would not be broken.[19]

This was Saturday, September 19. Stimson was leaving that day

17. Kido diary, Sept. 19, 22, Oct. 1, 1931; Saionji-Harada diary, Sept. 23, 24, Oct. 2, 1931. The Library of Congress has made available, through purchase from the Photoduplication Service, microfilms of the complete Saionji-Harada diary (Baron Kumao Harada was Saionji's secretary) and portions of the Kido diary, in Japanese or in rough English translation. There is a published Japanese edition of the Saionji-Harada diary: *Saionji Kō to Seikyoku* (Prince Saionji and the Political Situation), 9 vols. Tokyo, 1950–52.

18. Sept. 19, 1931.

19. Conversation with Hornbeck, Jan. 4, 1952; Stimson diary, Sept. 19, 1931; memorandum of press conference by the Department press officer, Michael J. McDermott, Sept. 19, 1931, *FR: 1931, 3,* 15–16.

for a week end on the Rapidan with Hoover, so he gave instructions to Hornbeck to see the Japanese ambassador the next day. Ambassador Debuchi on Sunday stressed, off the record, the difficult struggle within the Japanese government, and told Hornbeck all he knew of the incident, which was not much.[20] Hornbeck afterward prepared a memorandum for Stimson arguing that the Japanese army had violated the Kellogg Pact, and also that any American protest should not appear as part of traditional American Far Eastern policy but as cooperation with the international movement for world peace.[21]

Stimson at the Rapidan camp was thinking of other matters. During his week end, an enormous relief from the summer heat in Washington, he mixed business and pleasure. Sunday morning the twentieth, while Colonel Itagaki was making history in Manchuria, the secretary relaxed with Allen Klots' little son Binkie and taught him to cast for trout. The rest of the day went in hiking and quiet reading. The secretary had a troubled night; a marine officer routed him out of bed about midnight, bringing a message from the British embassy telling what the different exchanges were going to do next morning when Britain left the gold standard (the British exchange would close, the French were thinking about closing).[22] Only after returning to Washington on Monday, September 21, did he begin to sense the seriousness of the Mukden Incident.

In a diary entry for the twenty-first he noted that the situation had grown worse, though he could not tell how far the Japanese government was implicated. It did look, though, as if the War Ministry was "in pretty deep," and that made a "very serious situation." [23] As the machinery of international diplomacy began to turn at the League of Nations in Geneva, where the League Council happened to be in session, Stimson nonetheless remained uncertain

20. Memorandum by Hornbeck of a conversation with Debuchi, Sept. 20, 1931, 793.94/1888.

21. Memorandum by Hornbeck for Stimson, on "Mukden Incident," Sept. 20, 1931, 793.94/1889.

22. Stimson diary, Sept. 20, 1931.

23. Ibid., Sept. 21.

of his course.[24] He heard from the American minister in China, Nelson Johnson, that the Nanking foreign minister, C. T. Wang, was preparing a note to the American government invoking the Kellogg Pact, as Dr. Wang had done in 1929.[25] The Chinese note arrived immediately, but its content happily did not come up to expectation; the Chinese did not request action under the Kellogg Pact, but only expressed a sentiment that the United States as sponsor of the pact's sacred engagements would be deeply interested in its deliberate violation.[26] Pressure momentarily threatened from another quarter: the American minister in Switzerland, Hugh Wilson, asked in the name of the secretary general of the League of Nations, Sir Eric Drummond, whether Stimson believed the Kellogg Pact was involved in Manchuria. Next day the secretary answered that the United States was watching the Far Eastern situation with concern; he did not say whether he believed the Kellogg Pact involved.

Tuesday, September 22, marked the first cabinet discussion of the Manchurian developments, although whether the cabinet considered Manchurian affairs seriously appears questionable. As Stimson recalled in his diary: "At Cabinet this morning I brought up the Manchurian situation which has now reached a very threatening condition. . . . The President is pretty well occupied with other things now, and this was just an additional chore, but he saw that it represented a major emergency and agreed with my propositions. My problem is to let the Japanese know that we are watching them and at the same time to do it in a way which will help Shidehara, who is on the right side, and not play into the hands of any Nationalist agitators on the other. After I had made my talk on Manchuria the President brought up the question of saving the banks of the country." [27]

Next morning, the twenty-third, was extraordinarily busy. The

24. See below, Ch. 9.

25. A similar appeal would go to the League. Johnson to Stimson, Sept. 21, 1931, 793.94/1811.

26. Hornbeck called this important nuance to Stimson's attention in a memorandum of Sept. 21, 793.94/1903. For the Chinese note, see the Chinese chargé, Yung Kwai, to Stimson, Sept. 21, 1931, *FR: 1931, 3,* 24.

27. Diary, Sept. 22, 1931.

American consul at Geneva, Prentiss Gilbert, cabled that according to the League representatives of the powers the United States was the hope of the world during the grave Far Eastern situation; the powers wished the American government to take action. Hugh Wilson also cabled that Drummond in the most tentative way had suggested that the United States send a representative to sit on the Council (the secretary general thought this the boldest and perhaps most effective maneuver), or else the Council might appoint a small committee with American representation. Then, as Stimson afterward recalled, "Pretty soon I got a long-distance telephone from Geneva. It was a call from Norman Davis, who was there, and he had been dragged into the Manchurian situation and had some rather wild propositions . . ."[28] Stimson, conversing over the transatlantic telephone with Davis and Hugh Wilson (who soon joined the conversation), heard the former say that "I never in my entire life have seen a situation which I think is so loaded with dynamite and where there is such great opportunity to do something perfectly wonderful." The secretary refused to do anything wonderful. He recalled for Davis his earlier experience in the Chinese Eastern Railway dispute, and explained to him the diplomatic virtue of caution.[29]

28. Diary, Sept. 23. At that time Davis was an American member of the organizing committee for the World Economic Conference.

29. Memorandum of a transatlantic telephone conversation between Stimson and Undersecretary Castle and Norman H. Davis and Wilson, Sept. 23, 1931, *FR: 1931, 3*, 43–7. Hugh Wilson wrote to Stimson, Sept. 24, 1931: "It is impossible to give you a picture of the strain under which everybody is working here. This seems an odd remark to make to you who are laboring under a heavier individual responsibility than any of these men here . . . They look on this episode as the test case for the League of Nations and counsels of despair are not lacking which urge that the Council pass a resolution that the League can do nothing about this and ask the United States to take it over. Other rumors are that the League should invite the United States to sit on the Council in spite of our attitude and either force our hand or make us assume responsibility for the future. I do not think these counsels will prevail but a state of extreme nerves and apprehension exists in which anything is possible." 793.94/1944 1/2. Wilson in his memoirs recalls how "I was dragged out of the Assembly to answer the telephone from Washington, I had constant conferences with members of the Council, the press was clamorous." *Diplomat between Wars*, p. 262.

Next day, the twenty-fourth, brought no end to propositions. The secretary, receiving advice from everyone, was getting thoroughly tired of it. Even former Secretary of State Kellogg offered a course of action. In a telegram Kellogg advised: I BELIEVE IT IS THE DUTY OF EVERY COUNTRY PARTY TO PARIS PACT AS WELL AS FOUR POWER PACIFIC TREATY TO MAKE REPRESENTATIONS TO BOTH COUNTRIES. . . . AM SURE YOUR REPRESENTATIONS IN CASE OF THREATENED CONFLICT BETWEEN RUSSIA AND CHINA WERE VERY EFFECTIVE.[30] The League, too, was "nagging" the secretary to know whether he would appoint an American member to an investigating committee. Stimson's mood of irritation emerges clearly from his diary: the League was "just bound to do something . . . they are trying to butt in and do something. So after luncheon I went over and had a talk with the President about it and found that he thoroughly agreed with me in my caution." [31]

3

Thus a week had passed since, in distant Manchuria, Colonel Itagaki and his fellow officers had engineered their incident. Stimson had reacted with extreme care, with much less vigor than he displayed two years before in the Chinese Eastern Railway dispute. During the first week of the far more important Mukden Incident he refused to do anything. Besieged by "nagging" requests, he would not be moved. His military aide, Captain Regnier, told Dr. Hornbeck that "the chief" hated to get into the new Manchurian affair. The secretary, Regnier explained, was like some small boy who early in the spring proposes to go swimming: the boy puts his toe in the water and says, "You know, it's awfully cold." [32]

30. Kellogg to Stimson, Sept. 24, 1931, 793.94/1861. Stimson replied, with care, that he appreciated Kellogg's telegram and that the steps he was taking grew out of the traditional American policy of amicable settlement of international disputes which Kellogg had so effectively furthered. Stimson to Kellogg, Sept. 25, 1931, 793.94/1861.

31. Diary, Sept. 24, 1931.

32. Conversation with Hornbeck, Jan. 4, 1952.

In retrospect Stimson's caution appears quite sensible and levelheaded—much more so, certainly, than the proposals emanating from Geneva and Nanking. The secretary realized that for an "outside" power to interfere in China proper was, to the Japanese, tolerable if annoying, but that for such a power to interfere in Manchuria was insufferable. To indulge in some well-meaning policy such as a committee of investigation organized without consent of Japan would have roused the patriotism of Japanese citizens of all political views, who would see foreign nations attempting to interfere with Japan's life line. In his *Far Eastern Crisis* Stimson argued that history was full of lessons which pointed to the dangers of fanning nationalist sentiment through interference: one hundred and fifty years before, in the French Revolution, intervention by the European allies had proved disastrous.[33] The secretary was not going to have a 20th-century French Revolution in the Orient. He of course did not know the depths of political-military maneuvering in Japan. Certainly he had little understanding in 1931 of the conservative, feudal nature of the Japanese social structure, as it had continued to prevail after the Meiji Restoration despite the so-called modernization of the country. He could not know that ten years later in a second World War the Japanese people would employ Western industrial techniques in an effort to dominate all of Asia. He sensed at the outbreak of the Mukden Incident that the forces of disorder in the Far East were not easy to understand, that it was better not to intervene until he knew what was going on.

A word remains to be said about American intelligence of the Mukden Incident. One might wonder how such a large military operation could have started without warning of some sort to American authorities. Was it necessary for Stimson, and for that matter his Western counterparts, to have been taken by surprise in September 1931?

The then head of the Far Eastern division has said that intelligence was as good as could have been expected.[34] The American minister to China, Nelson Johnson, was an able foreign service

33. *Far Eastern Crisis*, pp. 36–7.
34. Interview with Hornbeck, Jan. 4, 1952.

officer who had served a number of years in China, spoke the language, and only recently had returned to the Far East after his Department assignment as assistant secretary of state; he was one of the better men the Department could have chosen for the Peking legation. Even so, an ineffective intelligence situation did exist in China. Despite the change in the Chinese capital from Peking to Nanking as a result of the Kuomintang victory of 1927–28, embassies and legations of the powers had remained in the comfortable old buildings in the diplomatic quarter of Peking, and conducted business with the Nanking government in a second-hand fashion through the Nanking consulates. Johnson frequently went down to Nanking for extended periods of time, but when he was in Peking the consul general in Nanking had to send telegrams in code to the legation, where they were decoded and answers, if such were necessary, coded and sent back: hardly an efficient situation.

The American embassy in Tokyo likewise was somewhat ineffective, but for a different reason. The ambassador, W. Cameron Forbes, was a good-natured appointee, a man of high native intelligence but leisurely habits, without elementary knowledge of Japanese history and politics. The grandson of Ralph Waldo Emerson, "Cam" Forbes had devoted his life to polo and pleasant living. He eventually received an honorary Phi Beta Kappa key from Harvard, but he would never have earned a real one. This indolent Brahmin might have ably represented his country in less frenzied times, but Forbes was hardly the right man in the Tokyo embassy in 1931. Of all moments he chose September 19, 1931, for sailing back to the United States to make a routine report to the State Department and visit his polo ponies in Wyoming. The head of the Mitsui interests in Japan, Baron Takumo Dan, intimated that he should not sail. Forbes sailed. Despite a hasty return—the round trip required six weeks—he never displayed initiative and imagination in his dispatches and constantly had to be prodded to cable fuller reports.[35] Forbes nonetheless had

35. Comment by Leon Hubbard Ellis, in 1931 second secretary of the legation in Peking: "Cameron Forbes, while Ambassador to Japan, visited Peking. Soon after his arrival Minister Johnson called all career secretaries

capable assistants in the Tokyo embassy; and despite cumbersome communication in China between the legation and Nanking the minister and consuls there were an able group. American representation in the Orient was far better than the United States Government had a right to expect, considering the low remuneration of diplomatic and consular officers and the language barriers of the Japan and China services.

Somehow everyone was caught off guard by the Mukden Incident. And anyway, the American government could not have used a warning had there been one: nothing could have been done, given the temper of the time—bank failures at home, uncertainty abroad because of the collapse of sterling. In such circumstances the Japanese army found it a relatively easy matter to, as Stimson put it, "gallop across the grass." [36]

---

to his office in his residence near the chancery. I was one of the group. Minister Johnson introduced us to Ambassador Forbes and said that the Ambassador wished to hold several conferences with us so that he could learn more of China and so that we could have a clearer picture of Japanese politics. At that first meeting it was all too evident that the Ambassador knew nothing of Chinese history or politics. Aside from four or five names, such as Chiang Kai-shek, Sun Yat-sen, Chang Tso-lin, etc., he was at a complete loss to know whom we were talking about. We constantly had to explain to the Ambassador who such-and-such a political figure was. After the first meeting we never had another. Nevertheless, at that one meeting we learned that Forbes [who once had been governor general in the Philippine Islands] had introduced polo into the Philippines and had spent large sums of money on polo fields in the islands. He was a charming gentleman."

36. To Charles P. Howland, Oct. 27, 1931, Stimson MSS.

Chapter Nine: THE LEAGUE OF NATIONS AND THE LYTTON COMMISSION

The first few days of the Mukden Incident passed in confusion and uncertainty, with neither Secretary of State Stimson nor anyone else knowing quite what to do. No one understood what was going on in Manchuria, and it was impossible to form a policy on the basis of ignorance. Stimson had in mind his experience of two years before with the affair of the Chinese Eastern Railway. Then there was the Great Depression, the decisive fact of foreign relations in the years after 1929; because of the Depression there could be no Western diplomatic démarches in Eastern Asia that would run the risk of war. In view of these difficulties the secretary waited cautiously to see what might happen.

As it became obvious that the incident was not going to receive any control from Tokyo, that the military would be able to exploit the incident, and that the situation was therefore serious, Stimson had to revise his tactics. He was much disturbed by this new state of affairs. The United States since the turn of the 20th century had been elaborating a Far Eastern policy based on the Open Door notes of John Hay, especially the second note, which referred to the preservation of Chinese territorial and administrative entity. In support of this policy the great powers including Japan had made naval and territorial and consultative agreements at the Washington Conference. Japan at the request of the United States had signed the Kellogg-Briand Pact in 1928. The Japanese, taking unilateral action against China after the Mukden Incident, seizing Chinese territory contrary to such solemn international engagements as the Kellogg Pact and the Nine-Power Treaty, struck at some of the basic policies of American diplomacy.

To Stimson there came all sorts of forebodings. He knew that the Japanese government was supporting its troops in Manchuria, making subtle diplomatic excuses to the representatives in Tokyo of the Western powers. He asked himself if it was possible that a great power could let its armed forces get out of control and bring about a situation which might force a second world war only a dozen years after the Great War. Not that the secretary immediately anticipated world war from the conflict in Manchuria, but who could tell the result, once war in any form appeared in the world? Remote conflicts, in out-of-the-way places, could grow into conflagrations. A quarrel between Serbia and Austria had frightful results in 1914. In the 20th century when so many delicate bonds of commerce and finance linked all nations, and when the industrial systems of the nations could so easily get out of kilter —when the world was so interrelated as in 1931—war anywhere and of any size presented immediate and grave possibilities. The year 1931 was not 1831 or 1731, and the capricious freedom of nations in the 19th and 18th centuries to resort to war over small matters, with knowledge that war probably would not cause great national dangers, no longer existed in the 20th century.

Stimson knew by the end of September 1931 that he would have to do something about the Mukden Incident to keep it in hand, and his first thought was to cooperate with the League of Nations. In the autumn of 1931 he trusted that the League would take the Manchurian matter under consideration and do something. In this hope he sent to the mid-October meeting of the League Council at Geneva the American chargé d'affaires in Switzerland, Prentiss Gilbert,[1] with instruction to take part in Council sessions whenever a question arose over invocation of the Kellogg-Briand Pact in the Sino-Japanese dispute. A second effort to work with the League came in mid-November 1931, at another Council meeting, this time in Paris, when the secretary sent over on special mission his ambassador in London, Charles G. Dawes.

1. Minister Wilson had left his post to return to the United States, in connection with the forthcoming World Disarmament Conference.

The real work of preserving international peace, Stimson and his contemporaries believed, would take place within the foreign offices of the powers (for, among other reasons, no power such as Japan would accept advice from so heterogeneous an international body as the League of Nations). Nonetheless it was no little relief to the American secretary of state that he could pass to Geneva the diplomatic initiative in the Manchurian dispute. There is something politic about giving a problem to a committee. In business politics, academic politics, in just about any branch of human activity, committees protect individuals from the onus of unpopular decisions. In the history of the League of Nations during the 1920's the powers on a number of occasions worked out among themselves solutions to disputes and covered those solutions with the prestige of the League. Moreover, the League occasionally had done something on its own. In the State Department and among some members of the European foreign offices in 1931 there existed a vague feeling that the League might succeed in Manchuria where individual nations might falter. How the League was itself to solve the Manchurian dispute no one knew, but the hope remained.

1

In attempting to settle peacefully the Sino-Japanese outbreak, through an American policy of cooperation with the League of Nations, Stimson faced at the outset the problem of enlisting the support of his superior, President Hoover. The rapidly deteriorating economic situation had now seized the complete attention of the president and the members of his administration. For the American government, the days and weeks after the incident of September 18, 1931, were scarcely propitious for international cooperation toward preserving peace in so faraway a place as Manchuria. "The situation in Wall Street," Stimson dictated to his diary on October 1, "has been very bad again for the last two days, and very bad reports are coming again." Three days later the government once more was in receipt of depressing news. The banking situation had grown more difficult than ever, and there was a conference going on that morning at Ogden Mills' house.

Next day was "very bad." The banking situation was "very tough, and we seem to be on the brink of a serious crash." [2] It was about this time that the secretary set down in his diary his firm conviction that American diplomacy in solving the Sino-Japanese dispute should cooperate with the League but prevent Geneva's "leaving any baby on my doorstep." [3] No responsible member of the American government desired initiative for the United States in solving the Sino-Japanese troubles. Hoover had completely "immersed" himself in the domestic crisis, unable to look even for a moment at the Far East. A cabinet discussion on October 9, 1931, provoked a bitter outburst from the president, whose chief concern in regard to the Far Eastern Crisis, Stimson discovered, was not to allow "under any circumstances anybody to deposit that baby on our lap." [4]

Finally Stimson was able to persuade Hoover that the United States had to make some contribution to world peace, and the president gave the secretary permission to authorize one of "our men in Switzerland" to sit with the Council of the League of Nations at its meeting of mid-October 1931.[5] Stimson at once authorized Prentiss Gilbert to take part in Council sessions should there arise any discussion of the Kellogg-Briand Pact.

Gilbert appeared at a session on October 16. The effect of his appearance seems to have been beneficial. The governments of France, Britain, and Italy on October 17 cabled Japan and China invoking the Kellogg Pact. The French government notified the pact's other signatories and adherents, in the hope that they, too, would send notes to the disputants in Manchuria, putting pres-

2. Diary, Oct. 4, 5, 1931.

3. Ibid., Oct. 6. Stimson himself appears to have been the author of this expression. In later years credited to Hoover, the phrase (with variations, such as "dumping" or "depositing") appears in Stimson's diary as early as Oct. 5, 1931.

4. Ibid., Oct. 9. Former Ambassador Nelson T. Johnson, in reading a draft of this present chapter, commented: "President Hoover and his Cabinet were becoming more and more absorbed in the domestic economic situation. . . . they felt very sincerely that it was no time for the Chinese to be shrieking bloody murder under their windows."

5. Ibid., Oct. 10.

sure upon China and Japan so that the two Oriental nations would realize that they had been violating their pledges under the Kellogg Pact.[6]

From the outset of American cooperation with the League, however, it was difficult for Stimson and his harried chief, Hoover, to avoid feeling that the various nations represented at the League Council in Geneva were passing responsibility for the Manchurian matter back to the United States. There was certainly a distinct effort by Council members to draw Prentiss Gilbert into the entire network of League discussion, not merely the subject of the Kellogg-Briand Pact. The Council members magnified out of all proportion Gilbert's presence at their sessions. Rumor began to appear that the United States had joined the League of Nations, and that any action taken by the Council would receive the complete support, even military support, of the United States. Uneasily Stimson wondered whether representation at the Council sessions, some of which were *in camera,* was a wise policy. He instructed Gilbert on October 19 to cease attending meetings, and to take a seat away from the council table, reverting to the status of an observer. After strong objection via a special telephone call from the British foreign secretary, Lord Reading,[7] he agreed that Gilbert could attend one more secret session and one open session. This instruction he in turn amended, after discovering that there were no seats for observers in the Council room, so that Gilbert could continue at the horseshoe table but say nothing. Deeply irritated by what rapidly was becoming a ridiculous situation, Stimson described to his diary how "there came a telephone call from Geneva from Gilbert, bringing up again this infernal question of his seat at the table. Briand seemed to think that if we moved his seat from the table it would upset the whole stability of Europe, and then Gilbert read me a terrible long message from Briand on the subject. . . . finally I decided that so long as Gilbert kept out

6. The American government sent a note to Japan and China on Oct. 20.

7. Arthur Henderson left the MacDonald cabinet with the fall of the Labor government in August 1931. Lord Reading became foreign secretary, and held office until after the October elections, when Sir John Simon took his place.

of secret meetings . . . I would let him go on sitting at the damned table. He is, however, to keep his mouth shut . . ." [8]

The Council, lacking further assistance from Gilbert and Stimson, on October 24, 1931 voted a resolution calling upon the Japanese and Chinese to compose their differences, adjuring Japan to evacuate the occupied Manchurian areas, expressing hope that this might occur before the Council's next meeting on November 16.

Such was the outcome of Stimson's first attempt to cooperate with the League in regard to Manchuria. The presence of Gilbert, despite speculation that surrounded it, had been little more than a gesture, abandoned as soon as it began to appear inconvenient and embarrassing. The Council then went on, under its own power, to pass a resolution calling for withdrawal of the Japanese from the Chinese territory.

The situation in Manchuria continued to deteriorate. The Japanese army moved forward, rather than backward, in its campaign against the Chinese, and apparently was intending to take all Manchuria. The original purpose avowed by the Japanese, that of punitive action against the soldiery of Young Marshal Chang Hsueh-liang, disappeared completely as seizure of Manchurian towns and cities continued apace. Stronger action by the League seemed necessary—although again no one quite knew what to do. Secretary Stimson undertook to continue his diplomacy of supporting the League, and for the meeting of the Council scheduled to begin November 16, 1931, he chose as his representative General Dawes, a more important and forceful person than Prentiss Gilbert.

2

Dawes in many ways was a good choice. Despite private tendencies to clownishness and foolery, he was usually careful in conducting his public duties. His experience in American politics stretched back to the era of William McKinley. His connection with American diplomacy was rather recent, but he rightfully enjoyed the confidence of the Hoover Administration. Unfor-

8. Diary, Oct. 20, 1931.

tunately he knew nothing about Far Eastern problems. Since the outbreak of the Mukden Incident he had had little time or, in view of his diplomatic assignment in Great Britain, reason for learning the intricacies of Sino-Japanese rivalries in the Orient. As ambassador in London he had been worrying over the sterling crisis, and not Manchuria.[9] Dawes approached his new assignment with a knowledge of Far Eastern matters so limited that he would have to devote his first days and possibly weeks—if the task lasted that long—to acquainting himself with the general problems involved, not to mention the particular issues at stake in Manchuria in the dispute of 1931. "Sit down, Dr. Sze," Dawes allegedly said to the Chinese representative in Paris. "I know absolutely nothing about this business, or about diplomacy, either. So sit down and tell me all about it." [10]

Nor was Dawes' ignorance of the matter at hand the only difficulty. The League had gotten itself into trouble with its resolution of October 24, a sort of ultimatum to Japan assuming that the Japanese would evacuate occupied Manchuria by the time the Council met again, November 16. When the Kwantung Army refused to halt military action against Chang Hsueh-liang's troops and withdraw back into the South Manchuria Railway Zone and the Leased Territory of Dairen, the question arose: What was the League going to do about it? To restore League prestige, so unwisely risked at the October meeting of the Council, would be no easy matter.

When the Council opened its meeting at Paris on November 16, 1931, Ambassador Dawes hopefully was on hand, ready to do his best. He established himself in a suite at the Ritz, and to his rooms there came a steady stream of diplomatic callers, seeking advice. The diplomats streamed in and out, and rumor had it that in Paris Dawes had set up a league of his own—that while the Council at the Quai d'Orsay sought to make the Covenant effective, he held court at the Ritz on behalf of the Pact of Paris. His mysterious activities gave him wide press notice in the United States. Reading the daily roster of diplomats who entered and left

9. See *Journal as Ambassador*, pp. 390–410.

10. Pearson and Brown, *The American Diplomatic Game*, p. 321.

his hotel suite, hearing rumors about what went on inside, many Americans assumed that something important was going on. One wishful young college student way out at Whitman College in Walla Walla, Washington wondered whether "a story written about you and the interesting things that happen in your suite at the Ritz would be as entertaining a classic as the biography of Disraeli." [11]

Dawes was busy enough, of that there could be no doubt. The general later wrote that he had little time to leave the Ritz and attend sessions of the Council, even had he desired. His time was too occupied, he said, preparing cables, conversing with diplomats, receiving telephone calls from Hoover and Stimson, giving interviews to journalists, listening to delegations of American peace leaders.[12] At the Ritz he was "virtually a prisoner."

But as for his purpose in Paris, his mission of cooperating with the League Council, the general soon discovered that there was little that he could do. He abandoned his hopes of action by the Council, for as he informed Stimson over the transatlantic telephone, the League was just a town meeting.[13] Everyone wanted to talk. In the heat of argument and counterargument the Chinese representative, Dr. Sao-ke Alfred Sze, had become almost as unyielding as his opposite, Ambassador Kenkichi Yoshizawa, and the Council had reached a stalemate. Dawes did manage to exert some influence over Sze through the Chinese representative's American adviser, Robert E. Olds. A former undersecretary of state at the moment retained by the Chinese government, Olds kept Dawes informed of Sze's dispatches and on occasion acted as intermediary in passing Dawes' ideas to Sze.[14] Olds and Dawes nonetheless had a

11. Robert S. Cathey to Dawes, Dec. 5, 1931, Dawes MSS.

12. ". . . those time wasters—the self-appointed guardians of the peace of the world, whose numbers multiply in times of business depression." *Journal as Ambassador*, p. 431 (diary entry for Dec. 20, 1931).

13. Castle diary, Nov. 21, 1931. Often when the general talked over the telephone he became quite voluble, and Stimson once had to shout at him, "Please Dawes, can't you stop just long enough for me to tell you what I rang you up about." *Loc. cit.*

14. Memorandum of transatlantic telephone conversation between Stimson and Dawes, Nov. 21, 1931, *FR: 1931, 3*, 515–22.

most trying task "keeping the Chinese junk from rocking too much." [15] The Council continued helplessly to meet, adjourn, and meet again, everyone talking and no one capable of proposing a suitable course of action.

Day followed day with interminable conversation and no result. Dawes, still "prisoner of the Ritz," began to squirm ever more impatiently. League diplomacy was not to his taste. As he wrote to Colonel Frank Knox in Chicago, he was having a "most exacting assignment." "If things go right here, they go wrong in Manchuria; and if they go right in Manchuria they often go wrong here." [16] He remembered a line in a poem, pertaining to a certain woman: "She is never twice alike any one time and never once alike twice." [17] Dawes' irritation at the slowness of diplomacy had to find an outlet, and when on one occasion his good friend Tsuneo Matsudaira, the Japanese ambassador in London, came to call, the general momentarily lost his temper. Angered with what he deemed Chinese intransigence at Council meetings, he undiplomatically sputtered to Matsudaira that "the Chinese are altogether too cocky. What you people need to do is to give them a thoroughly good licking to teach them their place and then they will be willing to talk sense." [18]

The tedium of diplomacy at Paris lifted momentarily when the Japanese delegate at the Council session on November 20, 1931, proposed suspension of hostilities in Manchuria and appointment of a neutral investigating commission. Upon word of the Japanese proposal reaching Washington, Secretary Stimson was delighted, and described to his diary this "most wonderful news." [19] But

15. Olds to Nicholas Murray Butler, Feb. 5, 1932, Butler MSS, Low Memorial Library, Columbia University.

16. Dawes to Knox, Dec. 6, 1931, Dawes MSS.

17. Dawes to Owen D. Young, Dec. 6, Dawes MSS.

18. Former Ambassador Nelson T. Johnson commented here: "For once Dawes was speaking his mind. From Shanghai to Washington the Westerner (businessman, lawyer, industrialist) was put out that the Chinese should be disturbing him at this time. Why did the Chinese not submit and let the world alone? If the Japanese would just take the Chinese out and spank them!!!!"

19. Entry of Nov. 20, 1931.

Chinese intransigence appeared at once, for in Paris Dr. Sze balked at the Japanese proposition. When Stimson so advised President Hoover, the latter, enormously irritated, thought Sze an "awful fool," and wanted to know whether there was some way of apprising Sze of the fact. Two days later, according to reports from Dawes, Sze was still "off the reservation," refusing the Japanese proposal.[20]

Perhaps the Japanese, proposing a commission, were only seeking to offset the bad press occasioned by their taking of the strategic North Manchurian town of Tsitsihar on November 19, 1931. The Paris proposal of November 20 acted as a damper on Western resentment. Stimson in Washington noticed that in Manchuria another military operation was quietly under way—that the Kwantung Army was beginning to move again, this time into South Manchuria, toward the important city of Chinchow. The secretary had obtained explicit assurances from Foreign Minister Shidehara that the Japanese government contemplated no such operation. Deeply angered, he warned Ambassador Debuchi about further military action—that if the Japanese army attacked Chinchow it would "upset the whole applecart," and "nobody would trust Japan again." [21] By November 27 Japanese troops had advanced south so rapidly that Stimson went to the White House and asked Hoover to reconsider certain arguments in favor of an embargo, economic sanctions against Japan. The president at

20. Stimson diary, Nov. 21, 23, 1931.

21. Ibid., Nov. 22. In his diary for Nov. 26 he again reported the continuing danger of the Japanese advance. This, he believed, would "upset the applecart . . . It makes me feel that I cannot trust the sons-of-guns now. Their army is as hard-boiled as anything can be. They seem to think that they can go ahead and defy the whole world." On the 27th he received "the startling news . . . that the Japanese Army has picked up its duds and is marching on to Chinchow in direct violation of its superiors in Tokyo. . . . Confidentially, it seems that the Japanese Army is running amuck . . . Everything is now on the knees of the gods . . ."

Ambassador Johnson commented: "Apparently the Japanese authorities had taken an accurate measure of American fears and preoccupations, and were playing them up and down, to suit themselves and their plans."

the moment was unwilling to do so, although when Stimson saw him a few days later he was "not absolutely and to the last resort" against an embargo.[22]

Dawes in Paris kept steadfastly to his hotel, busy with his interviews and conversations. As the general informed Stimson, he did not attempt to get out to see the foreign diplomats, for if he "ran around making a spectacle of himself" it would do no good.[23] At the Quai d'Orsay Palace, where the Council was meeting, lights burned late at night as assistants studied reports and memoranda and *projets* directed toward solution of the Far Eastern dispute. Over the Paris deliberations hung uncertainty and the threat of new aggression from Japan.[24] Finally, after more than three weeks of debate, the Council took action. Unanimously, including the Chinese and Japanese representatives, it decided on December 10 to follow the original Japanese suggestion, made on November 20, and send out to the Far East a commission of investigation.

The result of the Council meeting at Paris was appointment of the famous Lytton Commission. The Council members decided in favor of the commission hoping that it would get to the root of

22. Ibid., Nov. 27, Dec. 6, 1931. The "poor old President," Stimson had informed his diary on Nov. 27, was in a bad plight—"As he says, he has been making speeches against actions of force all this time and he cannot reverse himself." Stimson wondered pensively if Hoover might have outstripped the progress of the world in taking too high a position. "Who knows? We are all thinking it over pretty hard."

Stimson and several of his advisers—Rogers, Klots, Hornbeck, Castle—held a vigorous meeting at Woodley on Dec. 6 on the question of what could be done if the proposed League resolution for a commission of inquiry failed. Rogers, Klots, and Hornbeck were for an embargo. Castle opposed. "I was against it," the latter wrote in his diary, "and, although I was pretty hard boiled I think the Secretary was inclined to agree. Certainly the President would." Castle diary, Dec. 7, 1931.

23. Memorandum of a transatlantic telephone conversation between Stimson and Dawes, Dec. 7, 1931, 793.94/3095 1/2.

24. ". . . over the whole atmosphere of these last two or three days has been hanging the uncertainty in Paris and this threat of new aggression from Japan, and every moment of my time is full of that. It is a desperate situation and many people are getting impatient and urging drastic steps or words upon me." Stimson diary, Dec. 8, 1931.

the tangled situation in Manchuria, that it would sort out claim and counterclaim and bring in a report around which men of good will could unite. Once the real facts of the Sino-Japanese dispute became known, the Council members hoped, a final solution of the affair might be more evident than it was at the moment.

The Council also hoped that military operations would come to a halt while the commission of inquiry was in the Far East. Such a hope consisted more of assumption than assurance, and members of the Council did not like but could not effectively object to a careful reservation which Ambassador Yoshizawa made in his nation's consent to creation of the Lytton Commission—that the League resolution establishing the commission of inquiry would not prohibit future Japanese military action. The Lytton Commission later discovered that the Japanese after this reservation "continued to deal with the situation in Manchuria according to their plans." [25] The Japanese army had no intention of halting operations until the League had completed its inquiry.

This recalcitrance became evident only in the months after adjournment of the League meeting at Paris. Western diplomatists in early December 1931 had accomplished the diplomatic task of the moment. The League Council had taken action, even if that action were only of an investigative nature. Ambassador Dawes returned to his post in London confident that he had assisted in the maintenance of international peace. The contribution of Dawes' diplomacy may, in fact, have been more substantial than it appears in retrospect. In any event the Council of the League of Nations, sending out a commission of inquiry, momentarily relieved the American government of initiative in trying to settle the Sino-Japanese dispute.[26]

25. *Lytton Report*, p. 77.

26. One of Ambassador Dawes' assistants at Paris was G. Howland Shaw, who in a letter to the author of May 29, 1957, recalled his experience in 1931: "I have often wondered why I was sent to Paris. I was on duty as Counselor of the Embassy in Turkey having some five months before completed an assignment to the Department as Chief of the Division of Near Eastern Affairs. I had had no experience of the Far East and knew next to nothing about the problems with which Ambassador Dawes was to deal. Out of a clear blue sky I was directed to proceed to Paris at once to take charge

of the Embassy and with utmost secrecy stop over for twenty-four hours in Switzerland to confer with Prentiss Gilbert. My Chargeship was one of the strangest in American diplomatic history as except for a few minutes at nine o'clock every morning I was never at the Embassy, but always in attendance on Ambassador Dawes at the Ritz. After an initial brisk exchange of views concerning the Foreign Service, of which the Ambassador had with a few exceptions a poor opinion, we got along beautifully and I enjoyed the assignment. From the outset it was perfectly clear that the Ambassador didn't want my views even if I had been in a position to offer any that were worth while. My role was that of a sympathetic listener and in that capacity I learned something about what was going on and even more about Greek and Roman history to which the Ambassador constantly referred to illustrate the proceedings in Paris. I had only one bad time and that was when the frightful possibility presented itself that Ambassador Edge might return from leave before Ambassador Dawes had left for London. The latter had informed me most emphatically that he would not make the first call. I was of course perfectly aware that if an incident took place the Department would blame me. Fortunately, Ambassador Dawes left on the 'Golden Arrow' at noon and Ambassador Edge arrived on the boat train at 2 P.M. The first thing he asked me was: 'Where is Ambassador Dawes?' "

Chapter Ten: THE STIMSON DOCTRINE

The League had decided to send a commission of inquiry, and Stimson gladly concurred, but early in December 1931 the secretary began to wonder if the Kwantung Army would remain stationary while the investigation went on. If the Japanese sent troops to Chinchow in South Manchuria where there was no pretext for the few Japanese residents to request protection, it would constitute, Stimson believed, a clear-cut act of aggression against Chinese sovereignty. It would break solemn treaties—decisive proof that Japan had committed an international crime. Would some sort of immediate counteraction then be necessary? How many months would the Lytton Commission need to make its investigation and present its report? Meanwhile what counteraction could Stimson devise? Obviously only such diplomatic devices (the secretary would insist upon calling them weapons) as would not provoke Japan to war. He was not sure what he could do, but he was already turning over in his mind a diplomatic doctrine, a device, a negative formula: nonrecognition of the fruits of aggression.

Dr. Hornbeck told the secretary early in December that the powers would either have to "put up or shut up"—the Japanese were suspecting that the West did not mean business.[1] Chargé Perkins in Peking reported that Chinese authorities saw only two remaining alternatives, to fight or accept Japanese demands.[2] Stimson determined not to act unless Chinchow was taken; he chose only to point out to Ambassador Debuchi that if the "Honjo

1. Memorandum by Hornbeck, "Manchuria Situation: A. Present Problem," Dec. 5, 1931, 793.94/3117.

2. Perkins to Stimson, Dec. 10, 1931, 793.94/3154.

army"—the Kwantung Army under command of Lieutenant General Shigeru Honjo—marched southward, a painful situation would arise.[3]

An added reason for hesitating was the recent change of government in Japan, and a series of new Japanese domestic policies the meaning of which was in doubt to Western observers.[4] The cabinet change had the immediate effect of taking Japan off the gold standard, allowing the yen to slide down till it reached a point where sufficient foreign sales could establish some sort of equilibrium in the balance of payments.[5] Currency control came on December 13. Four days later, and still unknown to Stimson, the new cabinet of Premier Tsuyoshi Inukai decided in favor of Japan's occupying all the provinces of Manchuria, including Jehol, in accord with a plan drawn up by the new Japanese war minister, General Sadao Araki.[6] The world learned of this expansionist policy on December 23, 1931, when a Chinese brigade gave up its position above Chinchow before advancing units of the Kwantung Army. The Japanese moved south with perfect regularity, meeting hardly any resistance because Chang Hsueh-liang's forces were following the general order to retreat. Chinchow fell on January 2, 1932. Japanese forces continued to the Great Wall at Shanhaikwan, refraining for the moment from crossing into Jehol.

When Chinchow fell, Stimson was furious. Three and a half months of past American policy, which frequently had acted as

3. Memorandum by Stimson of a conversation with Debuchi, Dec. 7, 1931, *FR: 1931, 3*, 629–30.

4. Undersecretary Castle advised waiting to see. Memorandum to Stimson, Dec. 5, 1931, 793.94/3117,

5. The supposedly "sound" fiscal policy of the Wakatsuki cabinet was soon proved—at least in currency matters—erroneous, for dropping the gold standard made for great and successful changes in the structure of Japan's foreign trade. In the case of raw silk, unfortunately, foreign demand proved inelastic, but a general equilibrium was restored by the rise in exports of manufactured goods, including products which under previous price conditions had sold abroad scarcely at all, but for which demand proved elastic at the new range of prices. G. C. Allen, *Japanese Industry: Its Recent Development and Present Condition* (New York, 1940), p. 10.

6. IMTFE, *Proceedings*, pp. 28139–40.

a brake on world pressure against Japan, had proved futile. With the capture of Chinchow it was apparent that despite League remonstrance, mild American objection and warning, and setting up of the Lytton Commission, Japanese appetite had improved with eating. It did not help when Hornbeck truthfully told the secretary of state that Chinchow was like the last dish in a set of dishes—that the secretary had watched Japan break dish after dish, and why should he now become so angry when the Japanese broke the last dish? Stimson nearly lost his temper. Hornbeck feared for a while that the chief of the Far Eastern division might "receive his walking papers." [7] After some time the secretary cooled down and turned his mind to the diplomatic device, the state paper which would carry his name into history.

1

Stimson in later years realized that a policy toward Japan of nonrecognition of the fruits of aggression had been a mistake—that such a policy could not have stopped the Japanese army in Manchuria. By 1947 he readily admitted that nonrecognition had been a failure.[8] In 1931–32, however, he was looking for some way to halt the long-drawn-out process of note-writing which had produced such insignificant results, and he hoped that formal refusal to recognize aggression in Manchuria would wind things up "with a snap," putting Japan on notice much the same way that his predecessor, Secretary William Jennings Bryan, had done in 1915 at the time of the Twenty-One Demands.[9]

Bryan in 1915 had first sought to persuade France, Britain, and Russia to intercede with him against Japan, to no avail. All those nations were busy in Europe with the War. They also felt no special concern for the plight of China. In the words of the Russian foreign minister, Sergei Sazonov, Russia at that time could not in any way have made representations to Tokyo, for Japan was

7. Interview with Hornbeck, Jan. 4, 1952.

8. *Far Eastern Crisis,* p. 92; *On Active Service,* pp. 261–2.

9. *Far Eastern Crisis,* p. 92. Stimson was a much different individual in taste and background from Bryan, and he should have felt keenest embarrassment in joining company with a pacifist and composer of words, the erstwhile "boy orator of the Platte."

giving a great deal of assistance in the war and the Allies expected more. Then, too: "Fifty years from now there won't be any China. Some of its provinces may continue to exist as independent states, together or separately, but there will be no Chinese nation as there is now." [10] Rebuffed by the powers, Bryan had turned to unilateral action. When the then counselor of the Department, Robert Lansing, suggested a note of nonrecognition of any Japanese treaty infringement upon Chinese sovereignty, little needed to be done except to send Lansing's draft to the White House for the consent of President Wilson, which was quickly forthcoming, and then cable the note. "In view of the circumstances of the negotiations which have taken place and which are now pending between the Government of Japan and the Government of China," Bryan announced, "and of the agreements which have been reached as a result thereof, the Government of the United States has the honor to notify the Imperial Japanese Government that it cannot recognize any agreement or undertaking which has been entered into or which may be entered into between the Governments of Japan and China, impairing the treaty rights of the United States and its citizens in China, the political or territorial integrity of the Republic of China, or the international policy relative to China commonly known as the open door policy." [11]

"Filing a notice"—this is the phrase that Bryan used privately to describe his note.[12] No responsible person in the American government in 1915 regarded nonrecognition as other than a weak and temporary expedient. Even the harassed Chinese gave it slight attention. The Japanese foreign minister airily dismissed it as "impudent." Bryan's busy mind then had turned to other more pressing problems, especially American neutrality toward

10. Letter to Bryan from the American ambassador in St. Petersburg, George T. Marye, May 9, 1915, 793.94/374.

11. Bryan to the American ambassador in Japan, George W. Guthrie, May 11, 1915, *FR: 1915*, p. 146.

12. "Having filed our notice of May 11, 5 p.m., with both parties . . ." Bryan to the American minister in China, Paul S. Reinsch, May 15, 1915, *FR: 1915*, p. 147.

Germany and the Allied powers. A German submarine torpedoed the *Lusitania* on May 7, 1915, four days before the note went off to Japan, and in the resulting crisis Bryan broke with Wilson and resigned.

Seventeen years later Stimson filed his notice, and made it the pivot of American foreign policy.

He had been thinking of a doctrine of nonrecognition as early as November 9, 1931, when President Hoover suggested it in cabinet.[13] Hoover had toyed with the idea of withdrawing Ambassador Forbes from Tokyo, or proposing to Japan and China a viceroy for Manchuria, but by early November he had come to believe that the "main weapon" should be to announce the nonrecognition of any treaty extorted from China by force. When Stimson discussed Hoover's proposal with Department officers there was incomplete enthusiasm, Hornbeck dissenting, but the secretary believed that if all nations announced nonrecognition it would exert a potent effect.[14]

Acquiring the idea of nonrecognition from President Hoover in early November 1931, Stimson a month later was ready to expound the subject by cable to Ambassador Dawes, then in Paris, for the edification of European diplomats.[15] After consulting various members of the Department, he gave up this scheme in favor of waiting for the Japanese occupation of Chinchow, which occurred on January 2, 1932.

At the State Department that morning Stimson revealed to Ambassador Claudel what he had in mind, nonrecognition, and spent the rest of the day on the golf course and showing movies to friends at Woodley. After retiring he grew restless thinking of Manchuria; and at six o'clock the following morning he arose with his mind clear on what he wished to do. He went downstairs

13. Stimson diary, Nov. 9, 1931. On the diary margin Stimson later penciled, "First germs of nonrecognition."

14. Ibid., Nov. 9. "Hornbeck had advanced the rather common idea in the Department that this remedy didn't amount to anything because we had tried it in 1915. But there the situation was wholly different as I pointed out. Under present circumstances, particularly if the disavowal is made by all of the countries, it ought to have a very potent effect."

15. Ibid., Dec. 2, 3.

to the library and wrote out in longhand a brief note to the Chinese and Japanese governments, based largely on the note of 1915. He had had in mind a longer note with a historical résumé, but now he decided to make the note as brief as possible. Later in the day he telephoned Ambassador Debuchi and excused himself from the ambassador's dinner of the next evening, pleading a diplomatic illness, having told the ambassador beforehand that he would not come if the Japanese took Chinchow. On Monday, January 4, 1932, there was long discussion at the Department over the draft of the previous morning at Woodley, and the secretary was happy to discover that his text stood the test of argument. In the evening he consulted the president, whom he found hard at work in the Lincoln study. The deteriorating economic crisis was much occupying Hoover. Nonetheless Stimson showed him two draft notes, the first being the general statement he had drawn at Woodley, and the second the longer historical discussion. "H.H." read the notes. Stimson explained their difference. There was no hesitation. "I agree with you," Hoover said. "Let us put it on the broad basis." [16] The secretary indicated the dangers which might occur if the Japanese "called" the American position, so to speak, and annexed Manchuria. The president was willing to run the risk.[17]

At breakfast next day, Tuesday, January 5, Stimson spent some time with Allen Klots and Captain Regnier in a "polishment" of the note. Later at the Department the British ambassador happened in and the secretary told him about the proposed move; Sir Ronald Lindsay [18] seemed favorable and said he would report to London at once. Claudel appeared again, and read the note, which the French ambassador diplomatically pronounced very strong.[19] Next day, the sixth, saw a final Department session in which Hornbeck fought tenaciously against a definite statement [20]

16. *Far Eastern Crisis,* pp. 95–6.

17. Stimson diary, Jan. 4, 1932. The two men talked about various subjects for almost an hour and a half, chiefly the possibility of a new bank crash.

18. Lindsay had replaced Sir Esme Howard in March 1930.

19. Stimson diary, Jan. 5, 1932.

20. Hornbeck sought in vain to convince Stimson that nonrecognition would not work because the world was full of rascals. Interview of Jan. 4, 1952.

and Stimson, although finding his adviser's alternate wording a little weak, did consent to soften the note. A form at last appeared which seemed to satisfy everyone. The chief of the Western European division, J. Theodore Marriner, said the tone now resembled Lord Curzon at his best.[21] The note was short, and to the point:

> With the recent military operations about Chinchow, the last remaining administrative authority of the Government of the Chinese Republic in South Manchuria, as it existed prior to September 18, 1931, has been destroyed. The American Government continues confident that the work of the neutral commission recently authorized by the Council of the League of Nations will facilitate an ultimate solution of the difficulties now existing between China and Japan. But in view of the present situation and of its own rights and obligations therein, the American Government deems it to be its duty to notify both the Imperial Japanese Government and the Government of the Chinese Republic that it cannot admit the legality of any situation *de facto* nor does it intend to recognize any treaty or agreement entered into between those Governments, or agents thereof, which may impair the treaty rights of the United States or its citizens in China, including those which relate to the sovereignty, the independence, or the territorial and administrative integrity of the Republic of China, nor to the international policy relative to China, commonly known as the open door policy; and that it does not intend to recognize any situation, treaty, or agreement which may be brought about by means contrary to the covenants and obligations of the Pact of Paris of August 27, 1928, to which Treaty both China and Japan, as well as the United States, are parties.[22]

Undersecretary Castle suggested notifying the members of the Nine-Power Treaty group so that they could send similar notes. Stimson thought this a good idea, although he had based his note

21. Castle diary, Jan. 8, 1932.
22. *FR: Japan* 1931–41, *I*, 76.

on the Kellogg Pact and not the Nine-Power Treaty. Consulted by telephone, Hoover also agreed.

The great day arrived, Thursday, January 7, 1932. The secretary had Hornbeck send off the notes, and conferred with all the ambassadors and ministers representing the parties to the Nine-Power Treaty. He began with Debuchi, "who took the shot with the pleasant stolidity of a Japanese." "The Chinaman, Dr. Yen," did not give much expression one way or the other, although Stimson believed Yen had reason to be pleased.[23] Reactions of the other diplomatists appear to have been diplomatic. They did not give the secretary reason to believe that his new policy might prove unsuccessful.

2

The first inkling that matters were amiss came the same day the notes went out.

At a dinner that night at the Czechoslovak legation Ambassador Claudel told Stimson that Briand, requesting the British to join a protest against the capture of Chinchow, had met with refusal: the British foreign secretary, Sir John Simon,[24] found the moment inopportune. Evidently the British government would not go along with Stimson and send a supporting note of nonrecognition to Japan.

This development did not worry the secretary of state. He had hoped that a nonrecognition doctrine would—to use Washington's words at the Federal Convention in 1787—raise a standard to which the wise and the honest might repair, the event being in the hand of God. But he knew that disorders in India and a continuing financial crisis at home were plaguing the British, and he did not especially blame them when, as he discovered within a few days after January 7, 1932, they sought to "play it safe" in foreign policy, acquiring the benefits of an American diplomatic move without taking any risk.

It was only when the Foreign Office allowed the London press

23. Stimson diary, Jan. 7, 1932.

24. Simon had replaced Lord Reading in November 1931.

on January 11, 1932, to publish an unenthusiastic official communiqué that Stimson became considerably irritated. The British announcement, dated January 9, bore no mention of preserving the territorial and administrative entity of China, or the Kellogg-Briand Pact, or nonrecognition of the fruits of aggression. It dealt with the single problem of Anglo-Chinese trade relations. In a lead editorial published the same day the London *Times* undertook to supply affirmative interpretations of the communiqué's omissions. The British government, the *Times* explained, had "acted wisely" in refusing to follow Stimson, for it was not the "immediate business" of the Foreign Office to defend the administrative integrity of China until that integrity was something more than an ideal ("It did not exist in 1922, and it does not exist today").[25]

Actually, the Foreign Office had not intended its communiqué as a rebuff to the United States. The communiqué was a faux pas of British diplomacy, and Foreign Office officials later openly admitted as much. It had received only the slightest attention at the Foreign Office. Sir John Pratt, who then headed the Office's Far Eastern section, later revealed that the permanent officials had drafted and approved it in haste at 1:00 P.M. on Saturday the ninth, just before getting off to their week end holidays. They did not realize until the following Monday that it read like a rebuff to America.[26] Stimson afterward would remark that a slightly different version of the published communiqué,[27] dated the ninth, did not get to him until the twelfth. This also was a result of the week end habit: the British ambassador in Washington presented the aide memoire at the State Department on Monday the eleventh, and Stimson, off on a long week end, did not see it until Tuesday.

In later years much misunderstanding arose over the British

25. London *Times,* Jan. 11, 1932.

26. Sir John T. Pratt, *War and Politics in China* (London, Jonathan Cape, 1943), pp. 275–6, reprinting a letter to the London *Times,* Nov. 30, 1938.

27. The difference was mostly an explanation that Britain's position as a member of the League precluded her from sending a note on the lines suggested. *FR: 1932, 3,* 22–3.

reaction to Stimson's announcement of nonrecognition, for it came to be a popular belief that the American secretary of state in January 1932 had made a definite offer to restrain Japan, and Britain had refused the offer. There was, in truth, no offer of any kind in January 1932. Stimson had gone ahead on his own, to announce nonrecognition, and had not solicited support. Before sending the note he had merely read it to the British and French ambassadors, asking them to communicate his intention to their governments. He did not ask reply but "waited for results." [28] The ambassadors did not receive copies of the note for transmission until after it had gone out to China and Japan. Such was the "offer of co-operation." Sir John Simon a month later, during events leading up to the so-called Borah Letter of February 23, 1932, did refuse immediate cooperation with Stimson under the terms of the Nine-Power Treaty, but this was something entirely different from the British response to the doctrine of nonrecognition.[29]

Official British disinterest in his note pained Stimson greatly, and the answer of Japan, given January 16, 1932, was far worse. Its veneer of elegant irony thinly covered a base of solid insolence. The nonrecognition note, the Japanese Foreign Office assured Stimson, had received the most careful attention in Japan. Reaffirming the policy of the Open Door, "a cardinal feature of the politics of the Far East," Japan regretted the unsettled conditions prevailing in China. Concerning the possibility that the Japanese might be using improper means in Manchuria, contrary to the Pact of Paris, "It might be the subject of an academic doubt whether in a given case the impropriety of means necessarily and always voids the ends secured; but as Japan has no intention of adopting improper means, that question does not practically

28. *On Active Service,* p. 237.

29. See below, pp. 180–3. For this matter of Stimson's "offer of co-operation," see Pratt, *War and Politics in China,* pp. 226–8, 279–80; also the interesting letter, perhaps by the same author, in Thomas Jones, *A Diary with Letters: 1931–50* (London, 1954), pp. 399–402. This question is thoroughly explored in Reginald Bassett, *Democracy and Foreign Policy, A Case History: The Sino-Japanese Dispute, 1931–33* (London, 1952), pp. 5, 75–6, 83, 92, 130 ff.

arise." As for the Nine-Power Treaty, the Japanese invoked something perilously close to *rebus sic stantibus:* "the present unsettled and distracted state of China is not what was in the contemplation of the high contracting parties at the time of the Treaty of Washington." The note concluded with a sarcastic thrust: that the United States had always been "alive to the exigencies of Far Eastern questions"—meaning annexation of Hawaii and the Philippines and perhaps the attempt in 1900 to secure Samsah Bay.[30] In this stinging *réplique* from a power beginning the conquest of China, Stimson to his dismay found a section which made almost literal use of the January 11 editorial in the London *Times.*

In following weeks Sir John Simon began to realize that Stimson took the doctrine of nonrecognition far more seriously than he, Sir John, had thought possible,[31] and Simon exerted himself at the League of Nations to make nonrecognition a principle accepted by that international body. Especially did Simon labor at the League after he and Stimson once more crossed notes, so to speak, over Stimson's effort in mid-February to invoke the Nine-Power Treaty. As a result of the British foreign secretary's work, the League's Committee of Twelve (the Council, excepting representatives of China and Japan) on February 16, 1932, addressed a note to Japan declaring that no violation of Article 10 of the Covenant "ought to be recognized as valid and effectual by the Members of the League of Nations." And the Assembly itself on March 11 resolved in favor of Stimson's policy.[32] Most of the

30. After having sponsored the second Open Door Note affirming the territorial and administrative entity of China, John Hay at the behest of the War and Navy departments had approached Japan about the possibility of an American coaling station at Samsah Bay in the Chinese maritime province of Fukien. The Japanese government reminded Hay of his Open Door Doctrine, and the American secretary of state in embarrassment dropped the subject.

31. "Rightly or wrongly we attached little importance to this *démarche.* Non-recognition was a peculiarly American technique, the fruit of American isolationism, and it was wholly out of harmony with the British tradition in international affairs." Pratt, *War and Politics in China,* p. 226.

32. For this declaration see below, p. 183. It is perhaps worth noting that

nations of the world thereafter stood behind the nonrecognition of "Manchukuo." Japan, of course, recognized the new Manchurian state on September 15, 1932, and later Manchukuo exchanged envoys with the Vatican (1934), El Salvador (1934), the Dominican Republic (1934), Italy (1937), Franco Spain (1937), Germany (1937), Poland (1938), Hungary (1939), and Slovakia (1939). Russia recognized in 1935, incident to selling to Japan, nominally Manchukuo, the Soviet interest in the Chinese Eastern Railway.[33] But in general, the League countries supported nonrecognition, and Manchukuo during its thirteen years of existence remained rejected and almost friendless, a waif outside the family of nations.[34]

3

What can one say in conclusion about the doctrine of nonrecognition of the fruits of aggression, which was undoubtedly

---

on Jan. 28, 1932, the Committee of Twelve completed a draft declaration on the Sino-Japanese dispute which made specific reference to the nonrecognition note of Jan. 7, and stated that it would be impossible for the League to recognize any settlement secured by methods contrary to international obligations. The president of the Council, Joseph Paul-Boncour, reported the declaration to the Council on Jan. 29. This episode, however, disappeared from view because of the general confusion caused by the Japanese attack, on Jan. 28, 1932, upon Shanghai.

33. Russian recognition proved only slightly embarrassing at the Tokyo war crimes trial after the second World War. The trial sought to demonstrate among other things that Japan had broken the Kellogg-Briand Pact; Stimson's note considered nonrecognition inherent in the pact; to recognize the fruits of aggression (as did Soviet Russia) therefore constituted an illegal act punishable under the charter of the Tokyo tribunal. But such an argument was avowedly theoretical and legalistic and could serve no useful purpose, since no one was prepared to hale Russia into court. It did indicate the large amount of politics often involved in applications of international law.

34. The Stimson Doctrine unfortunately failed for Ethiopia, Austria, Czechoslovakia, and Albania. The conquest of those nations by Italy and and Germany received recognition by most of the states of the world. The Kellogg-Briand Pact fell into discard. When President Roosevelt raised the question of the Pact with Italy, anent the conquest of Ethiopia, Mussolini told him (according to FDR) to "go to hell." Dorothy Detzer, *Appointment on the Hill* (New York, Holt, 1948), p. 186.

Stimson's most memorable diplomatic step while secretary of state? Despite his final realization that the doctrine, under the extraordinary international circumstances of 1932–45, exerted little influence in maintaining the peace of the world, did such a principle contain anything essentially worth while for the practice of American diplomacy in less frenzied times? And even if nonrecognition could have no immediate effect in diplomatic intercourse, was it a contribution to international law, to the eventual reign of justice among nations?

First of all, a clarification. The Stimson Doctrine applied only to boundary changes accomplished by force, whereas most questions of recognition concern changes of regime, not boundary. It is easy to confuse these two quite different issues.[35]

Stimson always maintained that his device of nonrecognition was something new in diplomacy, particularly if adopted by the nations of the world and made to include, in contrast to the Bryan note of 1915, not merely treaties but any "situation *de facto*" such as obtained in Manchuria in 1932. Yet it is difficult to see wherein the Stimson Doctrine was novel either in form or practice. The expediency of employing recognition as a diplomatic weapon had occupied the minds of diplomatists for many years, without any clear consensus. Few subjects in international law had encouraged so much investigation. International lawyers had chewed over the question of recognition of new states and new governments, *naissance et reconnaissance,* until there was scarcely anything left to masticate. But the practice of states always prevented the scholars from reducing recognition to a few easy formulas. Usually recognition served as a diplomatic method of exerting pressure—an instrument of national policy—though procedure varied according to circumstance.[36] This was particularly true of recognition of a state carved out of another state,

35. For Stimson's policy of political recognition in Latin America see below, pp. 218–20. Stimson abandoned in Latin America the moralistic recognition policy of Wilson.

36. This is the conclusion of Ross N. Berkes, "The Use of the Power of Recognition as an Instrument of Diplomacy," an unpublished doctoral thesis (1942) at the University of Southern California.

the situation Stimson had in mind, as opposed to recognition of a government involving no change of boundary. During the Peace of Amiens, for example, Great Britain in return for retention of Malta, immunity of Turkey, and French evacuation of Holland and Switzerland, had offered to Napoleon recognition of the Bonapartist Italian states. In American history notable instances of recognition as a diplomatic weapon were the independence of Latin America, 1800–30, the Texas question of 1835–45, and, of course, the recognition of Panama in 1903.

As one might have expected from the voluminous annals of American diplomatic practice, there were also precedents favoring codification of what later came to be labeled the Stimson Doctrine—or was it the Hoover Doctrine? Secretary of State James G. Blaine in 1889 had laid before the first conference of American states a proposal to prevent conquest: no state should recognize transfer of territory except after an arbitral decision. Years later came the Bryan note to Japan. Another declaration of nonrecognition occurred in 1921 when the American government informed Japan that it could "neither now nor hereafter recognize as valid any claims or titles" arising out of Japanese occupation and control of eastern Siberia, and could not acquiesce in any action taken by the government of Japan which "might impair existing treaty rights, or the political or territorial integrity of Russia." [37] Then, too, after the Paris Peace Conference the United States had refused to recognize Rumania's conquest of Bessarabia from Russia. But by 1932 there was still no clear American policy of nonrecognition of forceful territorial change. Expediency had dictated that practice be kept fluid.

It was not difficult to argue that nonrecognition of the fruits of aggression had generally proved an unrewarding means of diplomatic pressure, requiring a supplementary sanction to be effective. Japan, for example, had been put back in leash after the first World War not by virtue of Bryan's pronouncement of 1915 or the declaration on Siberia in 1921 but through arrangements at the Washington Conference following an American threat to outbuild the Japanese navy.

37. *FR: 1921, 2,* 704.

It certainly was true that an announced doctrine of nonrecognition compared unfavorably with the devices for peaceful settlement and change already possessed by the League of Nations. Stimson in an address of August 8, 1932, before the Council on Foreign Relations in New York City suggested that the Kellogg-Briand Pact represented a "more sweeping step" than the Covenant in the direction of restricting war, and that the American government in its note of nonrecognition was moving even further ahead.[38] Such a view was naive. Article 10 of the Covenant had gone at least as far as Stimson's note.[39] Article 11 provided for calling a conference in event of threat of war, on the ground that such a threat was a matter of concern to all League members. As for the admitted loopholes in Article 15,[40] whatever their size they were smaller than the reservation of self-defense that accompanied renunciation of war under the Pact of Paris. It was incorrect to say, as Stimson did in his address of August 1932, that the Covenant "left unrestricted a zone in which . . . wars might occur without reprobation." The whole tenor of the Covenant opposed such an idea. Nonrecognition, carrying none of the arrangements for conciliation, discussion, and compromise provided by the Covenant, was in many respects weaker than provisions of the League already constituting the public law of Europe and most of the world.[41] Stimson's insistence upon his Doctrine resembled Kellogg's advocacy in 1928 of a multilateral peace pact, for in both instances the United States presented to the world broad principles of international behavior well below standards already in general acceptance.

It is true that the Stimson Doctrine, even after a lapse of more

38. "The Pact of Paris: Three Years of Development," *FR: 1932, I*, 575–83.

39. "The Members of the League undertake to respect and preserve as against external aggression the territorial integrity and existing political independence of all Members of the League."

40. If the Council failed to agree unanimously upon solution of a dispute, individual states concerned could take action; war also was permissible in any dispute declared by a party to be a matter of domestic jurisdiction.

41. See the sparkling discussion by C. G. Fenwick, " 'The Implication of Consultation' in the Pact of Paris," *American Journal of International Law, 26* (1932), 787–9.

than twenty eventful years, has considerable merit if looked at from the vantage point of an international lawyer. One of the best recent statements in its favor has come from Professor Hersch Lauterpacht, who like most writers on the subject—except a few pessimists such as the late Edwin M. Borchard—is an indefatigable seeker after precedents favoring the eventual world rule of law. "The instrument of nonrecognition," Lauterpacht writes, "is admittedly an imperfect weapon of enforcement. However, in the absence of a regularly functioning international machinery for enforcing the law, it must be regarded as a supplementary weapon of considerable legal and moral potency. It prevents any law-creating effect of prescription. It constitutes a standing challenge to the legality of the situation which results from an unlawful act and which, in relation to the courts of the non-recognising State, is a mere nullity." [42]

Despite this favorable view, students of American foreign policy writing under the deepening shadows cast by the second World War have been industriously removing the luster from the principle of nonrecognition. Authorship of the note of January 7, 1932, has become something less than an unqualified historical asset. George F. Kennan, in Stimson's time an underling in the State Department, has reproached his one-time chief for too legalistic a view of international relations—too much concern with the "juridical tidiness of international life." Kennan deplores the legalistic doctrinal approach to international problems.[43] He of course would not agree with an earlier diplomatic practitioner, Charles Maurice de Talleyrand, who once gravely announced

42. L. Oppenheim, *International Law,* ed. H. Lauterpacht (8th ed. 2 vols. New York, Longmans, Green, 1955–), *1,* 145. See also Malbone W. Graham, *In Quest of a Law of Recognition,* Berkeley, Calif., 1933; Percy E. Corbett, *Law and Society in the Relations of States* (New York, 1951), p. 103; Robert Langer, *Seizure of Territory: The Stimson Doctrine and Related Principles in Legal Theory and Diplomatic Practice* (Princeton, 1947), p. 290.

43. *American Diplomacy,* p. 95: ". . . I see the most serious fault of our past policy formulation to lie in something that I might call the legalistic-moralistic approach to international problems. This approach runs like a red skein through our foreign policy of the last fifty years."

that the best principle was to have none. But the point is well taken that statesmen should not encumber themselves with too many fixed ideas and special schemes of thought. Principles, often serving to clarify, may also obscure and deceive; they may, furthermore, tie one's successor's hands against the unknown contingencies of the future.

Kennan may have carried his point too far in inveighing against use in diplomatic negotiations of principles of a broad, moralistic sort. According to Kennan and such other recent students as Hans Morgenthau, a "realistic" foreign policy should divorce itself from moral injunctions, but in practice this is simply impossible, even if it were desirable. The analogy between the nation and the individual, by which a nation as a corporate body receives attributes of personality, is unavoidable; people are too accustomed to describing a corporate body such as a nation in moral terms, calling it just or generous or cowardly or unscrupulous—which is to say, treating it as if it were an individual.[44] Such manner of speech was in vogue long before Hegel announced that the state was the highest embodiment of morality. Woodrow Wilson utilized it to the utmost in his crusade during the first World War. "We are at the beginning of an age," he told Congress on April 2, 1917, "in which it will be insisted that the same standards of conduct and of responsibility for wrong shall be observed among nations as among the individual citizens of civilized states." When in July 1918 Colonel E. M. House was meditating on a possible league of nations, the first article of his draft ran as follows: "The same standards of honor and ethics shall prevail internationally and in affairs of nations as in other matters." [45] The moral approach to foreign policy is rooted deeply in the traditions and thought of Western civilization, particularly in the main currents of American democratic thought.[46] Critics of

44. E. H. Carr, "The Moral Foundations for World Order," in *Foundations for World Order* (Denver, 1947), pp. 55–75.

45. Ibid., p. 58.

46. Ralph H. Gabriel, *The Course of American Democratic Thought,* New York, 1940; 2d ed. 1956.

Stimson's "moral approach" to international relations have usually condemned it because of the impossibility of its complete success. They overlook the lack of any acceptable substitute.

Morality in politics, a noble goal well worth striving for, has in addition a certain practical use in the workaday politics of democratic nations. If one is dealing with or between democracies it is extremely realistic to invoke high principle. There will always tend to be a high moral content in the policy of any democratic nation where diplomatists are directly responsible to their fellow citizens. Dexter Perkins has remarked that the mass of men in America are inclined to think that they know something about the conduct of foreign relations; generally, he believes, this mass will have opinions even on complicated subjects and tend to focus attention on easily remembered diplomatic slogans; hence the high moral content in American diplomacy.[47]

But it is unlikely that Stimson before promulgating his Doctrine made any calculation of the American psyche. Had he been a more reflective individual he might have done so. Not given to playing up to the foibles of the American people, he seems to have acted out of his own experience and preference. Skilled in the law, and a highly moral man, an aristocrat in temperament and in manner of life, he was the product in more ways than one of the late Victorian Age. An announcement of nonrecognition was for him a natural moral and gentlemanly thing to do. Japan would be left outside the moral code of the Western world, if she couldn't act up to it.

The Stimson Doctrine, reflecting its author's predilections, was in content unoriginal, in announcement hardly epoch making. In some ways it constituted a backward step in international behavior. It is curious therefore to observe the later rivalry between Stimson and Hoover over its authorship. Stimson liked the term "Stimson Doctrine," for it had a ring similar to Monroe Doctrine, and Hoover's secretary of state had a sense of history.[48] But Hoover,

47. *The American Approach to Foreign Policy* (Cambridge, Mass., 1952), ch. 4, "The Moralistic Interpretation of American Foreign Policy."

48. Undersecretary Castle remarked in his diary of Feb. 18, 1932, that "The President said a couple of days ago that for the coming election he must have

too, wished to go down to posterity with a Doctrine, and for the 1932 presidential campaign he needed all the credit he could secure. "I have projected a new doctrine into international affairs," he said in his acceptance speech of August 11, 1932.[49] The idea of nonrecognition so attracted him that despite defeat in November he afterward asked some cabinet members to prepare testimonial letters on the subject, which they did, in the interest, as Hoover later put it, of "accuracy of historic fact." [50] Stimson, on the other hand, in his *Far Eastern Crisis* left authorship of nonrecognition uncertain. In his memoirs of a decade later, written after other laurels had come his way, he clearly gave Hoover credit. By that time the phrase "Stimson Doctrine" had become an accepted historic label for the American diplomatic note of January 7, 1932.[51]

---

all the support he can get. He wants Stimson . . . to make a speech somewhere and proclaim this as the Hoover doctrine. . . . It would hurt his [Stimson's] feelings terribly to have this called the Hoover doctrine because he thinks of it as one very important star which history will put to his credit."

49. Ray Lyman Wilbur and Arthur M. Hyde, *The Hoover Policies* (New York, Scribner's, 1937), p. 585.

50. *Memoirs of Herbert Hoover: The Cabinet and the Presidency,* p. 373. For the letters see Myers, *The Foreign Policies of Herbert Hoover,* pp. 163 ff. See also Hoover's statements in an interview in 1947 with Alexander DeConde, *Herbert Hoover's Latin-American Policy* (Stanford, Calif., 1951), pp. 34–5.

51. There has been some debate over whether there were actually two doctrines, the Stimson Doctrine and the Hoover Doctrine, the latter not embodying sanctions. See Charles A. Beard, *American Foreign Policy in the Making* (New Haven, 1946), p. 116 n. Richard N. Current in a lucid and carefully reasoned article, "The Stimson Doctrine and the Hoover Doctrine," *American Historical Review, 59* (1953–54), 513–42, has used the Stimson and Castle diaries to support this thesis. There is no question that Stimson occasionally pressed Hoover for sanctions, and in the Stimson diary there are random statements favoring sanctions. Even so, Stimson after outbursts of anger against Japan would cool down in realization that sanctions during the Great Depression were politically impossible. Hoover, having to give more attention than Stimson to political matters, was more steady in opposition to sanctions. Hoover was no pacifist, nor was Stimson as belligerent in 1929–33 as he became in later years. In reality the two men agreed far more than they disagreed, and it was only in the latter 1930's that they began to differ radically over issues of foreign policy.

Chapter Eleven: THE SHANGHAI INCIDENT AND THE LETTER TO SENATOR BORAH

The doctrine of nonrecognition of the fruits of aggression, the Stimson Doctrine, so hopefully advanced as a moral and legal sanction against Japan in Manchuria, was the best-known diplomatic action taken by Henry L. Stimson as secretary of state. Most American statesmen, so it seems, have cherished during their careers the possibility that they may become authors of Doctrines. Stimson succeeded. It is another matter whether Doctrines, once promulgated and written into the history books, have any special influence on the course of events; and we have seen that the Stimson Doctrine was far less effective than its author hoped. People tended to forget this. They forgot especially—and there was some reason for this oversight because the chronology of events in China in January-February 1932 is difficult to keep in mind—that the Stimson Doctrine was *followed,* not preceded, by the most outrageous act of Japanese aggression in the history of the entire Far Eastern Crisis, the attack of late January 1932 on the great Chinese port city of Shanghai.

During the Far Eastern Crisis no single military event proved so alarming to Western statesmen as did the fighting between Japanese and Chinese troops at Shanghai. The Shanghai Incident, as the Japanese delicately called it, broke out toward the end of January 1932 and lasted well over a month. To American diplomatists this outbreak of virtual war in Central China was most disheartening because it came just three weeks after announcement of the Stimson Doctrine. It stirred the other Western powers far more than had Japanese operations in Manchuria, because in Shanghai the Western nations, chiefly Great Britain, possessed business investments worth not far from a billion dollars, about a third of the total foreign holdings in China. There was, indeed, an uproar among the foreign offices of the West when Japanese marines attacked this bastion of Occidental enterprise.[1]

Since the Shanghai Incident was the most provocative act of Japanese aggression during the Far Eastern Crisis, one might have thought it would have produced a new sharpness in Western policy toward Japan. One might have assumed that the righteous indignation with which diplomatists of the West condemned this new action of Japanese troops, the force with which representatives of the great powers announced to Japan her duties under the Covenant of the League of Nations, the Nine-Power Treaty, and the Kellogg-Briand Pact, was prelude to some signal Western move against Japan that would have brought the Japanese government up short, forcing that government to re-examine its entire international behavior since the Far Eastern Crisis had commenced several months before. At the time of the Shanghai affair diplomatists of the United States, Great Britain, France, Germany, and Italy might have stood together and said to the Japanese, "There shall be no more aggressive acts in China, and we expect you to withdraw from Shanghai immediately." Unfortunately for the future peace of the world, the Shanghai Incident produced no such policy. The Great Depression, once again, restrained all thought of action. The Western nations in early 1932 were sinking

1. Investment statistics for China are not too reliable, but according to the careful compilation of Charles F. Remer, *Foreign Investments in China* (New York, 1933), pp. 97–8, British direct business investments in Shanghai in 1931 totaled $737,400,000 out of the total British investment in China of $963,-400,000. American direct business investments in Shanghai were $97,500,000, out of a total American investment in China of $150,200,000. Remer estimated the total Anglo-American investment in Manchuria at no more than $40,000,-000. Japan's Manchurian investment came to $550,200,000, Russia's to $261,-800,000. British investment in Shanghai alone was nearly as much as the combined Japanese investment in Shanghai and Manchuria. All the above figures, incidentally, are for direct business investments only and exclude other holdings. British direct business investments in China in 1931 comprised 81 per cent of total investments; the United States, 78.8.

deeper and deeper in the slough of the Depression. There was constant internal crisis—increasing unemployment, bank failures, contraction of industrial production. No responsible statesmen in the Western world would run the risk, at such a time, of a Far Eastern war. The nations made public statements and read various lectures to the Japanese, and trusted privately that, somehow, the League of Nations would discover a formula for peace in the Orient, and that, if the League could not do so, then perhaps Mr. Stimson, the secretary of state of the United States, would do so.

The powers of Europe did virtually nothing. And Secretary Stimson, deserted by his colleagues abroad, had no certainty of support within the cabinet of President Hoover at home. Everyone in the cabinet was dealing with problems of the Depression. Hoover himself had told Stimson little more than a month before that he wanted to "get out of" international affairs temporarily in order to attack domestic economic problems. There was little that Stimson could do about the Shanghai Incident. He finally resorted to writing a public letter to the chairman of the Senate Committee on Foreign Relations, Senator William E. Borah.

1

In view of the undoubted international importance of the Shanghai Incident—whether that importance lay in its threat to Western business interests, or (as Stimson believed) to the world's machinery of peace—it is curious to note that the Japanese attack at Shanghai was actually something of an accident: the attack was in large measure an impromptu affair, its consequences unforeseen. At the outset of the Shanghai Incident, and even for some time afterward, most informed observers including the world's diplomatists believed that the affair at Shanghai was part of a general Japanese plan of aggression directed against Nationalist China. It seemed logical that the Mukden Incident had been the first step in this Japanese plan, and that the second move was an occupation of Shanghai, which then would inaugurate "preventive" occupations stretching northward to Nanking and southward (the Kwantung Army had occupied Chinchow on January 2, 1932) to Peking.

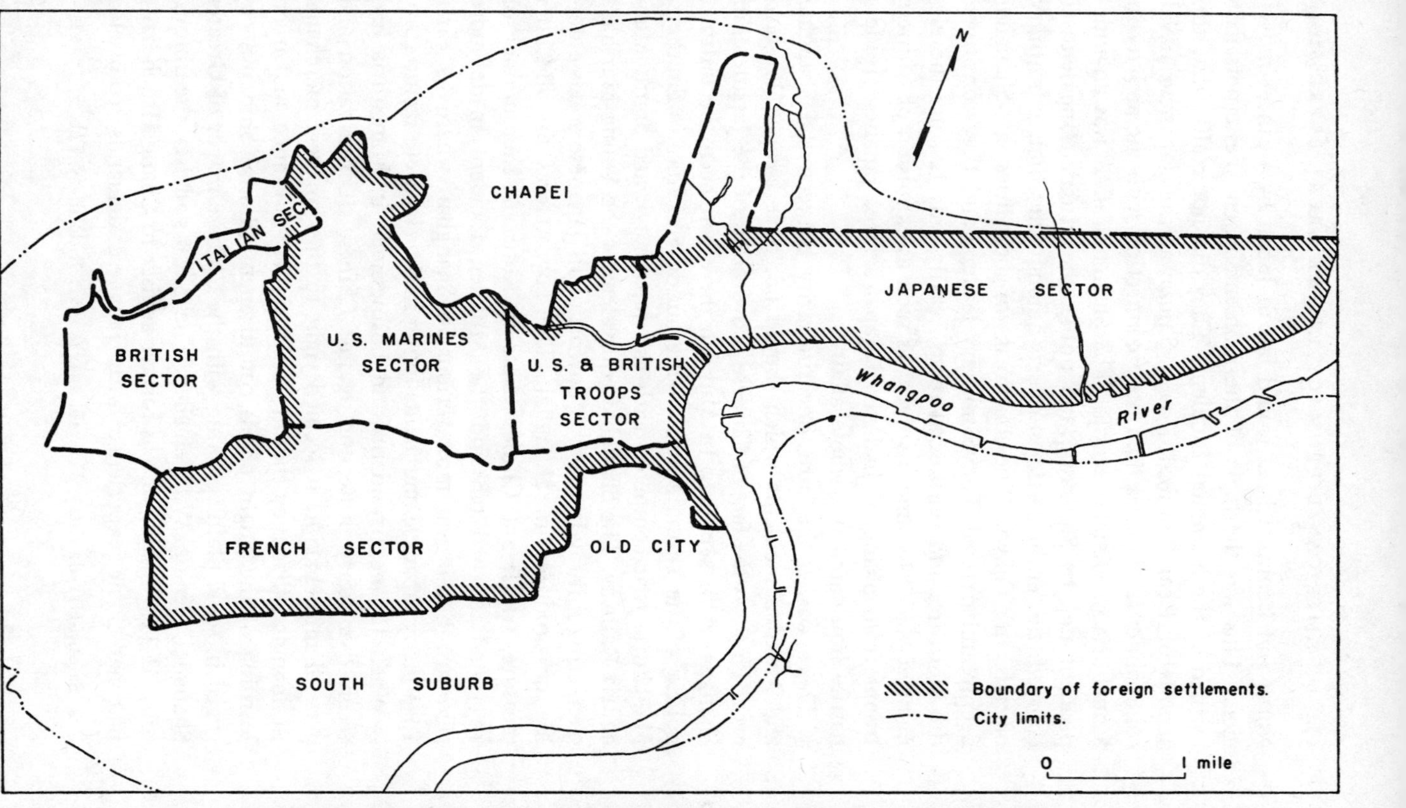

Greater Shanghai in 1932—International Settlement, French Concession, and the Chinese City

North and Central China would fall to Japan by a pincer movement. This was the logic of the moment, when Westerners first learned of the Shanghai Incident. They did not realize that the actions of Rear Admiral Koichi Shiozawa, the Japanese naval commander in the area, had little connection with the activity in Manchuria of General Honjo. The Shanghai affair was an independent step by Shiozawa, and unlike the Mukden Incident, it enjoyed no enthusiastic support among the higher military officials in Tokyo. The outbreak of hostilities at Shanghai deeply embarrassed Tokyo military leaders, and they continued the hostilities and reinforced them heavily only because the element of "face" became involved: as soon as expulsion of Chinese troops from Shanghai had saved Japan's face, Japanese leaders hastily liquidated the whole affair.[2]

There was, to be sure, one similarity between the Shanghai and Mukden incidents which should not have escaped Western eyes. This was the fact of Chinese provocation of the Japanese, in Shanghai as in Mukden. In Mukden there had been the railroad politics of the Young Marshal—the building of lines in Southern Manchuria that competed with the Japanese-owned South Manchuria Railway. The Shanghai equivalent of the Young Marshal's competing railway lines was a boycott of all Japanese goods entering or produced in Shanghai. The boycott was an all-China measure, which anti-Chinese riots in Korea in the summer of 1931 had touched off, and the Mukden Incident made more rigorous; but it was most serious in Shanghai, where by early 1932 many Japanese merchants living in the city were facing ruin.

When Japanese residents and businessmen in Manchuria had received military protection against Chinese discrimination and general misbehavior, it seemed right to the Japanese merchants in Shanghai that they should obtain similar assistance, and upon learning of the plight of his countrymen Admiral Shiozawa engaged in some plain speaking with the Chinese mayor of Greater Shanghai, General Wu Teh-chen. The mayor's adviser, the ubiquitous W. H. Donald, who as former adviser to Chang Hsueh-liang had had some experience with Japanese demands, counseled

2. Saionji-Harada diary, Feb. 16, 23–24, 1932; Kido diary, Feb. 5, 17, 21.

General Wu to close the local boycott societies.[3] This gesture, taken after considerable hesitation, came too late. Admiral Shiozawa, convinced that the Chinese were bent upon driving out of Shanghai the 27,000 Japanese residents in the city, had decided to take action. The American newspaper correspondent Hallett Abend, who happened to be visiting aboard Shiozawa's flagship on the afternoon of January 28, 1932, suddenly heard the admiral say that although the Chinese had accepted a Japanese ultimatum, at 11:00 P.M. that evening he would send marines into Chapei, a large Chinese quarter of the city, to preserve order and protect the 6,000 Japanese nationals residing there. The astonished Abend answered that the Chinese would resist. Shiozawa only replied, "Well, you see the army had to protect our interests in Manchuria. There is no Japanese army in Shanghai, so the navy will have to take over a similar job here." [4]

In such circumstances and reasoning did the Shanghai Incident

3. Selle, *Donald of China,* pp. 272–3.

4. Abend, *My Life in China,* pp. 186–7. After cabling this conversation to the New York *Times,* Abend telephoned the American consul general in Shanghai, Edwin S. Cunningham, who advised that the conversation was a "scare story," unnecessarily upsetting to the *Times'* readers, and that it should not be cabled. Abend, pp. 187–8.

Payson J. Treat in an interesting article entitled "Shanghai: January 28, 1932," *Pacific Historical Review, 9* (1940), 337–43, contends that the Japanese actually were innocent in their movement into Chapei, and that fighting with the Chinese began over a misunderstanding of Japanese intentions. According to this interpretation, Japanese troops were moving into Chapei in compliance with a general defense plan for the protection of the International Settlement and the French Concession: because of threats from Chinese extremists, the municipal council of the Settlement had proclaimed a state of emergency, and on the afternoon of January 28 all foreign forces began to take up their allotted positions under the formal plan of defense decided upon several weeks before in event such an emergency should arise; when the Japanese took up their designated position in the Chapei quarter, later in the evening, they met the Chinese troops. Treat's contention of Japanese innocence is technically plausible but overlooks the previous Japanese blustering. It seems certain that Shiozawa was moved by aggressive intentions, else he would have avoided implementing the Shanghai defense plan only a few hours after acceptance by the Chinese of his ultimatum. There is a lucid discussion of this situation in Stimson's *Far Eastern Crisis,* pp. 117–23.

take its origin. The Japanese admiral's marines advanced into Chapei shortly before midnight on January 28, 1932. Chinese troops in the area, the Nineteenth Route Army, resisted. Shiozawa sent bombing planes over Chapei, to destroy the positions of the Chinese by setting fire to them. This inhuman tactic proved insufficient to defeat the Chinese, and the Japanese army finally brought in three full divisions to do the job.

The bombing of Chapei, let it be added, proved deeply shocking to Western opinion, which was then unaccustomed to indiscriminate air attacks on civilian populations. Hundreds of Chinese died in the fires of Chapei, and thousands rushed headlong into the International Settlement, having lost all their property and personal belongings in what soon became a completely gutted area. Newspaper correspondents, of whom there were always large numbers in Shanghai, watched the roaring fires from their hotels in the Settlement, and for two or three days jammed the Shanghai cables with their accounts of disaster. In terms of "public relations" the Chapei bombing was a bad Japanese blunder. Not to mention the fact that it was militarily ineffective.

There is no reason to describe in the following pages the various maneuvers and battles that occurred before the Japanese had driven Chinese troops out of Shanghai and, having done that, proved willing to conclude an armistice. The purpose of this present chapter is to set forth, in brief compass, the origin of the Shanghai Incident, and then to analyze the diplomatic moves and countermoves of the Western powers as the incident proceeded toward its conclusion: retirement of Japanese troops from the Shanghai area. In passing, however, it might be worth while to notice the peculiar military circumstances, on the Chinese side, that attended the hostilities at Shanghai. As mentioned, the Nineteenth Route Army defended the city, and out of this fact arose some complications in Chinese domestic politics which had diplomatic repercussions. The Route Army, so it happened, was the personal force of the Chinese revolutionary and political leader, Wang Ching-wei. Wang usually controlled Shanghai, and on occasion took part in Chinese politics in Nanking. At the moment the Japanese attacked, Wang was in power at Nanking, due to a temporary "retirement" of Chiang Kai-shek because of embarrassments of the Mukden Incident. Chiang was not unhappy to observe the Japanese attacking the forces of his domestic rival. This peculiar circumstance of Chinese politics accounts for the lukewarm diplomatic and military assistance which the Nationalist government, soon back in possession of Chiang Kai-shek, accorded the hard-pressed forces at Shanghai. For weeks Chiang's personally trained 87th and 88th divisions camped at the rear of the Nineteenth Route Army, refusing to assist the southerners in the fight against the Japanese, standing ready to disarm the Route Army should it retreat. This circumstance explains in part why the Japanese, after expelling the Route Army from Shanghai, refrained from pursuing their success. It was a strange political confusion which reigned during the Shanghai Incident, for as the Japanese well knew, if they pushed the Nineteenth Route Army too hard they would only send it into the arms of the hostile troops of the regime of Chiang Kai-shek.[5] Curiously, a Chinese defeat could become a Chinese victory.

These ramifications of the affair at Shanghai passed largely

5. Kido diary, Feb. 17, 1932; Selle, *Donald of China,* p. 273. Admiral Montgomery Meigs Taylor, in command of the American Asiatic Squadron, wrote to the chief of naval operations, Admiral William V. Pratt, from Shanghai, Apr. 4, 1932, that Chiang Kai-shek wished to see the Nineteenth Route Army weakened as much as possible. "He now has them between his own troops and the Japanese, a very unenviable position"; moreover, Chiang refused to allow the representative of the Nineteenth Route Army on the peace council (at that moment in session) to resign, so that the Route Army would have to bear the onus of any agreement with the Japanese. Taylor MSS in the Library of Congress. The Nationalist Chinese interpretation of the fighting at Shanghai was, of course, quite different. The official biography of Chiang Kai-shek by Hollington K. Tong (*Chiang Kai-shek: Soldier and Statesman,* 2, 338–41) asserts that the Nationalist 87th and 88th divisions really bore the brunt of the fighting at Shanghai, with the result that a third of the men of these divisions were killed. Stimson apparently took at face value these Nationalist claims, for in *The Far Eastern Crisis,* p. 130, he wrote that "this threat from a common foe healed the old antagonisms and the two armies [Nationalist and Nineteenth Route Army] now fought shoulder to shoulder with equal ardor."

unnoticed by Western diplomatists, who saw only the fact of Admiral Shiozawa's attack on a Chinese garrison in the principal port city of China.

2

In Washington at the State Department the last days of January 1932 went by in hectic disorder as the Shanghai Incident got underway. Cables arrived from the Far East like snowflakes in a blizzard. There was trouble merely in keeping the record straight, sifting in a preliminary way the mass of information and speculation that arrived over the wires from Shanghai, Tokyo, and Nanking.[6] Ambassadors and ministers accredited to Washington besieged the Department for word of what was going on and what the American government intended to do about it. The press clamored for news. "With Shanghai boiling," Undersecretary Castle wrote in his diary, "the days are almost as full as they were last summer" during the moratorium negotiations.[7] Without hesitation, consultation, or much deliberation President Hoover dispatched the Thirty-First Infantry Regiment together with four hundred marines from the Philippines to Shanghai, to reinforce the marine contingent permanently stationed in the International Settlement. He ordered to Shanghai all American naval vessels available in the Orient. Officials of the State Department actually took under consideration the advantages of a full-fledged naval demonstration against the Japanese. Undersecretary Castle asked himself if "a really important naval demonstration" would be worth while, "or would it simply stir up the Japanese to fury? Would it be wise to evacuate everybody from Shanghai or would this merely be a sign of impotence? It certainly would put an end to extraterritoriality and to American trade with China and there would be years of reconstruction, if indeed that would ever be possible. The Secretary is feeling very belligerent, and nobody can blame him for his fury against the Japanese . . ." [8]

One of Stimson's moves, taken on February 2, 1932, at the

6. Castle diary, Jan. 29, 1932.
7. Ibid., Jan. 30.
8. Ibid., Feb. 3.

suggestion of President Hoover, was to propose that the Western powers make joint representations to the Chinese and Japanese to stop fighting and open direct negotiations in the presence of neutral observers. As Undersecretary Castle described this maneuver in his diary, the idea was

> to get the British to go along with us on it and to ask them to try to get the French and Italians to join. So we rang up MacDonald at ten o'clock [on the morning of February 1, 1932] and read him what we proposed to say to Japan and China, asked whether the British would join and would ask France and Italy. The Prime Minister said it sounded good, that he would consult his colleagues and telephone back later. In an hour or so Sir John Simon rang us up, said they had studied the matter, made certain suggestions as to verbal changes which we accepted, arranged as to the time tomorrow of presenting the notes, said he already had messages ready for Paris and Rome and the matter was closed. It was the quickest and most modern bit of diplomacy which I have ever seen.[9]

This was the initial action—a joint proposal of good offices. The Japanese government on February 4 repulsed it. There was some reason to believe that the Japanese military had used the intervening time to send reinforcements to Shanghai, and that the government had shielded this action by negotiating with the Western powers.[10] Stimson, angered by rejection of his proposal, wanted to change his tactics at once and say "Go to the devil" to Japan, allowing the Japanese thereafter to "sizzle in a pretty sharp disapproval" by world public opinion.[11] The secretary nonetheless discovered upon consulting Sir John Simon that the British government wished to string out negotions, rather than cut them, and in the State Department Hornbeck and Castle insisted that the

9. "Japan may not agree but refusal will be to set the whole world against Japan. In order to get off the messages promptly the Secretary and I had luncheon in his office. Hornbeck is, of course, horrified at such tactics but except for screams of agony plays the game rather well." Castle diary, Feb. 1, 1932. See also Stimson diary, Feb. 1.

10. Stimson diary, Feb. 4, 1932; *Far Eastern Crisis,* pp. 150–1.

11. Castle diary, Feb. 5; Stimson diary, Feb. 5.

sharp note then under consideration for sending to Tokyo should allow for further negotiations rather than sending Japan to the devil; with the result that Stimson abandoned all thoughts of rebuttal.[12]

After the secretary "digested" the situation he tried another approach, an invocation with Great Britain of the Nine-Power Treaty of Washington. He desired to bring Japan to an international conference. The idea of a conference, he knew, was only implicit in the Nine-Power Treaty; there was no express stipulation that in event of danger of war in the Far East any of the signatories should call a conference; but there was a statement in Article 7 that "whenever a situation arises which in the opinion of any one of them involves the application of the stipulations of the present Treaty, and renders desirable discussion of such application, there shall be full and frank communication between the Contracting Powers concerned." Stimson hoped that through a joint Anglo-American invocation of the treaty the Japanese would prove willing to attend an international conference where Japan might air her grievances against China.[13] Then, too, there was another advantage to invoking the Nine-Power Treaty. If the Japanese government turned down a request for a conference under that treaty, there might arise among the nations the question of sanctions against Japan—sanctions, say, in the form of an embargo upon Japanese goods. Such a measure, Stimson calculated, would have more chance of passing Congress after invocation of the Nine-Power Treaty than if the League of Nations recommended it under the provisions of Article 16 of the Covenant.[14] This was a fond hope of Stimson's—that the nations of the world might engage in sanctions against Japan—for none of the powers would have taken such action during the Great Depression, least of all the United States under the administration of President Hoover. But Stimson afterward claimed that the possibility of sanctions, even if remote, entered his calculations in seeking invocation with Britain of the Nine-Power Treaty. There

12. Castle diary, Feb. 5, 6, 1932; *Far Eastern Crisis,* p. 161.
13. *Far Eastern Crisis,* p. 160.
14. Ibid., p. 161.

thus seemed advantages in invoking the Nine-Power Treaty, and so Stimson dictated the first draft of a joint declaration on the afternoon of February 9, 1932,[15] and during the following week discussed the proposed démarche in detail with Sir John Simon in five transatlantic telephone calls.

There developed a labyrinthine discussion between Stimson and Simon, in which the British foreign secretary resorted to one equivocation after another. Stimson wished to invoke the treaty. Sir John apparently did not. According to Stimson's diary account for February 11, 1932, Simon said that day, speaking from Geneva where he was attending a League meeting, that "at present and tentatively he was with me. He favored this matter certainly in principle, but he wanted to consult the Foreign Office in London and would telephone me tomorrow at eleven o'clock and let me know the situation." [16] Next day Sir John called and agreed in principle but wished to talk with MacDonald; he would get back to London on Sunday night and let Stimson know on Monday.[17] After several days of such tergiversation the American secretary of state concluded that the British were "soft and pudgy" on the whole matter, "very coldfooted," shopkeepers more interested in peddling their wares than saving the world in a grave international emergency.[18] Impatiently he decided upon a formal statement of principle by the United States alone.

The exchange of views between Simon and Stimson in February 1932 in regard to invocation of the Nine-Power Treaty would seem to be a fairly clear-cut matter, in which Stimson favored using the treaty and Simon did not. Still, Sir John Pratt has written that his chief at the Foreign Office was in fact seeking to assist Stimson in invoking the treaty, and that only when Stimson

15. Stimson diary, Feb. 9, 1932.

16. Ibid., Feb. 11.

17. Ibid., Feb. 12. On this same day Simon made an off-the-record speech to the Anglo-American press in Geneva, and undiplomatically remarked that China was a "geographical expression." Stimson, much hurt by this pronouncement, informed his diary that the remark was, "to put it mildly . . . rather out of the spirit in which I was making my proposal" for invocation of the Nine-Power Treaty. Loc. cit.

18. Ibid., Feb. 15, 1932.

became impatient and wanted everything done at once—and the British foreign secretary could not move so rapidly—did there result an American unilateral pronunciamento.[19] This point of view relies on a communication which Simon sent to Stimson on February 16, 1932, in which Sir John stated that the Committee of Twelve of the League Council, then meeting in Geneva, was going to adopt the nonrecognition doctrine in a note to Japan and China, and that he, Simon, preferred an invocation of the Nine-Power Treaty after the League had taken this preliminary measure. In his note Simon stated that he was "hopeful that the adherence of the Powers now at Geneva to the declaration proposed to be made by the Council [the Committee of Twelve] of the League on Wednesday might predispose those of them who are signatories to the Nine-Power Treaty to associate themselves with the American demarche also." [20] According to Stimson's diary account, Simon believed that if the League did this, the nations signatory of the Nine-Power Treaty would inevitably have to do the same thing under that treaty.[21]

The secretary of state was not so certain about the inevitability of invocation of the Nine-Power Treaty. As he commented in his diary, he hoped that Simon while "rounding up" the League would also "round up the recalcitrants in his own Cabinet." [22] And here, perhaps, Stimson had singled out the real difficulty in invoking the Nine-Power Treaty: Sir John could not get cabinet approval. Former President Hoover has stated in his memoirs, without giving the source of his information, that the British government stood unanimously against invocation of the Nine-Power Treaty.[23]

19. Pratt, *War and Politics in China*, pp. 270–4, 281–6.

20. Ibid., p. 285. For the League action of Feb. 16 see above, p. 161.

21. Stimson diary, Feb. 15, 1932.

22. Ibid.

23. *Memoirs of Herbert Hoover: The Cabinet and the Presidency*, p. 376. In Simon's memoirs, *Retrospect* (London, 1952), there is no information on this point, and not much on the entire Far Eastern question. Stimson seems to have realized that Simon could not act without cabinet approval, as witness his diary entry for Feb. 15, 1932. Yet the secretary believed that Simon had far more freedom of action than was the case. Stanley K. Hornbeck in conversa-

It was not altogether unconnected with Sir John Simon's disappointment of Stimson, coming hard upon failure the month before to support the doctrine of nonrecognition, that the British government vigorously continued its efforts at the League of Nations. Having obtained (on February 16) a nonrecognition note from the Committee of Twelve, Simon on March 11, 1932, secured from the Assembly a resolution in support of Stimson's doctrine of nonrecognition: "it is incumbent upon the members of the League of Nations not to recognize any situation, treaty or agreement which may be brought about by means contrary to the Covenant of the League of Nations or to the Pact of Paris." [24]

3

By this time Stimson had already gone ahead on his own to make another unilateral declaration somewhat similar to his nonrecognition doctrine of January 1932.

A declaration of principle appealed strongly to the secretary, for a formal statement of the case against Japan, he felt, would "put the situation morally in its right place." [25] Something of this sort

---

tion on Jan. 4, 1952, said that twenty years before he had sought to tell Stimson that Simon would need express cabinet consent to any promise of joint invocation of the Nine-Power Treaty, but Stimson preferred not to believe this.

24. It is true that Stimson on Mar. 4, 1932, instructed the American minister in China to abstain from attending further sessions of a League *ad hoc* committee, composed of the diplomatic representatives in China of the various Western powers, which was then meeting in Shanghai; and this refusal to cooperate, promptly explained by Stimson to Simon, convinced the British foreign secretary that the time had come to round up the League. *Far Eastern Crisis,* p. 178. But it seems also to be true that Simon was worried over his previous record of uncooperativeness, and was genuinely eager to please Stimson on that score alone. It is difficult, of course, to explain precisely why Simon chose to work so ardently at Geneva in early March 1932.

Hoover's reaction to the good news of Mar. 11—the League resolution—is worth noting. Stimson in his diary related how, upon receiving the news, he went over to the White House to see the president: "The President was busy with other things and at first was not ready to rise to the enthusiasm of the occasion. But I stirred him up a little and told him he would have to be a little more lively." Diary, Mar. 11, 1932.

25. Stimson diary, Feb. 8, 1932.

was necessary to meet the Japanese challenge. As Stimson later recalled, "it seemed to me that in future years I should not like to face a verdict of history to the effect that a government to which I had belonged had failed to express itself adequately upon such a situation." [26] The only problem was the form of his announcement. He was fearful that if he drew up a note to the powers invoking the Nine-Power Treaty he would only receive "yellow-bellied responses." [27] He knew that he could make no statement that in any sense required an answer. He finally hit upon the solution to his problem while on a horseback ride in Rock Creek Park, on the morning of February 21, 1932, when he recounted his diplomatic difficulties to his riding companion, Assistant Secretary of State James G. Rogers. Rogers suggested a public letter, and the secretary at once recalled how Theodore Roosevelt had been wont to write letters to William Dudley Foulke of Indiana. He decided to write his letter to Senator Borah.

The resulting statement, the Borah Letter, dated February 23, 1932, Stimson afterward considered "in many ways the most significant state paper" he ever composed.[28] Much of it he wrote himself, although he had the assistance of Department officers, especially Hornbeck, Klots, and Rogers. The letter strongly affirmed American rights in the Far East under the Nine-Power Treaty and the Kellogg-Briand Pact. In many ways it was similar to the note of nonrecognition of January 7, 1932, but it differed from that note in two particulars: it explicitly mentioned and emphasized the Nine-Power Treaty; it contained an implicit threat that further Japanese conquests in the Far East might compromise the American promise at Washington in 1922 that the United States would not further fortify Guam and the Philippines.[29] The

26. *Far Eastern Crisis,* p. 157.

27. Stimson diary, Feb. 21, 1932.

28. *On Active Service,* p. 246. The complete text of this document appears at the end of this chapter.

29. As Stimson afterward explained in his memoirs, this delicate threat to the Japanese was the strongest statement he made during the Manchurian crisis. Ibid., p. 256.

Nine-Power Treaty, Stimson said in his letter, had "crystallized" American foreign policy and the policy of all the powers in the Far East; it had given "definition and precision" to the principle of the Open Door which included respect for Chinese territorial and administrative entity. The Nine-Power Treaty was "a carefully developed and matured international policy" in regard to China. After some judiciously selected comments of approbation of the Nine-Power Treaty, by such personages as Secretary Hughes, Lord Balfour, and Baron Shidehara, Stimson passed on to his implied threat:

> It must be remembered also that this Treaty was one of several treaties and agreements entered into at the Washington Conference by the various powers concerned, all of which were interrelated and interdependent. No one of these treaties can be disregarded without disturbing the general understanding and equilibrium which were intended to be accomplished and effected by the group of agreements arrived at in their entirety. . . . The willingness of the American government to surrender its then commanding lead in battleship construction and to leave its positions at Guam and in the Philippines without further fortification, was predicated upon, among other things, the self-denying covenants contained in the Nine Power Treaty . . .

The Borah Letter, so ingeniously addressed to an American senator, was an excellent example of the sort of legalistic state paper in which Stimson always excelled. Extremely well drafted, its statement of the American diplomatic position was sharp and yet not irritating. The note was careful, comprehensive, and likely to convince any individual who read it with an open mind and clear conscience. Stimson intended his letter, so he recalled in his *Far Eastern Crisis,* for the perusal of at least five unnamed addressees: he hoped it would encourage China, enlighten the American public, exhort the League, stir up the British, and warn Japan.[30]

30. *Far Eastern Crisis,* p. 175.

The only question one might have raised about the letter was whether its unnamed addressees took it seriously. There is reason to believe that they did not. It seems to have exerted no effect at all in Japan.[31] The American public, at least judging from contemporary newspaper comment, approved the declaration and forgot about it.[32] As for Great Britain and the Borah Letter, the British seem to have taken it as another example of American diplomatic sermonizing; Sir John Pratt considered it "trivial." [33] In China the note became lost in the swirl of domestic politics. Its sole discernible effect upon the League of Nations may have lain in the passage by the Assembly of the resolution of March 11, which was the special work of Sir John Simon, and which probably would have passed anyway.

The letter had scarcely appeared in print when Stimson was arguing with President Hoover against issuance of a public declaration that under no circumstances would the United States go to war with Japan—a declaration which would have destroyed most of the effect of the missive to Borah, certainly the letter's only sharp statement, the implied threat of fortifying Guam and the Philippines.[34] Stimson knew that the possibility of further fortifying the Pacific islands was bluff, for the Hoover Administration was in no position to make so provocative a proposal to Congress. He knew also that President Hoover possessed not "the slightest element of even the fairest kind of bluff." [35] He hoped that Hoover would not give his diplomatic hand away by a self-denying statement such as the president desired. As he wrote to a friend, "There is no point in telling your enemy that you have less ammunition

31. The voluminous and comprehensive Saionji-Harada diary does not mention the Borah Letter.

32. Shortly after Stimson published his letter there occurred in Paris the spectacular suicide of the Swedish match king, Ivar Kreuger, heralding the downfall of Kreuger's empire of bogus stocks and bonds, many of which were held in the United States. At the same time there was the kidnapping of the Lindbergh child, which occupied the front pages of American newspapers from March to May 1932.

33. *War and Politics in China,* p. 228.

34. Stimson diary, Feb. 25, 1932. See also entries of Feb. 26, Apr. 3.

35. Ibid., Jan. 26.

than he thinks."[36] Through the spring of 1932 Hoover "incubated" on the self-denying statement, and finally insisted upon a speech by Undersecretary Castle in May 1932 affirming that the United States would always employ peaceful means in international affairs. Stimson at the moment was in Europe attending the World Disarmament Conference, and could do nothing to prevent the release of this information.

The Shanghai Incident meanwhile had run its course. For the Japanese high command in Tokyo the conquest of Manchuria was enough military action for the time being, and the leaders of the army and navy proved anxious to bring the Shanghai affair to an end. After a face-saving expulsion of the Chinese forces from Shanghai, the Japanese virtually disavowed the aggressive tactics of Admiral Shiozawa, and proved eager to settle the Shanghai Incident diplomatically and return the situation to the status quo ante hostilities. Negotiations between Chinese and Japanese plenipotentiaries commenced in Shanghai in April 1932, assisted by a League of Nations *ad hoc* committee composed of the diplomatic representatives in China of the various Western powers. A formal Sino-Japanese armistice agreement, signed on May 5, 1932, stipulated for complete evacuation of the Japanese forces which at their peak strength had numbered upward of 50,000.[37]

Western diplomatists took comfort in the fact that the hostilities at Shanghai had not resulted in a formally declared war between China and Japan, and that the world's peace machinery had not come thereby to an ultimate and conclusive test. Secretary Stimson, relieved at the final solution of the difficulties at Shanghai, disappointed that in his efforts toward a peaceful settlement he had received such slight assistance from the Western great powers, in particular Britain, was satisfied that in the letter to

36. "I agree with you as to the dangers of a boycott, and since January 7 we have tried to stake out an alternative policy which would not involve its dangers. But I see no advantage as yet in saying that under no circumstances would we ever use any particular weapon . . ." Stimson to Henry P. Fletcher, Feb. 27, 1932, Stimson MSS.

37. Details of the settlement at Shanghai—the negotiations carried on by Western representatives with the Chinese and Japanese—are in the Nelson T. Johnson MSS deposited in the Library of Congress.

Senator Borah he had summed up the moral aspects of the Shanghai Incident and presented those moral aspects unofficially to the several parties concerned. Here, for the moment, the secretary rested his case anent Japanese aggression in the Far East, while he turned his thoughts to the World Disarmament Conference.

THE LETTER TO SENATOR BORAH, FEBRUARY 23, 1932 *

You have asked my opinion whether, as has been sometimes recently suggested, present conditions in China have in any way indicated that the so-called Nine Power Treaty has become inapplicable or ineffective or rightly in need of modification, and if so, what I considered should be the policy of this Government.

This Treaty, as you of course know, forms the legal basis upon which now rests the "Open Door" policy towards China. That policy, enunciated by John Hay in 1899, brought to an end the struggle among various powers for so-called spheres of interest in China which was threatening the dismemberment of that empire. To accomplish this Mr. Hay invoked two principles (1) equality of commercial opportunity among all nations in dealing with China, and (2) as necessary to that equality the preservation of China's territorial and administrative integrity. These principles were not new in the foreign policy of America. They had been the principles upon which it rested in its dealings with other nations for many years. In the case of China they were invoked to save a situation which not only threatened the future development and sovereignty of that great Asiatic people, but also threatened to create dangerous and constantly increasing rivalries between the other nations of the world. War had already taken place between Japan and China. At the close of that war three other nations intervened to prevent Japan from obtaining some of the results of that war claimed by her. Other nations sought and had obtained spheres of interest. Partly as a result of these actions a serious uprising had broken out in China which endangered the legations of all of the powers at Peking. While the attack on those legations

* *FR: Japan,* 1931–41, *I*, 83–7.

was in progress, Mr. Hay made an announcement in respect to this policy as the principle upon which the powers should act in the settlement of the rebellion. He said

> The policy of the Government of the United States is to seek a solution which may bring about permanent safety and peace to China, preserve Chinese territorial and administrative entity, protect all rights guaranteed to friendly powers by treaty and international law, and safeguard for the world the principle of equal and impartial trade with all parts of the Chinese Empire.

He was successful in obtaining the assent of the other powers to the policy thus announced.

In taking these steps Mr. Hay acted with the cordial support of the British Government. In responding to Mr. Hay's announcement, above set forth, Lord Salisbury, the British Prime Minister expressed himself "most emphatically as concurring in the policy of the United States."

For twenty years thereafter the Open Door policy rested upon the informal commitments thus made by the various powers. But in the winter of 1921 to 1922, at a conference participated in by all of the principal powers which had interests in the Pacific, the policy was crystallized into the so-called Nine Power Treaty, which gave definition and precision to the principles upon which the policy rested. In the first article of that Treaty, the contracting powers, other than China, agreed

> 1. To respect the sovereignty, the independence and the territorial and administrative integrity of China.
>
> 2. To provide the fullest and most unembarrassed opportunity to China to develop and maintain for herself an effective and stable government.
>
> 3. To use their influence for the purpose of effectually establishing and maintaining the principle of equal opportunity for the commerce and industry of all nations throughout the territory of China.
>
> 4. To refrain from taking advantage of conditions in China

in order to seek special rights or privileges which would abridge the rights of subjects or citizens of friendly states, and from countenancing action inimical to the security of such states.

This Treaty thus represents a carefully developed and matured international policy intended, on the one hand, to assure to all of the contracting parties their rights and interests in and with regard to China, and on the other hand, to assure to the people of China the fullest opportunity to develop without molestation their sovereignty and independence according to the modern and enlightened standards believed to maintain among the peoples of this earth. At the time this Treaty was signed, it was known that China was engaged in an attempt to develop the free institutions of a self-governing republic after her recent revolution from an autocratic form of government; that she would require many years of both economic and political effort to that end; and that her progress would necessarily be slow. The Treaty was thus a covenant of self-denial among the signatory powers in deliberate renunciation of any policy of aggression which might tend to interfere with that development. It was believed—and the whole history of the development of the "Open Door" policy reveals that faith—that only by such a process, under the protection of such an agreement, could the fullest interests not only of China but of all nations which have intercourse with her best be served.

In its report to the President announcing this Treaty, the American Delegation, headed by the then Secretary of State, Mr. Charles E. Hughes, said

> It is believed that through this Treaty the "Open Door" in China has at last been made a fact.

During the course of the discussions which resulted in the Treaty, the Chairman of the British delegation, Lord Balfour, had stated that

> The British Empire delegation understood that there was no representative of any power around the table who thought that the old practice of "spheres of interest" was either advo-

> cated by any government or would be tolerable to this conference. So far as the British Government was concerned, they had, in the most formal manner, publicly announced that they regarded this practice as utterly inappropriate to the existing situation.

At the same time the representative of Japan, Baron Shidehara, announced the position of his government as follows:

> No one denies to China her sacred right to govern herself. No one stands in the way of China to work out her own great national destiny.

The Treaty was originally executed by the United States, Belgium, the British Empire, China, France, Italy, Japan, the Netherlands and Portugal. Subsequently it was also executed by Norway, Bolivia, Sweden, Denmark and Mexico. Germany has signed it but her Parliament has not yet ratified it.

It must be remembered also that this Treaty was one of several treaties and agreements entered into at the Washington Conference by the various powers concerned, all of which were interrelated and interdependent. No one of these treaties can be disregarded without disturbing the general understanding and equilibrium which were intended to be accomplished and effected by the group of agreements arrived at in their entirety. The Washington Conference was essentially a disarmament conference, aimed to promote the possibility of peace in the world not only through the cessation of competition in naval armament but also by the solution of various other disturbing problems which threatened the peace of the world, particularly in the Far East. These problems were all interrelated. The willingness of the American government to surrender its then commanding lead in battleship construction and to leave its positions at Guam and in the Philippines without further fortification, was predicated upon, among other things, the self-denying covenants contained in the Nine Power Treaty, which assured the nations of the world not only of equal opportunity for their Eastern trade but also against the military aggrandizement of any other power at the expense of China. One cannot discuss the possibility of modifying or abrogating those provisions of the Nine Power Treaty without considering at the same time the other promises upon which they were really dependent.

Six years later the policy of self-denial against aggression by a stronger against a weaker power, upon which the Nine Power Treaty had been based, received a powerful reinforcement by the execution by substantially all the nations of the world of the Pact of Paris, the so-called Kellogg-Briand Pact. These two treaties represent independent but harmonious steps taken for the purpose of aligning the conscience and public opinion of the world in favor of a system of orderly development by the law of nations including the settlement of all controversies by methods of justice and peace instead of by arbitrary force. The program for the protection of China from outside aggression is an essential part of any such development. The signatories and adherents of the Nine Power Treaty rightly felt that the orderly and peaceful development of the 400,000,000 of people inhabiting China was necessary to the peaceful welfare of the entire world and that no program for the welfare of the world as a whole could afford to neglect the welfare and protection of China.

The recent events which have taken place in China, especially the hostilities which having been begun in Manchuria have latterly been extended to Shanghai, far from indicating the advisability of any modification of the treaties we have been discussing, have tended to bring home the vital importance of the faithful observance of the covenants therein to all of the nations interested in the Far East. It is not necessary in that connection to inquire into the causes of the controversy or attempt to apportion the blame between the two nations which are unhappily involved; for regardless of cause or responsibility, it is clear beyond peradventure that a situation has developed which cannot, under any circumstances, be reconciled with the obligations of the covenants of these two treaties, and that if the treaties had been faithfully observed such a situation could not have arisen. The signatories of the Nine Power Treaty and of the Kellogg-Briand Pact who are not parties to that conflict are not likely to see any reason for modifying the terms of those treaties. To them the real value of the faithful performance of the treaties has been brought sharply home by the perils and losses to which their nationals have been subjected in Shanghai.

That is the view of this Government. We see no reason for abandoning the enlightened principles which are embodied in these treaties. We believe that this situation would have been avoided had these covenants been faithfully observed, and no evidence has come to us to indicate that a due compliance with them would have interfered with the adequate protection of the legitimate rights in China of the signatories of those treaties and their nationals.

On January 7th last, upon the instruction of the President, this Government formally notified Japan and China that it would not recognize any situation, treaty or agreement entered into by those governments in violation of the covenants of these treaties, which affected the rights of our Government or its citizens in China. If a similar decision should be reached and a similar position taken by the other governments of the world, a caveat will be placed upon such action which, we believe, will effectively bar the legality hereafter of any title or right sought to be obtained by pressure or treaty violation, and which, as has been shown by history in the past, will eventually lead to the restoration to China of rights and titles of which she may have been deprived.

In the past our Government, as one of the leading powers on the Pacific Ocean, has rested its policy upon an abiding faith in the future of the people of China and upon the ultimate success in dealing with them of the principles of fair play, patience, and mutual goodwill. We appreciate the immensity of the task which lies before her statesmen in the development of her country and its government. The delays in her progress, the instability of her attempts to secure a responsible government, were foreseen by Messrs. Hay and Hughes and their contemporaries and were the very obstacles which the policy of the Open Door was designed to meet. We concur with those statesmen, representing all the nations in the Washington Conference who decided that China was entitled to the time necessary to accomplish her development. We are prepared to make that our policy for the future.

Chapter Twelve: A WORLD DISARMAMENT CONFERENCE

1

Incongruous events have a way of happening at the same time, in the course of international affairs, and such certainly was the case in early February 1932: the World Disarmament Conference met in Geneva while the Japanese and Chinese carried on an undeclared war in Shanghai. Diplomatists had not planned events this way. The Shanghai Incident was not planned at all. As for the Disarmament Conference, it had been planned too long—since the year 1925—and the statesmen of the world would have abandoned it if they dared. In early 1932 the Disarmament Conference was an unmitigated nuisance, but there was no chance of postponing it any longer, even because of the Far Eastern Crisis. Popular hopes for disarmament had risen too high. The conference of 1932 was the largest international assemblage held up to that time. Delegates attended from fifty-nine different nations. Cynics could describe the Geneva meeting as a fools' paradise, a universal embrace. Diplomats recalled the injunction of Frederick the Great, that diplomacy without armaments was like music without instruments. Common people everywhere hoped that so grand a meeting, so crowded with delegations, might perchance discover a solution to the world's ills where previous smaller conferences had failed. They hoped that the World Disarmament Conference would provide, through a treaty of disarmament, a solvent for national rivalries. Was not the year 1932, they asked, a good year for such a solvent?

Popular hopes for peace through disarmament were many and large. In anticipation of the conference, peace leaders such as

Viscount Cecil had announced that war was an international vendetta which ought to be stopped.[1] Sir Edward Grey had already told the British public that "great armaments lead inevitably to war. . . . The enormous growth of armaments in Europe . . . made war inevitable." [2] Military leaders of the World War were themselves making startling confessions; Field Marshal Sir William Robertson was saying that "War hurts everybody, benefits nobody but the profiteer, and settles nothing." The pleas of the disillusioned soldiers, political leaders, and peace leaders mingled with demands of taxpayers who found the expense of armaments burdensome. One amateur economist calculated that the nations of the world had been spending annually on arms the equivalent of $4.89 per minute since the birth of Christ. President Hoover announced in mid-1931 that annual world arms expenditure came near to five billions of dollars, an increase of about 70 per cent over the hectic years before the World War; the world's armies in 1931, he declared, greatly exceeded those of the prewar period: nearly 5,500,000 men were under arms, and 20,000,000 more stood available in reserves.[3] Including the huge benefits to veterans, the American government in 1932 spent more on wars, past and future, than any other nation—about 75 per cent of the budget. People wanted relief in some form from such military taxation. In many quarters, moreover, the disarmament conference had linked itself to the question of intergovernmental debts. The debts could not be written down or off, Americans thought, without a disarmament agreement, because debt relief would merely shift European budgetary appropriations so as to bring greater expenditure on armaments.[4] For all these reasons, people everywhere looked forward to the World Disarmament Conference.

Despite such widespread popular support, it had been no easy

1. Viscount Cecil, "Facing the World Disarmament Conference," *Foreign Affairs, 10* (1931–32), 14.

2. Viscount Grey of Fallodon, *Twenty-Five Years: 1892–1916, 1,* 89–90.

3. Speech before the International Chamber of Commerce in Washington, May 4, 1931, *Memoirs of Herbert Hoover: The Cabinet and the Presidency,* p. 353.

4. Allen W. Dulles, "Progress toward Disarmament," *Foreign Affairs, 11* (1932–33), 65.

task of diplomacy to bring the conference together. Behind it lay years of careful diplomatic labor. The League of Nations since its first meeting in 1920 had debated disarmament, promising annually to do something about it. The Covenant did not itself require action, Article 8 committing the nations to disarm only to an extent consistent with national safety. This latitudinarian wording made the article a dead letter. Still, in the preamble to Part V of the Versailles Treaty there was another such statement that after limitation of German arms the nations should limit their own weapons.[5] This latter injunction could not be brushed lightly aside despite the fact that a preamble has little legal weight, because every year the German government reminded the erstwhile Allies of their "promise," and German unrest made for Allied unrest, and the result was a vicious circle of unrest which needed to be broken. When Germany joined the League after signing the Locarno treaties, the nations consented to organization of a preparatory commission, looking toward the future Disarmament Conference. Most League members together with the United States and Soviet Russia sent representatives to this commission, and after six meetings a session in late 1930 drew a tentative disarmament convention and adjourned.

The preparatory commission ended its labors after five years of acrimony. It had considered many questions—reserves, war material, publicity of war material in reserve, supervision, escape clauses, consultation, holidays. Disarmament was no simple matter. Such apparently minor details as "quantitative" and "qualitative" disarmament had turned into touchy political problems. Qualitative disarmament—abolition of offensive weapons—attracted

5. "In order to render possible the initiation of a general limitation of the armaments of all nations . . ." When the German delegation at Paris first received the peace treaty, they made the following observation upon Part V: "Germany is prepared to agree to the basic idea of the army, navy, and air regulations . . . provided this is a beginning of a general reduction of armaments." To which the Allied powers replied that their requirements were "the first steps toward that general reduction and limitation of armaments which they seek to bring about as one of the most fruitful preventives of war, and which it will be one of the first duties of the League of Nations to promote."

the British government, which liked the idea that disarmament, while not ending the possibility of war, could bring within narrow limits the possibility of sudden attack; but qualitative disarmament did not commend itself to the French, who by limiting their powers of sudden offense would only reduce themselves toward the weak situation of Germany—and Germany in a long war would have the advantage of a huge war potential.[6] Such details had to be explored, and the exploration lent itself to wordy arguments. Descents into the vast mechanical paraphernalia of war-making confused laymen, and proved difficult for experts. The possibilities for delay at the meetings of the preparatory commission were patent, and one must suspect that some of the more interested nations encouraged obscurantism. The chairman of the commission, the diplomatist-publicist Salvadore de Madariaga, later asserted that a subcommittee alone used 3,750,000 sheets of typescript, enough to permit the League's Polish or Swedish delegations to walk home on a path made of League paper.[7] Observing the endless committee meetings from Washington, Undersecretary Castle believed that "time and again, when the Commission took a recess, it was apparent that the labor of months had issued in just exactly nothing. As time dragged on, the representatives of the different nations became more interested in the details of gun construction than in the broad purpose for which the Commission had been assembled, that of mapping out a plan of limiting armament for the sake of world peace. The disease of trivialities was contagious. Even in the Department of State, those doing the spade work found themselves discussing the size of tanks to be permitted . . ." The commission "lived too long. Or perhaps it might be better to say that it died of inanition, but was given a false appearance of continued vitality instead of decent interment because the Governments supporting it were afraid of the reaction of the people at home if the death of the Commission

6. Moreover, the French had great stocks of material left over from the World War. Jordan, *Great Britain, France, and the German Problem,* p. 164.

7. Alfred Zimmern, *The League of Nations and the Rule of Law: 1918–1935* (London, 1936; 2d ed. 1939), p. 377.

were admitted. President Coolidge often thought of recalling the American delegates . . ."[8] But after a welter of discussion the commission arrived at a provisional plan, and received a decent interment.

Such was the diplomatic preparation for the Geneva Disarmament Conference by the end of the year 1930, when the preparatory commission finished its work. In following months the State Department continued to assemble masses of data on armaments and to draw together its ideas in preparation for the coming conference.[9] This essential preconference work was still going forward by the autumn of 1931, with only a few months left before the beginning of the conference in February 1932, when Premier Pierre Laval of France announced that he would travel to the United States for preliminary pourparlers.

2

Laval's visit followed the precedent by Ramsay MacDonald two years earlier. The French premier desired to come to the United States; he expressed his desire delicately through diplomatic channels; the American government made known its pleasure over the prospect of receiving him. It could hardly do otherwise after what a Department officer in 1929 had told the French ambassador when questioned about MacDonald's previous visit—that the president was receiving the British minister just as he would have received Premier Raymond Poincaré, had the latter desired to come to America.

Unfortunately, autumn of 1931 was an exceedingly busy time. The Far Eastern Crisis had just developed. The British financial crisis was making trouble. In the United States the last quarter of 1931 saw more banking failures than any previous period of the Hoover Administration. No one in high government circles thought much about Laval's visit until the premier was virtually

8. William R. Castle, manuscript book on American foreign relations, pp. 167–8.

9. In the Department, Pierrepont Moffat worked on preparation for the conference. See Nancy H. Hooker, ed., *The Moffat Papers: Selections from the Diplomatic Journals of Jay Pierrepont Moffat,* Cambridge, Mass., 1956.

on the high seas. Stimson at Woodley on the morning of September 30, having awakened earlier than usual, lay sleeplessly in bed: "As I was awake early this morning," he afterward informed his diary, "I began to think about troubles which are ahead. The President is so busy over his domestic and financial troubles that he is not thinking out ahead the problems of international relations . . . and that throws more of the responsibility on me . . ." The situation required action, so on the way down to the State Department the secretary of state stopped at the White House and, as he put it, "moved in on" Hoover. The president was not the least interested: "the Laval meeting was evidently just a nuisance to him. As I told him after we had been going for awhile, it seemed to me all he was thinking about was how he could best stop Laval from picking his pocket while he was here." [10]

There were several reasons why Laval was coming to the United States, although none of them, of course, was as furtive as Hoover imagined. Not the least of the premier's purposes was to secure his political position in France by ostentatious international visiting. With his foreign minister, Briand, he had made a trip to Berlin, the first time a French premier had visited Germany since the International Conference at Berlin in 1878, and with other trips to Rome and London and Washington it was beginning to appear in France that Pierre Laval was a hard-working premier. Then at Geneva, at the World Disarmament Conference, the old problem of French security would arise, and Laval may have thought that he could persuade the leaders of the American government not to take a doctrinaire attitude toward France's European position—an attitude of the sort which had prevented France from adhering to the naval limitation agreements at the London Conference. Pierre Laval in the early 1930's served France well with his brilliant political talents and ability to charm and convince almost everyone he met. In the early 1930's Laval was a capable citizen of France, and his skill was badly needed in ex-

10. Stimson diary, Sept. 30, 1931. The British ambassador reported to the Foreign Office on Oct. 23, 1931, that Hoover in talking to a "well-known pacifist" about Laval, had said bluntly: "What has he come for, anyway?" *Documents on British Foreign Policy,* 2d ser., 2, 303.

plaining his country's international requirements to President Hoover (who, strongly anti-French, had allegedly spoken privately of Frenchmen as "frogs"). Perhaps Laval could convert Hoover. Because of the moratorium he at least would not have to speak of war debts, hitherto such a touchy subject with the president of the United States.[11]

Despite apparently faultless calculation of the possibilities, Laval in his American visit had not reckoned with the illogicalities of American international views. The United States Government did not regard the World Disarmament Conference as an opportunity to lead the European nations or even to help them much. The conference would have to deal primarily with land armament, which the State Department believed was a European—mainly French—problem. To the United States, disarmament had always meant naval limitation, and at Geneva the American government would offer only moral support, while the European countries themselves sought to limit their armies.

Moreover, there was another difficulty which the premier would discover upon his arrival in the United States. Secretary Stimson was beginning to see the World Conference as something bigger than a disarmament meeting—as a European peace conference, at which the nations would discuss all their problems, not merely disarmament, and out of the discussion would come political agreements making disarmament possible. The only way to get at the question of European peace, the secretary now thought, was to get at the underlying problems of the nations, particularly those between France and Germany.[12] This entailed a revision of the Versailles Treaty with concessions to Germany on the Polish Corridor and other matters. And here was a most dangerous proposal. As Laval well knew, to suggest to a large international conference in 1932 a revision of the Treaty of Versailles would

11. But see *Memoirs of Herbert Hoover: The Great Depression*, pp. 95–6, where Hoover accuses Laval of coming over to urge reduction in French debt payments: "As France had enough gold on deposit in the United States to cover future debt payments for five or six years, I was not very enthusiastic about that part of his errand."

12. Stimson diary, Sept. 20, 1931.

have stirred up grave international troubles in Europe. It would have made trouble elsewhere, for many non-European nations, observing an effort to change the most vital treaty of Europe, would wish to revise something or other, probably a boundary with a neighboring enemy, and discussion at the World Disarmament Conference would have gotten out of hand.

The premier quickly discovered, upon arrival in Washington on October 22, 1931, that he could do nothing to please the obtuse Americans except revise the Versailles Treaty in favor of Germany, which would not have increased France's own security, the prime object of his visit. On the subject of disarmament he informed Hoover that he could do little in Europe unless he had guarantees; France, he added, desired some type of consultative pact which would lead in that direction. Hoover responded that this was a political impossibility—the American people could not and would not guarantee the security of any country, and Americans would not involve themselves in any agreement that might lead to military consequences in Europe. The real security of France, the President insisted, rested upon the progress of world peace, which would greatly increase with an all-around reduction of armaments.[13]

The Hoover-Stimson-Laval discussions proceeded uneventfully

13. When Laval returned to Paris, the British ambassador, Sir William Tyrrell, asked what had happened during the Washington conversations. Laval said that at the first meeting he had said to the President: "It lies with you to stop war by a simple declaration that America will always be found opposed to the aggressor. The best way to give expression to such a policy would be for America to join in a consultative pact and reconsider her attitude on the freedom of the seas [that is, on co-operation with League sanctions under Article 16 of the Covenant]." To this Hoover had replied that public opinion in the United States was not yet sufficiently advanced to make such a general declaration, but that the United States, as in the past, would always be found siding against the aggressor. Tyrrell to the Marquis of Reading, Nov. 5, 1931, *Documents on British Foreign Policy,* 2d ser., 2, 317–18. See also Myers, *The Foreign Policy of Herbert Hoover,* p. 181; Stimson and Bundy, *On Active Service,* p. 275; Stimson diary, Oct. 23, 1931. Ogden Mills, M. Buisson (Laval's interpreter), Hoover, Laval, and Stimson talked from 3:30 P.M. until midnight on Oct. 23, with exception of an hour at dinner.

toward their foreordained end, and would have arrived there without further ado had it not been for Senator William E. Borah. The senator possessed a long nose for publicity, and from afar he scented a headline in the Laval visit. As chairman of the Committee on Foreign Relations his word carried weight abroad, although he was not an official member of the Administration. He could speak irresponsibly if the spirit moved him, which it frequently did. Public men and journals in the eastern part of the United States often counseled Borah that the best service he could perform for peace was to hold his tongue; [14] but to no avail, for the American people, particularly Midwesterners, liked irresponsibility when it was pitched in the high moral key usually employed by the Lion of Idaho. And so, while (as the Louisville *Courier-Journal* whimsically put it) the world audience was eagerly awaiting an act by Hoover and Laval, the majestic notes of the overture died away, the lights went down, the curtain rose, and there stood Senator Borah bowing in the spotlight. While the president and premier and the secretary of state were conferring at the White House, Borah summoned the press to his Senate office and indulged in an outburst which some newspapers later characterized as "childish, naive, simple-minded, ill-timed, raucous, mischievous, tactless, indiscreet, and immature." "I suppose I have likely started something," the senator wrote afterward to a friend. When he began his press interview he had asked the reporters, "Shall I speak frankly?" and of course the answer was "yes." What he actually said was not world-shaking except that he discussed openly and in his semi-official capacity what he knew Hoover and Laval were discussing secretly: revision of the Treaty of Versailles. There would have to be some changes in the treaty, he said, and that meant the Polish Corridor and the Hungarian frontiers. Reporters at once cabled his statement abroad, to the consternation of Polish and French opinion and the joy of all Germans and Hungarians.[15]

14. See the editorial in the New York *Times*, Sept. 26, 1931.

15. Claudius O. Johnson, *Borah of Idaho* (New York, 1936), pp. 320, 446, 448. Borah had talked to Hoover at the White House the day before Laval arrived in Washington. Ibid., pp. 445–6.

Such an irresponsible open statement could hardly have assisted the diplomacy then going on at the White House. When news of the "Borah Doctrine" was handed in to the conferees, Laval broke into a horrified laugh, raised his hands, and said, "Why the man lives in Mars!" But all was eventually forgiven when Stimson introduced Borah to Laval at Woodley. The two antagonists sat on a sofa in Stimson's library and talked amiably and at length. Master politicians, they were really kindred spirits, and their differing ideas about foreign policy could hardly separate them.[16] After dinner the next night at the French embassy, the premier played a joke on Borah by introducing him to a French deputy in Laval's party and describing him as *"un homme sauvage, qui est toujours contre le gouvernement."* The senator, who did not understand French at all, eagerly grasped the man by the hand.[17]

After his Washington conversations, Laval must have concluded that the time was ill-chosen for obtaining guarantees for France. Americans were in no mood to take part in European affairs. Dwight Morrow, ordinarily a strong friend of France, about this time told Undersecretary Castle that if the entire American continent disappeared under the surface of the ocean it would not greatly affect the questions which agitated Europe.[18] The undersecretary might have added: vice versa. Even Stimson now seemed to have made a *volte face* so far as concerned European politics. Castle noticed that the secretary was "rather hot" on the subject of the Disarmament Conference "because he thinks that nothing can possibly come of political questions in Europe." [19] For the moment, however, Laval's unsuccessful visit had to be glossed over, and when the premier departed he and Hoover issued a joint statement. "While in the short time at our disposal," they concluded, "it has not been possible to formulate definite programs, we find that we view the nature of these financial and economic problems in the same light and that this understanding on our part should serve to pave the way for helpful action by our respec-

16. Stimson diary, Oct. 24, 1931.
17. Ibid., Oct. 25.
18. Castle diary, Oct. 2, 1931.
19. Ibid.

tive governments." [20] Stimson acknowledged to his diary that this was a colorless communiqué.[21] Ambassador Claudel was furious, and afterward cornered Castle and "was unusually undiplomatic, in fact really outrageous. He was mad all through because he considered the communiqué . . . too thin." [22]

The vicissitudes of Franco-American diplomacy incident to the coming World Disarmament Conference at Geneva were followed by somewhat similar happenings in Italo-American diplomacy. Not to be outdone by the French, Italy sent over Count Dino Grandi, Mussolini's new foreign minister. Hoover was delighted by Grandi's visit, for it offered an opportunity "to use Grandi as a foil to the French." [23] But when the foreign minister finally got down to diplomatic business with the president, he found—as Laval had discovered before him—that he could get nowhere. Hoover spoke sharply to Grandi, as the following memorandum well indicates:

> The President . . . gave a summary of the attitude of the American man on the street. For a hundred and fifty years we had kept out of Europe; then in 1917 we had been dragged in in a great war. We had spent forty billions of dollars in the war, and we had added ten billions more in the shape of loans after the war. We were spending a billion dollars a year on our disabled men. And yet Europe was in a worse condition than she was before the war. This, he said, led to despair as to Europe and European affairs on the part of the ordinary American citizen, and now he just wanted to keep out of the whole business. This was the general attitude of the American public, and he did not see how the United States could take the leadership in any direction.[24]

Grandi gave up. His visit produced nothing except to permit Washington officials and their wives to become acquainted with

20. Statement of Oct. 25, 1931, *FR: 1931, 2*, 252–3.
21. Stimson diary, Oct. 26, 1931.
22. Castle diary, Oct. 28, 1931.
23. Stimson diary, Oct. 5, 1931.
24. Memorandum by Stimson of conversations between Hoover and Grandi, Nov. 18, 1931, Stimson MSS.

the count's attractive personality. Grandi had disguised his youth by a fine Old World beard, and with the beard went such Old World customs as kissing ladies' hands. At one White House dinner he kissed the hands of all the ladies present, which was perhaps more of a kissing party (opined the veteran head usher) than the Executive Mansion had seen in forty years.[25]

Such was the result of diplomatic visiting to the United States in the autumn of 1931.

In the time that remained before the opening of the Disarmament Conference, Stimson and Hoover assembled the American delegation. First choice for chairman of the delegation was Dwight W. Morrow, who accepted with small enthusiasm on October 2, 1931. Three days later came Morrow's sudden death. Charles G. Dawes then received an invitation to be chairman, and he consented, although the proposition "left him cold." [26] He soon stepped down to become head of the new Reconstruction Finance Corporation in his own country. The eventual solution was to have Stimson as chairman and entrust most of the duties of the post to Hugh Gibson. Gibson had the assistance of Norman Davis, Hugh Wilson,[27] and Senator Claude Swanson, the latter being the ranking Democrat on the Foreign Relations Committee.[28] These four delegates represented four types: "Mr. Gibson, friendly, witty, somewhat cynical; Mr. Wilson, thoughtful, quiet, hard-working, not overoptimistic; Senator Swanson, genial, warm-hearted, *extremely nationalistic;* Mr. Davis, eager to go all the way, but realizing that it is a condition, not a theory, which

25. Irwin H. Hoover, *Forty-Two Years in the White House,* p. 212. Stimson concluded that on the whole Grandi's visit was extremely tactful and made a "very wonderful impression." Diary, Nov. 21, 1931.

26. Dawes, *Journal as Ambassador,* pp. 431–2 (diary entry for Dec. 21, 1931).

27. Wilson was an alternate.

28. Swanson was a colorful figure, and his Southern oratory nonplussed his auditors at Geneva. His wit amused the press correspondents, especially when dispensed from a Geneva bar. "The great press—" he used to drawl, "that phrase amused me, sir, even when I was governor of the great state of Virginia. I was inspired to search the classics of Greece and Rome and to delve into the Holy Scriptures for the first mention in antiquity of you gentlemen of the press. And I found it, sir; turn to the Good Book and there you will find in Luke 19:3 how they sought to see Jesus 'and could not for the press.' " John T. Whitaker, *And Fear Came* (New York, Macmillan, 1936), p. 131.

confronts us, bringing all his international experience, which is great, to bear on these questions, caring only for accomplishment, not an iota for recognition." Mr. Davis' friend, who wrote these lines, was the fifth member of the delegation, Dr. Mary E. Woolley, president of Mount Holyoke College.[29] Hoover had suggested that it would be a good thing to send a woman to the conference, and Stimson agreed if it were possible to get a sensible one and not a member of the Women's Party. The choice devolved upon Dr. Woolley.[30] The delegation, less Stimson who arranged to go later, left for Europe in mid-January 1932 after instruction by the secretary and Hoover, both of whom impartially stressed the grounds for hope of the mission and also the grounds for "conservatism." [31]

3

The World Disarmament Conference opened in Geneva with great solemnity on February 2, 1932. "The very simplicity of that opening day helped to make it impressive; even more, the great audience, representing almost all the peoples on earth; and most of all the significance, the realization of the hopes and the possibilities centered in that gathering . . ." [32] Arthur Henderson in the leading address told the delegates that they were the chosen

29. Mary E. Woolley to a friend, Mar. 11, 1932, Jeannette Marks, *Life and Letters of Mary Emma Woolley* (Washington, Public Affairs Press, 1955), pp. 140–1.

30. Stimson diary, Dec. 13, 1931. Dr. Woolley had the support of American peace workers. See Detzer, *Appointment on the Hill,* pp. 105–8; Marks, *Life and Letters of Mary Emma Woolley,* pp. 125 ff. There is a piquant passage in the Moffat diary for December 23, 1931: "the Secretary summoned me to his office. He was very brief. 'Dr. Woolley,' he said, 'has been offered the post of Arms Delegate by the President, and has just told me over the telephone that she would accept. She is a woman of 69 years of age, and knows nothing about the subject. I assume, however, that she knows how to read, so will you please send her, before the day is out, enough necessary documentation for her to have a reasonable background . . . ?'" Diary of Jay Pierrepont Moffat, deposited in the Houghton Library at Harvard.

31. Stimson diary, Jan. 5, 1932.

32. Mary E. Woolley to a friend, Feb. 13, 1932, Marks, *Life and Letters of Mary Emma Woolley,* p. 136.

spokesmen of hundreds of millions of people. Most of his auditors, however, were really their nations' regular members of the League Assembly. In a sense the Disarmament Conference was a fiction by which the United States was brought into a League meeting. The initial session had to be postponed for an hour so that members of the Council might answer an emergency call to discuss the Japanese attack on Shanghai.

The conference's first three weeks consisted of speeches by the delegations and presentation of petitions by leaders of the international peace movement.[33] Eventually there began to emerge the disarmament views of the great powers.

André Tardieu—who had replaced Laval as premier of France—on February 5, 1932, submitted a French plan for an international police force, reminding the delegates that "no substantial reduction of armaments can be brought about by empirical and technical means." A few days afterward Hugh Gibson presented a nine-point American program for limitation of armaments, recognizing no connection whatever with Continental security. The conference quickly reached the familiar impasse, of French demands for disarmament through security and American demands for security through disarmament. This confrontation continued

33. Women peace leaders on Feb. 6, 1932, presented petitions numbering millions of names. See Marks, *Life and Letters of Mary Emma Woolley*, pp. 131–2, 136–8. What happened to them afterward was a matter of some comment. "They are not destroyed," Sir Eric Drummond explained to the press. "They are in storage with other documents." Someone asked if Sir Eric required considerable storage space. "Yes," Drummond replied, "most of the cellars of Geneva already are full of our documents." Pearson and Brown, *The American Diplomatic Game,* p. 196. Peace leaders in the United States had instituted a large campaign to obtain signatures to the petitions. There was, among other methods of publicity, a cross-country caravan of automobiles that took the petitions to Washington. Pierrepont Moffat watched from a window of the State, War, and Navy Building as the peace leaders reached the White House. "The Caravan arrived to present the monster peace petition to the President. Miss Jane Addams led the procession of cars which was over a mile in length and bore the scroll with hundreds of thousands of signatures. We watched them drive up to the White House and were slightly amused to see the Caravan preceded by military music." Moffat diary, Oct. 10, 1931.

until mid-April and the arrival in Europe of the American secretary of state.

Stimson found an ovation awaiting him when he passed through Paris en route to Geneva. Tardieu and Laval both appeared at the railroad station. The secretary noticed a sharp contrast to his reception in Paris on a European trip the previous year, when the French government had rudely snubbed him and made no fuss at all over his presence in the French capital.[34] After his new welcome he received a bid to the Quai d'Orsay for a *tête-à-tête* with Tardieu, where he stated "at length" what he and Hoover had told Laval the previous October: "I said I had always regarded it [the Disarmament Conference] as more in the nature of a European peace conference than anything in which we had direct responsibility." [35]

In Geneva next day he talked with Sir John Simon, and lectured Sir John on American views of the Far Eastern crisis. Simon gave every indication of agreeing and tried to assure Stimson that apprehension as to the attitude of the British Foreign Office was unfounded. After listening to the repeated protests of agreement Stimson became convinced that the foreign secretary at last had no doubt as to "any part of my position." [36] A few days afterward he talked with two representatives of the Empire and told them both about the Far East, stressing his troubles in obtaining effective cooperation from the Foreign Office. These men shortly afterward saw Simon.[37]

The secretary renewed his acquaintance with Louis Aubert of France: "I put up to him my conception of the function of the American Delegation at this Conference, namely, that having restricted our Navy and reduced our Army and being out of air range from Europe, we are not going to take a leading position . . . He brought up the security-for-France proposition and I found he stated it just as they had it two years ago. I told him that was France's affair with the British." Inspired by the turn of the

34. Stimson diary, Apr. 15, 1932.
35. Ibid.
36. Ibid., Apr. 16, 1932.
37. Ibid., Apr. 19.

argument, Stimson reviewed the American position on consultative pacts. The secretary said, further, that Aubert could see from American action in the Far East that the United States would cooperate with the League. The French diplomatist conceded that additional international guarantees of security could come only from Great Britain.[38]

Afterward Stimson lunched with Simon, and informed him of the Aubert conversation. Simon "told me flatly that Britain would not give any further promises of armed assistance to France. British opinion wouldn't stand for it. I, myself, felt this was true from what I had observed of British opinion two years ago. Simon said British opinion was now even stronger."

The secretary of state at this point concluded from his talks that he had found "an apparent clear-cut impasse" between France and Britain, which would block any true disarmament unless both nations found some way to solve it. He saw no immediate solution.

He explored further the French position. On Thursday morning, April 21, he hurried over the Hotel des Bergues, and encountered Tardieu (who had just gotten off the night train from Paris) in his bathrobe. The two statesmen held a ten-minute discussion on disarmament. Tardieu said that Gibson in a speech to the conference had forgotten the policy of interdependence of the three classes of armaments—air, land, and water (by which he meant that France would not limit her army unless Britain and the United States limited their navies). Stimson "punched that ancient heresy in the nose" by pointing out that the naval powers had limited their navies at the Washington Conference ten years before. "Furthermore, in view of the present situation in the Far East and our relation to it, it wasn't the time for us to do anything more . . ."[39]

Apropos the latter difficulty Stimson that same day told Sir Eric Drummond when Sir Eric "opened up on me with capital ships [Drummond wished more limitation of capital ships] . . . that he had better back up on that . . . I told him we were now preserving the stability of the Far East which would not be preserved

38. Ibid., Apr. 20.
39. Ibid., Apr. 21, 1932.

but for our efforts in having our fleet concentrated at Hawaii and not a single British ship at Singapore and he had better not juggle our elbows." [40]

The secretary later went over to MacDonald's villa and gave the prime minister the history of the negotiations with the Foreign Office over the nonrecognition proposal for the Far East. MacDonald in early 1932 had been ill, and he now told Stimson that he had known nothing of the difficulties with Sir John Simon, "and he raised his hands in horror when I told him of how I was driven to write the Borah letter because I could not get the British Government to go with me in a joint appeal under the Nine-Power Treaty." MacDonald confided to Stimson that he was going to stay ten days at Geneva and attempt "to get matters going." [41]

Then on Saturday evening, April 23, came the climax of Stimson's Genevan diplomacy. To place himself in a mood of relaxation the secretary played golf in the morning, and after luncheon he went with Mrs. Stimson for a drive to the Jura Ridge.

> In the evening, however, I did some serious business. I invited MacDonald and Simon to meet Gibson, Davis and myself at a 7:30 dinner and after dinner we reviewed the situation until after 10 o'clock. I had decided to squelch the consultative pact nuisance which has been cropping up again, so I brought that up first and after reminding MacDonald of the transactions which had taken place on the subject in London in 1930 I asked him these three points:
>
> First, I told him that Aubert had told me that the British would not give the extra security which the French desired and that they (the British) gave as the reason the fact that they could not tell what we would do in case of a major emergency and action by the League under Article 16. I asked him if this was so. He became very intense and said with the utmost seriousness that never had his Government made any such

40. Ibid., Apr. 21, 1932. The Navy Department had announced in the summer of 1931 that the fleet would hold its annual maneuvers off Hawaii. During the Shanghai Incident the fleet was concentrating in the Pacific. President Hoover agreed to allow the vessels to remain at Hawaii for a while.

41. Ibid., Apr. 21.

suggestion or statement to the French, that it was entirely untrue.

Second, I told him that I had from my observations reached the conclusion that the British Government, owing to the pressure of British public opinion, would not make any further commitments to the French as to additional security or armed assistance and that in their decision upon this matter no amount of assurance on our part that we would consult in time of emergency would have any influence whatever. I asked him categorically if I was right in this. He replied that I was. He said that British public opinion was very definitely against any such further commitments and that no covenants on our part as to consultation would have the slightest effect on it.

I finally said that I thought what I had done during the Sino-Japanese crisis in my cooperation with the League ought to give them satisfactory assurance that in any such major crisis any normal American Government would consult with them without any pledge of consultation beforehand, and I asked him whether he did not feel that way. He said he did and was perfectly satisfied.[42]

4

Upon conclusion of his Geneva visit Stimson looked back on his diplomacy there with some satisfaction. He felt that in two weeks he had accomplished a great deal. His coming had brought the leaders of the principal powers to Geneva. MacDonald came to the Disarmament Conference for the first time, and only because the American secretary of state was there. Tardieu came "solely because I visited him in Paris and brought him." Bruening and Grandi came back after absences. MacDonald and Stimson then finding that they both agreed there had been a "lamentable waste of time and stalling," there began the direct conversations which the European powers should have organized long before the conference met, but which as it happened had not started until more than two months after the conference got under way.[43]

42. Ibid., Saturday, Apr. 23, 1932.
43. Ibid., May 1, 1932.

Unfortunately the direct conferences inaugurated by Stimson had not been productive. As he discovered, an "impasse" existed between France and Britain over security, and as the secretary made abundantly known, the United States proposed to do nothing about it. The Franco-British conflict—or American aloofness, according to another interpretation—made impossible any international agreements on disarmament at the World Disarmament Conference.

At Geneva in 1932 there came no immediate end to the futile conference speeches and debates, only a gradual lapse of interest and expectation. People began to see that the mere size of an international conference could not ensure success, and in fact might well do the opposite. The only totally cooperative nation was Soviet Russia, whose economy was in flux, midway between the first and second five-year plans, quite unable to support the strain of a foreign war. Litvinov ingenuously declared his country willing to agree to "complete disarmament, partial disarmament, quantitative disarmament and qualitative disarmament," and "prepared to go any length in the direction of disarmament." [44] His hope was to pull the nations down to a Russian par, then close to zero; later, when the Soviet economy was on its feet again, armament could begin once more, to Russian advantage. None of the powers gave serious attention to this demagoguery.

President Hoover, to stop the conference from "dawdling," [45] proposed in June 1932 an all-round reduction of one-third in armaments, seemingly a simple plan. Italy, Germany, and Russia greeted the president's proposition enthusiastically, and the American government discovered itself the embarrassed leader of the revisionist bloc in Europe. In November the Herriot government of France offered a complicated scheme for an international police force, also ensuring French security.[46] The Herriot

44. Allen W. Dulles, "Progress toward Disarmament," p. 59.

45. *Memoirs of Herbert Hoover: The Cabinet and the Presidency,* p. 354.

46. National armies of Europe were to be reduced to a militia level, deprived of bombing aircraft and powerful mobile land material, especially heavy artillery and tanks. Restricted amounts of powerful mobile material would be retained by special contingents of long-term soldiers, to be maintained by

plan slipped into the special limbo reserved at Geneva for ambitious proposals. Ramsay MacDonald in March 1933 submitted a draft convention stipulating that any breach or threat to the Pact of Paris should result in an international conference; what would happen after the conference convened, he did not amplify. Not to be outdone, the United States in May 1933 offered consultation to the nations, providing they first agreed on a substantial reduction of armaments. This marked a complete reversal of the American attitude at the London Conference where Stimson had refused a consultative pact for the reason that the French might link it with disarmament. Nothing came of this gesture.

In truth the interminable discussions at Geneva seemed to place Germany's right to armaments in an ever more justifiable

---

each state and held at the disposal of the League for common action against an aggressor. Material in excess of restrictions would not be destroyed, but stored in each state under international supervision. If engaged in a war of legitimate self-defense, a state could regain full use of its League contingent of troops and of the stocks of material within its territory. This military organization would be crowned by the constitution of an organically international air force.

The Herriot plan provided for three sets of guarantees, each stronger and narrower than its predecessor. Guarantees would be made by (1) League and non-League members, by means of the Kellogg-Briand Pact; (2) League members, by the Covenant; (3) nations of the Continent, by the military provisions set forth above.

W. M. Jordan, in his *Great Britain, France, and the German Problem,* pp. 217–18, states that the Herriot plan "may justly be held to have constituted the most courageous and thorough attempt to work out an organization of collective security at once universal in scope and yet capable of immediate and effective operation within the continent of Europe." But did not the Herriot plan only ingeniously gloss over, in a haze of anonymity, the rivalry between France and Germany? German support of the plan was essential, and the Germans rightly considered the plan as one more French device to ensure the status quo in Europe. Not that the status quo was undesirable in Europe, but by November 1932 the time for adroit formulas was rapidly passing.

The Herriot plan did not cover the Far East, and this was a significant omission, for it showed something of the temper of Europe toward the Sino-Japanese conflict. One could argue that the peace of the world might have been maintained, however, if there had been no dangerous situation in Europe during the years after 1932.

light. German representatives at the conference never tired of pointing out that their nation had disarmed in accord with the Versailles Treaty, and that it now was the turn of the other nations. They meant, of course, the French nation, which was maintaining the only army on the Continent capable of protecting the peace of Europe from a resurgence of German power. The conference badly undermined France's position by making the French appear as "militarists" rather than protectors of European peace. When Chancellor Hitler in October 1933 announced Germany's withdrawal from the League and the Disarmament Conference it became evident that the grand meeting at Geneva had run its course. It lingered on for a while, and finally in 1934 disappeared from view, adjourning *sine die,* accompanied by diplomatic expressions of hope that it would meet again in the future.

Chapter Thirteen: LATIN AMERICA

During the years of the Hoover Administration, American diplomacy encountered several major crises and difficulties—chief of which was the Far Eastern Crisis—but there remained, throughout all trials, one area of achievement: Latin America.[1] The policy of the United States toward the other twenty independent republics of the Western Hemisphere changed considerably during the presidency of Herbert Hoover, and when the Quaker president left office in March 1933 he could justly feel that the nation's neighbors to the south were, for the first time in decades, fairly friendly in their estimates of *Tío Sam.*

President Hoover's change in the Latin American policy of the United States came after thirty years of unappreciated American supervision and policing of the affairs of the Hemisphere. Ever since the Cuban-Spanish-American War of 1898, the United States had been exercising what Latin Americans regarded as undue influence over the internal affairs of their countries. In pursuit of Caribbean security, and specifically for protection of the Panama Canal, the United States had not hesitated to intervene forcibly in the affairs of Panama, Cuba, the Dominican Republic, Nicaragua, and Haiti. Under President Wilson, American troops temporarily occupied Veracruz, and General Pershing led a punitive expedition into northern Mexico. In the years after the first World War there no longer appeared any possible European threat to the Panama Canal. "I felt sure," Secretary of State Kellogg told the Chilean ambassador in 1928, "that there was very little danger

1. For a succinct and detailed analysis of United States relations with Latin America from 1929 to 1933 see Alexander DeConde, *Herbert Hoover's Latin-American Policy,* Stanford, Calif., Stanford University Press, 1951.

of war in the Western Hemisphere . . ." [2] The Latin American nations, moreover, were becoming extremely sensitive to intervention in their affairs. Even intervention for the unexceptionable purpose of protecting the lives and property of American nationals no longer seemed politically wise. By the end of the 1920's it was clearly evident that the American government would have to change its policy. After several years of indifference President Calvin Coolidge in a burst of zeal sent Dwight W. Morrow to Mexico, Charles Evans Hughes to the Sixth Inter-American Conference at Havana in 1928, and himself went to Havana to deliver an address. Coolidge's concern for inter-American relations came too late to accomplish much. Hughes at Havana defended sturdily the United States's right of "interposition of a temporary character" in Latin affairs. With truth, but also with failure to appreciate the new sensibilities of Latin Americans, Hughes asked what the United States was to do "when government breaks down and American citizens are in danger of their lives? Are we to stand by and see them butchered in the jungle . . . ?" [3] It remained for Herbert Hoover, during the following four years, to place the relations of the United States with Latin America on the necessary new foundation, jettisoning the outworn policies of tutelage and forcible instruction, even at the expense of undoubted American rights. The attractive phrase "good neighbor," usually associated with the administration of Franklin D. Roosevelt, marked the new policy of Herbert Hoover, who hopefully employed it in addresses to the peoples of Latin America.[4]

2. Memorandum of a conversation between Kellogg and the Chilean ambassador, Sept. 20, 1928, 711.0012 Anti-War/414.

3. Dexter Perkins, *Charles Evans Hughes and American Democratic Statesmanship* (Boston, 1956), p. 135. The Havana Conference did result in a special conference in Washington in 1928–29, where representatives of a number of the American states worked out two treaties, a General Convention of Inter-American Conciliation, and a General Treaty of Inter-American Arbitration. The Argentine Republic refused to take part in the conference, and did not ratify either of the general treaties.

4. The phrase "good neighbor" goes back at least to the early 19th century. It was "one of the most familiar clichés in the language of international intercourse." Arthur P. Whitaker, *The Western Hemisphere Idea* (Ithaca, N.Y.,

1

Immediately after his election to the presidency in 1928, Hoover decided upon a pre-inauguration trip to Central and South America, and this journey, begun on November 19, 1928, and ended on January 6, 1929, gave broad indication of policies during his presidency. The ten-week tour took the presidential party to Honduras, El Salvador, Nicaragua, Costa Rica, Ecuador, Peru, Chile, Argentina, Uruguay, and Brazil. During the tour Hoover delivered some twenty-five addresses. In his first speech, in Honduras, on November 26, 1928, the president-elect employed the phrase "good neighbor," and in subsequent speeches the phrase appeared so frequently that it could not have avoided impressing the Latin Americans with Hoover's desire to place the relations of the United States with its Latin neighbors on a new basis. President Hipólito Irigoyen of Argentina, in a press interview after Hoover had departed his country, stated that the president-elect of the United States had even promised "that the United States under his coming administration would abstain from further intervention in the internal affairs of Latin America." This Hoover appears to have done, although at the moment some Latin skeptics expressed hope that the new administration might "prove the declaration more than wind blowing across the Pampas." [5] During his trip Hoover constantly indulged in statements of friendship and good will toward the peoples of the American republics, and when the battleship *Utah* finally brought him back to the United States at Norfolk, there was little doubt in the minds of most of the newspapermen who had accompanied him that the president-elect had enjoyed, in his Latin American journey, a considerable diplomatic triumph.[6]

Cornell University Press, 1954), p. 135 n. Franklin D. Roosevelt's first use of the phrase, in his inaugural of Mar. 4, 1933, was in regard to the entire world: "In the field of world policy I would dedicate this Nation to the policy of the good neighbor." Only later did it come to have its special meaning for his Administrations.

5. DeConde, *Herbert Hoover's Latin-American Policy,* p. 22.

6. Harry W. Hill, ed., *President-elect Herbert Hoover's Good-Will Cruise to Central and South America,* San Francisco, 1929; Mark Sullivan, "With Hoover

In the first few months and even the first year or so of office, President Hoover was unable to give much further attention to the affairs of the American republics. He was too busily engaged in getting his administration organized, and diplomatically these were the months of preparation for the London Naval Conference and then the conference itself. Likewise, Secretary of State Stimson spent most of his first year at the Department working on the London Conference, with some attention to the Sino-Russian dispute in Manchuria. It was in September 1930 that, with other matters out of the way, the Hoover Administration announced a new policy of recognition for Latin America, partly fulfilling in this manner the promises of good will and nonintervention made by the president during his tour a year and a half before.[7]

In a circular instruction to American diplomatic missions in Argentina, Bolivia, and Peru, Secretary Stimson on September 17, 1930, revoked the recognition policy toward Latin America that had prevailed since the administration of Woodrow Wilson. According to Stimson's circular, the chiefs of mission in the three states mentioned were "to resume normal diplomatic relations" with the provisional governments of those countries. There was, the secretary announced, a three-fold criterion upon which the United States thereafter would grant recognition to a new regime: (1) *de facto* control of the country: (2) intention to fulfill international obligations; (3) intention to hold elections "in due course." [8] This policy stood in contrast to Wilson's moralistic policy of recognition, enunciated in a public declaration of March 11, 1913. Wilson then had said that recognition was "possible only when

in Latin America," *Review of Reviews, 79* (1929), 53–7. For a somewhat disparaging account see Thomas L. Stokes, *Chip Off My Shoulder* (Princeton, 1940), pp. 247–51. Hoover paid the expenses of the trip out of his own pocket. DeConde, *Herbert Hoover's Latin-American Policy,* p. 16 n.

7. On the general subject of American recognition policy toward Latin America see William L. Neumann, *Recognition of Governments in the Americas,* Washington, 1947. Perhaps one should remark, once again, the essential difference between problems of political recognition in Latin America and the problem of recognition of boundary changes accomplished by force. It was the latter problem, of course, that gave rise to the Stimson Doctrine of nonrecognition of the fruits of aggression.

8. *FR: 1930, 1,* 387–9.

supported at every turn by the orderly processes of just government based upon law, not upon arbitrary or irregular force. We hold, as I am sure all thoughtful leaders of republican government everywhere hold, that just government rests always upon the consent of the governed, and that there can be no freedom without order based upon law and upon the public conscience and approval. We shall look to make these principles the basis of mutual intercourse, respect, and helpfulness between our sister republics and ourselves." [9]

One could argue that Hoover and Stimson in 1930 had no choice but to change the government's recognition policy, for there had been so many revolutions in Latin America in preceding months—and indications were that there would be more—that it no longer was possible to sit in judgment on the character of new regimes.[10] There is some truth in this, but it also seems true that Hoover, through Stimson's circular instruction of September 1930, was fulfilling his promises made on the Latin American tour. The fact is that until Hoover's presidency the United States had not worried greatly about Latin American opinions of the Colossus of the North, and had allowed relations to deteriorate to a point where something had to be done. Hoover saw this state of affairs clearly, during his trip, and took the problem in hand. His decision in this matter was in no sense a decision of expediency, forced by the kaleidoscopic series of revolutions that began to afflict Latin America soon after the beginning of the Great Depression. It was a decision of principle, taken out of understanding of the Latins and of the interests of the United States.[11]

One should mention, in passing, that not until after four years

9. *FR: 1913,* p. 7. Wilson inaugurated this policy in connection with the notorious Huerta regime in Mexico.

10. Stimson undeservedly received the sobriquet of "Wrong-Horse Harry" in October 1930 when, acting under a congressional resolution of 1922, he denied arms to rebel forces in Brazil, only to see those forces assume control of the Brazilian government. His detractors forgot that by similar action during a revolt in Mexico in the first weeks of the Hoover Administration, the United States had maintained in power the legitimate government and earned its gratitude.

11. See the explanation by Stimson in "The United States and the

did the new recognition policy extend to the five republics of Central America which had undertaken for themselves in a treaty in 1907, reiterated in 1923, a special recognition policy. These states, ridden by revolts and interventions across their several borders, had written out a code of proper revolutionary behavior, which even went to the length of stipulating what officials in a given government could and could not, by revolution, take office in a new regime. The United States, although not a signatory of the treaty of 1923, adhered to its specified recognition policy and followed the dictates of the treaty during revolts in Guatemala in 1930 and El Salvador in 1931. The Central American states themselves abandoned their agreement in 1934, at which time the United States Government reverted, for this area of the Western Hemisphere, to its general recognition policy in Latin America as laid down in 1930.

As another earnest of his new policy of the good neighbor, Hoover insisted upon withdrawal of American marines from Nicaragua, which he accomplished by January 2, 1933. When the last marine left Nicaragua at that date it was the first time in twenty years (with exception of a brief interlude in 1925–26) that no American troops had garrisoned that Central American state. Likewise the president prepared to withdraw troops from Haiti, and only the Haitian national assembly's refusal in 1932 to accept the American terms of withdrawal prevented an immediate exit of the marines. The stone that the assembly rejected, the treaty of 1932, became the foundation of an executive agreement with Haiti by the Roosevelt Administration in 1933, carried out in October 1934. It was ironic that the individual who in 1920 boasted that he wrote the Haitian constitution ("a pretty good constitution, too") should have presided over American withdrawal from that state in 1934; the honor should have gone to Hoover in 1932, and but for a quirk of Haitian politics it would have done so.

The final achievement of Hoover's new policy of friendship for Latin America was the Clark Memorandum. Hoover in 1930 di-

Other American Republics," *Foreign Affairs*, 9 (1930–31), i–xiv, a speech before the Council on Foreign Relations, New York, Feb. 6, 1931.

rected the Department of State to publish a memorandum prepared two years earlier by Coolidge's undersecretary of state, J. Reuben Clark, Jr., in which Clark had performed upon the Monroe Doctrine an act of major surgery.[12] Employing such sources as John Bassett Moore's *Digest of International Law* and *Digest of International Arbitrations,* Carlton J. H. Hayes' *A Political and Social History of Modern Europe,* the *Encyclopedia Britannica* (11th ed.), and the *Encyclopedia Americana,* Clark in 236 closely printed pages had dissected the Monroe Doctrine and discovered that the Roosevelt Corollary of 1905 had no place among the principles of James Monroe. In a seventeen-page covering letter to Secretary of State Kellogg he explained, in authentic Department of State passive-voice style, that "it is not believed that this corollary is justified by the terms of the Monroe Doctrine, however much it may be justified by the application of the doctrine of self-preservation." Clark thus did not deny that the United States possessed the right of "interposition of a temporary character" in Latin American affairs, but he denied that the Monroe Doctrine justified intervention. This notable memorandum, one of the most important statements of United States policy toward Latin America in the 20th century, received reinforcement in 1930 by statements from Stimson and Undersecretary Castle. Stimson declared that "The Monroe Doctrine was a declaration of the United States versus Europe—not of the United States versus Latin America." Castle explained that the Monroe Doctrine "confers no superior position on the United States." The era of tutelage and instruction by force was plainly over.[13]

12. J. Reuben Clark, Jr., *Memorandum on the Monroe Doctrine,* Washington, 1930. See the comments by Hoover in an interview of Aug. 5, 1947, with DeConde, *Herbert Hoover's Latin-American Policy,* pp. 48–9; also *Memoirs of Herbert Hoover: The Cabinet and the Presidency,* p. 334.

13. Stimson, "The United States and the Other American Republics," p. ii; William R. Castle, speech prepared for delivery at the University of Virginia, July 4, 1931, New York *Times,* July 5, 1931.

During his last weeks of office Secretary Kellogg prepared an instruction to American diplomatic officers in Latin America, Feb. 28, 1929, which he did not at the time send out. *FR: 1929, 1,* 698–719. The Kellogg instruction differed from the Clark Memorandum in that it separated the Roosevelt Corollary from

Announcement of the Clark Memorandum as American policy was again, like the new recognition policy, a decision of the president. The Clark Memorandum had reposed in the files of the State Department since its presentation to Secretary Kellogg on December 17, 1928. President Coolidge, despite his journey to Havana that year, was unwilling to abandon the Roosevelt Corollary, but Hoover did so a year and a half later, when the Clark Memorandum was conspicuously published by the Department of State.

It was in the liquidation of the protective imperialism of earlier years, then, that Hoover displayed not merely the good intentions but the resolution of his administration, and by 1933 there could be no doubt that there had been a distinct change of policy: the tour of 1928–29 had brought a new policy of recognition, withdrawal from Nicaragua, virtual withdrawal from Haiti, and the Clark Memorandum. The sister republics were quick to sense the new attitude of the *"Hooveristas"* in Washington. Hoover told his undersecretary of state in early 1933, that the Latin American press had stopped talking about United States imperialism.[14]

There were other problems in Latin America during these years. As already mentioned, the Great Depression produced a spate of revolutions and unsuccessful revolutions which, by 1933, totaled over fifty. Economic troubles brought these revolutions, usually, and in many cases the revolutions marked merely a change of actors, with the same old play going on: poverty and disease continued to harass the domestic affairs of Latin nations, and the politics of the capital cities often seemed to have little to do with what went on in the villages and countryside. Perhaps a change of United States policy could do little for the basic problems of Latin American life. Still, by making abundantly clear that the United States was no imperialist nation, the American government

---

the Monroe Doctrine only by implication; it did not mention the Roosevelt Corollary specifically, either by name or quotation from President Theodore Roosevelt's message of 1905. Hoover in 1930, upon a query by Kellogg through Stimson, decided that publication of the Kellogg instruction was at the moment unwise. Apparently the Department made no use of it. In the Department archives there is no further mark of what might otherwise have become the Kellogg Memorandum.

14. Castle diary, Jan. 11, 1933.

placed the Latins in a position where they could, perhaps, devote more attention to their internal problems, rather than fulminating about the threats of the Colossus. Too, once the thirty-year heritage of political antagonism was laid to rest, it might prove possible through cooperation for the United States to assist in ameliorating some of the economic and social difficulties of its Latin neighbors. Two major irritants of United States-Latin American relations during the 1930's did not assist the policy of the good neighbor: defaulting by Latin American governments of well over $1,000,000,000 of United States capital during the years after 1929, and the confiscation of United States investments in Latin America done under the false signboard of "nationalization." [15] But there was no intervention by the United States. And in the middle and later 1930's the results of the Hoover policy of good will and nonintervention, the policy continued by the Roosevelt Administration, became apparent in the solidarity of the republics of the Western Hemisphere toward the developing threat of Germany and Japan. By the time of the second World War, and despite expropriations and other lesser troubles, the policy of the good neighbor had proved its worth.

2

There remain, in any brief analysis of United States relations with Latin America during the Hoover years, two special problems of the time which tested the diplomatic ingenuity of all the American states, not the least the United States, which had been enunciating toward Central and South America the good neighbor policy and simultaneously, toward the Orient, a policy of nonrecognition of the fruits of aggression. These two special problems were the dispute between Paraguay and Bolivia over the Chaco, and the conflict between Peru and Colombia over Leticia.[16]

15. See Samuel Flagg Bemis, *The Latin American Policy of the United States: An Historical Interpretation* (New York, Harcourt, Brace, 1943), ch. 19, "Dollar Diplomacy in Reverse (1929–41)," pp. 331–42; ch. 20, "The Myth of Economic Imperialism," pp. 343–54.

16. There were two other boundary disputes in Latin America during the Hoover years. In one of them, that between Peru, Chile, and Bolivia, over the

In South America prior to the appearance of these disputes there had been few international wars. In the first century after liberation it was possible to point only to the war in 1865–70 between Paraguay on the one side, and Brazil, Argentina, and Uruguay on the other, and the Chilean War of the Pacific against Peru and Bolivia in 1879–83. Perhaps this century of abstention had led, by the time of Herbert Hoover's presidency, to a desire for trouble, but for whatever reason it is of interest that two international wars in South America did occur in the early 1930's. Both were over nearly useless pieces of jungle territory.

The explorer, Julian Duguid, published a book about the Chaco in 1931, and he appropriately described that pearl of Paraguayan-Bolivian desires as a Green Hell. An exotic area of South America, one of the last truly primitive places left on the globe, it was a land where purple orchids "studded the vast tapestry of green, poking their parasitic heads through the rotting forks of trees; lianas hung in slender loops and festoons; underbush cluttered up the ground in luxuriant profusion. Mystery and gloom lurked in every corner of the crowded wood, and the atmosphere was such that one half expected a snake to slither out of every bush. And over all hung a brooding, watchful silence, a thousand times more terrible than the silence of a crouching tiger." [17]

Why any nation would have fought over such a piece of real estate was difficult for Stimson to understand. He wrote in his diary in mid-1932, when hostilities were entering an acute stage, that a line could be drawn almost anywhere in the worthless Chaco with-

---

provinces of Tacna and Arica, "the Alsace-Lorraine of South America," discussions in Washington produced a treaty of June 3, 1929, between Peru and Chile; this treaty ended a fifty-year dispute stemming from the War of the Pacific in 1879–83. Secretary Stimson meanwhile brought together in Washington representatives of Honduras and Guatemala, who in a treaty of July 16, 1930, provided for arbitration of their disputed border; the Special Boundary Tribunal, presided over by Chief Justice Charles Evans Hughes, handed down its decision and award on Jan. 23, 1933. See DeConde, *Herbert Hoover's Latin-American Policy,* pp. 25–33.

17. Julian Duguid, *Green Hell: A Chronicle of Travel in the Forests of Eastern Bolivia* (London, Century, 1931), p. 183.

out affecting the rights of either of the quarreling nations.[18] Actually there were some oil possibilities in the Chaco; and to Bolivia, which in the 19th-century War of the Pacific had lost her seacoast to Chile, the Chaco offered an outlet to the Atlantic. The dispute, one should add, had enjoyed a long history prior to its violent reappearance in the summer of 1932, when on June 14 Bolivia seized the Paraguayan outpost of Fort Carlos Antonio López, bringing into question the treaty structure for world peace upon which Stimson and individuals everywhere in the Western world had placed such hopes and reliance.

Hostilities soon reached a point where, by the end of July 1932, Stimson believed some sort of appeal to the disputants was in order; a successful appeal, he hoped, would reinforce the doctrine of nonrecognition of the fruits of aggression, and would help materially in the situation with Japan. It was difficult, however, for the American government to take any sort of step in such a matter without support from the other Latin republics. In obtaining support there was danger of running afoul of the jealousies and humors of supporting states, not to mention the primary antagonism of Paraguay and Bolivia in the Chaco. A further complication was the fact that neither Bolivia nor Paraguay was a member of the Kellogg-Briand Pact, nor were four other of the Latin American states; an appeal could not be made under the antiwar treaty. Neither could it be made under the Covenant of the League of Nations, for Bolivia and Paraguay had not joined the League. The only structure of international promises available was the Union of American Republics and its secretariat, the Pan American Union. Stimson worked gingerly through the Union, with the help of his astute assistant secretary of state for Latin American affairs, Francis White. A Commission of Neutrals—the United States, Mexico, Cuba, Colombia, and Uruguay—already had been investigating the Chaco affair, under the aegis of the Union.[19] Francis White was chairman of the Commission.

18. Stimson diary, July 18, 1932.

19. The Inter-American Conference on Arbitration and Conciliation, meeting in Washington in 1929, created this Commission of Neutrals, which had attempted unsuccessfully to settle the Chaco conflict that year.

But before the Commission of Neutrals moved, it was necessary to get assurances that the large neighbor countries about Paraguay and Bolivia (Argentina, Brazil, Chile, Peru) would go along with the Commission. The secretary of state also hoped that the initiative for his diplomacy would come so far as possible from the Latin American countries. Fortunately the first suggestion of using the Stimson Doctrine in the Chaco came from the Mexican ambassador to the United States, José M. Puig Casauranc.[20]

During the crucial days of the negotiation, from July 30 to August 3, 1932, White reported every day to Stimson, and everything went well. An overture to the large nations bordering the Chaco disputants brought favorable responses. The nineteen nations thereupon dispatched a joint telegraphic appeal to the quarreling states on August 3, 1932, calling for cessation of troop movements and presentation of their cases to the Commission of Neutrals. The appeal closed with the warning that "The American nations further declare that they will not recognize any territorial arrangement of this controversy which has not been obtained by peaceful means nor the validity of territorial acquisitions which may be obtained through occupation or conquest by force of arms." [21]

This statement virtually adopted, for the Americas, the doctrine of nonrecognition of the fruits of aggression, the Stimson Doctrine.

The declaration of August 3, 1932, also accepted as a part of inter-American law, in everything but name, the Kellogg-Briand Pact: "Respect for law is a tradition among the American nations who are opposed to force and renounce it both for the solution of their controversies and as an instrument of national policy in their reciprocal relations. They have long been the proponents of the doctrine that the arrangement of all disputes and conflicts of whatever nature or origin that may arise between them can only be sought by peaceful means." [22]

20. Stimson diary, July 29, 1932.

21. *FR: 1932, 5*, 159–60.

22. Curiously, three of the nations adhering to this joint appeal—Argentina, El Salvador, and Uruguay—had not subscribed officially to the Kellogg-Briand Pact, nor did they do so afterward.

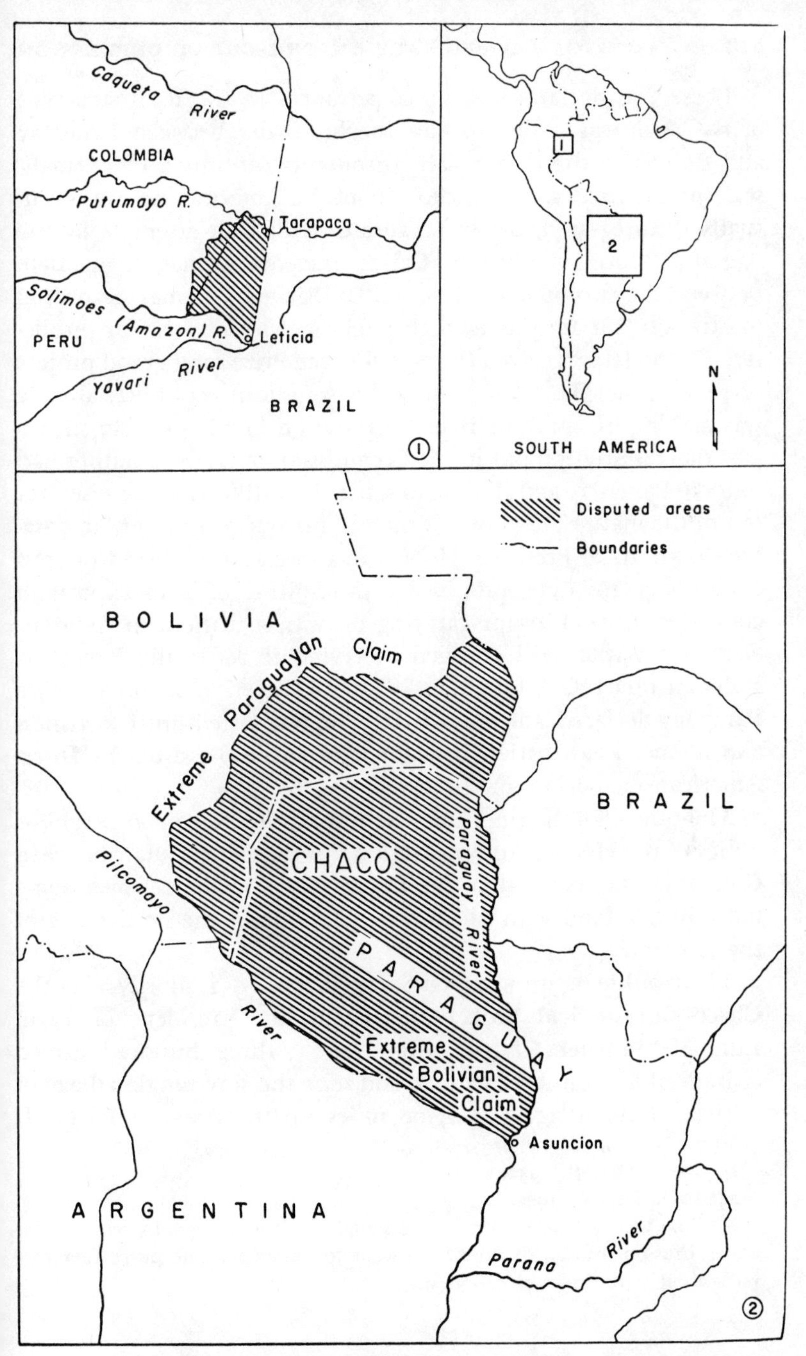

Border Disputes in Latin America, 1929–33—the Chaco and Leticia

These two declarations, signal advances in the legal structure of the Americas, failed to halt the hostilities between Paraguay and Bolivia in the Chaco. The disputants continued their small-scale jungle battles. The unanimity of the American nations eventually disintegrated, partly because of maladroit attempts by the Argentine foreign minister, Carlos Saavedra Lamas, to mediate between the two quarreling states. Dr. Saavedra Lamas, according to Stimson "an ambitious, flighty fellow, with an itch for publicity," [23] who later received the Nobel Peace Prize for a grand project of peace which he foisted upon the American republics, already was making his mark in 1932. Negotiation finally came to such a pass that, as Stimson put it, the Commission of Neutrals either had to force Paraguay and Bolivia to settle their differences or else "get out of the matter altogether, which is, of course, a rather lamentable situation." [24] President Hoover in a special message to Congress on January 10, 1933, proposed a prohibition of arms exports to countries threatening or carrying on war, as a help to Assistant Secretary White, still engaged in trying to settle the Paraguay-Bolivian quarrel. A few months after Hoover went out of office Paraguay declared war on Bolivia. The war lasted until weariness and financial exhaustion brought it to an end, assisted by Inter-American mediation, on June 14, 1935.[25]

The other South American war testing the new good neighbor policy of the Hoover Administration was the Leticia affair between Colombia and Peru—like the Chaco affair, a quarrel over some more jungle land with oil prospects, at one of the headwaters of the Amazon.

The trouble began when on September 1, 1932, shortly after the Chaco dispute had broken out again, the president of Peru, Luis M. Sánchez Cerro, allowed some three hundred armed citizens of his country to attack and seize the tiny jungle village of Leticia. This village was 2,700 miles up the Amazon River. It

23. Diary, Oct. 31, 1932.

24. Ibid., Dec. 14, 1932.

25. The ultimate peace terms were signed on July 9, 1938, by which, after an arbitration, nearly all the Chaco went to Paraguay. The peace therefore recognized some fruits of conquest.

consisted of about sixty-five crude huts, two-thirds of which boasted thatched roofs. For Colombia, Leticia meant the prestige of being an Amazonian power; for Peru, Colombian possession of Leticia meant sharing of commercial advantages with a rival nation.[26] For Stimson in Washington it meant—like the Chaco affair—a challenge to the treaty structure of international peace, especially in this case the Kellogg-Briand Pact, to which both Peru and Colombia had adhered, and which Colombia invoked soon after Peruvian seizure of Leticia.

President Sánchez Cerro of Peru at first took refuge under the fact that the Peruvians who seized Leticia were not members of the regular Peruvian army, but after a while he simply let it be known that he would not transfer sovereignty of the village back to Colombia. The Colombians fitted out an expedition of two small freighters which, in mid-February 1933, reached the neighboring village of Tarapacá and took it away from the Peruvians.[27]

Meanwhile there was much diplomatic maneuvering to avoid war and settle this problem by peaceful means. Stimson was incensed at the behavior of Peru. On the afternoon of October 14, 1932, he opened from Washington the new telephone line between the United States and Peru, and talked with the Peruvian foreign minister. "After we had exchanged our polite messages about the effect of this new line of communication upon the relations between us and South America and all that bunk, I took the Ambassador aside to say what I wanted to and I told him if I were to convey my real sentiments to his honorable chief, the Foreign Minister of Peru, I should have told him that if he didn't get his damned scoundrels out of Leticia without delay I'd string him up. Freyre looked a little aghast." [28]

Four months later, the dispute still on, Stimson convened at Woodley a conference of the ambassadors of the large powers,

26. Cooper, *American Consultation in World Affairs,* pp. 285–7.

27. Peruvian irregulars had seized Tarapacá along with Leticia.

28. "The Letician incident is still on, and it is perfectly indefensible on the part of Peru. Peru and Colombia are drifting into war over it and if they do, it will be one of the worst incidents to show how superficial all the peace work we are doing is." Diary, Oct. 14, 1932.

including the Japanese ambassador,[29] to endeavor to settle the quarrel in accord with the Kellogg-Briand Pact. Colombia had invoked the pact on January 23. The conference met promptly on January 24. White and Stimson laid before the ambassadors the history of the Peru-Colombia trouble and told them that the United States was going to send a note admonishing the disputants in the name of the antiwar pact. The secretary of state asked the ambassadors to communicate with their governments, so that the other nations also could send admonitory notes. Ambassador Claudel, the secretary recalled later, was rather pessimistic as to what could be done, mentioning that the United States had just failed with Paraguay and Bolivia. But all the ambassadors agreed that when Colombia had invoked the Kellogg Pact there was "nothing to do but to pay some attention to it." Ambassador Debuchi, Stimson noticed, remained silent during the proceedings. Claudel later told Stimson that at the Conference at Woodley he had suggested to Debuchi that Japan annex Leticia to Manchukuo.[30]

The secretary of state dispatched his note to Peru on January 25, 1933, informing President Sánchez Cerro that a violation of the Kellogg Pact "would entail a denial of the benefits furnished by that Pact to the signatory power which violated it."[31] A number of other states admonished Peru in one manner or another. The only great power not responding to the secretary's request was Japan. Shortly thereafter the dispute began to simmer down, with a peaceful solution appearing possible, a turn of affairs less the result of the Kellogg Pact than of the assassination in April 1933 of the Peruvian dictator, Sánchez Cerro. The new president of Peru, Oscar Benavides, worked beneficially for peace. The League of Nations settled the Leticia affair on June 19, 1934, returning the sixty-five jungle huts of Leticia to their original owner, Colombia.

29. "I did not want to leave him out, although the situation in regard to the Kellogg Pact in the light of the conduct of the Japanese Government during the last year and a half is rather anomalous, to say the least." Diary, Jan. 24, 1933.

30. Stimson in the margin of his diary described this as "Claudel's joke on Debuchi." Diary, Jan. 24, 26, 1933.

31. *FR: 1933, 4,* 426.

Chapter Fourteen: A MEETING AT HYDE PARK

During the Great Depression the treaty structure of world peace—erected at the Paris Peace Conference, supplemented for the Far East by the Washington treaties of 1921–22, sanctified by the Kellogg-Briand Pact—began to come apart. A distinctly downward turn of international affairs, resulting eventually in the second World War, first became visible during the years 1929–33 when the Depression was at its worst. Henry L. Stimson, more than the other members of the Hoover Administration, was in a position to confront this tragic turn in international affairs, and he was deeply worried. Japan by 1933 had scrapped the Covenant of the League of Nations and—what weighed more heavily on American hearts—those supplementary treaties, the Nine-Power Treaty and the Kellogg-Briand Pact. Stimson was well aware of the Far Eastern Crisis. But for the life of him he did not know what he could do to save the situation. He had exhausted against Japanese aggression the available devices of American diplomacy, feeble at the best—the doctrine of nonrecognition and the Borah Letter and the interminable diplomatic inquiries and protests which had gone on since September 18, 1931. When the Japanese on January 3, 1933, captured the little town of Shanhaikwan, just south of the great wall in China, the secretary of state could think of nothing more to say to Ambassador Debuchi than that Japan should "get out of" the League of Nations and the Kellogg Pact.[1]

1. Memorandum of a conversation with Debuchi, Jan. 6, 1933, *FR: Japan 1931–41, I,* 107–8. "And I made a careful explanation of our theories of what the movement against war meant since the Great War and that we were trying

After the presidential election, in which the Hoover Administration went down to defeat before the Democrats under Franklin D. Roosevelt, there came to Stimson's mind one further move. Not itself diplomatic in nature, it required the arts of diplomacy. He sought to arrange a personal conference, on the subject of American foreign relations, with Roosevelt; he would interview the president-elect and commit him to a policy of firmness in the Far East.

Because of Hoover's touchiness about any suggestion as to international cooperation (the defeated president was giving complete attention to the Great Depression in the United States and wanted no experiments in foreign affairs), and because of Hoover's rapidly increasing personal antagonism toward the president-elect,[2] it seemed desirable at first that Stimson should have some sort of pretext for seeing Roosevelt about foreign policy. Fortunately, an excuse—it was quite an important matter—presented itself immediately after the November election.

1

Semiannual debt installments to the amount of about $150,000,000 were coming due from the war associates of 1917–18 on December 15, 1932, the first payments since the moratorium of mid-1931. The debts were one issue on which European nations could unite with rare enthusiasm, and having made their gentlemen's agreement at Lausanne in July 1932, the debtors faced their creditor across the Atlantic in one solid, defaulting phalanx. Stimson and Hoover became much concerned. Solution of the debt problem, they believed, would assist in reviving prosperity in the United States. Payment of the installments on December 15 would, they thought, help balance the national budget. A balanced budget would increase faith in the solvency of the federal government. Faith in the government would stimulate businessmen to

---

to protect our civilization, and if Japan wanted to live on a different basis then the one we had chosen with those peace treaties she had better get out of the peace treaties and not break them. We would consider ourselves living in two different worlds." Stimson diary, Jan. 5, 1933.

2. See below, pp. 234–7.

invest and buy and produce. Which in the end might terminate the Depression. In retrospect this all appears as a highly unlikely sequence, the product of wishful thinking, an oversimplification of economic processes. Yet the fiscal views of Hoover and Stimson were the orthodox views of their generation. Economists usually considered business activity in terms of money supply (a strict acceptance of the 19th-century classical economic doctrines of Ricardo and Mill); a public debt was like a private debt, requiring payment, else there would follow national bankruptcy; a government had to balance its budget sooner or later, preferably sooner; it had to collect its foreign debts; the debtors had "hired" the money, hadn't they, as Calvin Coolidge allegedly remarked with a terseness which to his contemporaries sounded uncommonly sensible.

A later generation would lament the perverse ways of American politics, in refusing—by a high tariff—to accept payment of European war debts [3] in goods and services, necessitating payment in gold, which helped to wreck the gold covers of the various European currencies as soon as the Great Depression created for many nations unfavorable balances of trade. In the consequent frenzied efforts to prevent gold shipments,[4] governments blocked their currencies and made international trade exceedingly difficult —at the same time as Americans, themselves caught in the Depression, hoped to increase their own exports. It is of course far from certain that if there had been no high American tariff in the interwar years, the European nations would have paid their debts. Perhaps the tariff, one might conclude, only provided the debtors with a convenient excuse for not paying. Yet there can be no doubt that the tariff made payment difficult (if one granted, for the sake of argument, that there was willingness to

3. About a third of these debts were not "war debts" but peace debts, contracted after the Armistice of Nov. 11, 1918, for purposes of European reconstruction.

4. Shipments of gold occurred partly to cover adverse trade balances, partly because of fear that such nations would go off the gold standard and depreciate their currencies. Once the balance of payments turned adverse and the gold cover was thin, currency flights began.

pay), and the tariff was a result of American domestic legislation. Refusal of the United States to lower the tariff after the World War—and Congress' action in raising it twice, in 1922 and 1930—has been the subject of much discussion. Economists from the outset were aware of the contradiction contained in raising tariffs and simultaneously demanding large international payments. But politically tariffs were difficult to lower; and payment of the war debts was one issue on which the American people in the post-1918 era were solidly united; with the result that the foreign debtors eventually made rather unorthodox but nonetheless effective adjustments in the international balance of payments. European and other nations defaulted the debts, and for good measure joyously "nationalized" or otherwise trapped private American investments; private loans, because of the blocked currencies, simply were uncollectible.

The most violent of these unorthodox adjustments in the world trade position of the United States came during the Depression period with defaulting of the war debts. It consumed an inordinate amount of American diplomacy during the last two years of the Hoover Administration and created between the American people and their debtors a large portion of ill will.

At no time was the war debt problem so acute as in November-December 1932. It was the worst possible time for such a question to have come to the forefront of international relations. One of the two arch-tyrants of the 20th century was now maneuvering for power in Germany. Besides, in the United States the people had just repudiated the Hoover Administration at the polls, gravely weakening its position in international affairs. In the month after the election Stimson, Hoover, and Ogden Mills (who had succeeded the elderly Mellon at the Treasury in January 1932) conferred almost daily, and the president undertook to get in touch with the president-elect to obtain approval of the expiring government's debt policy. Success of the debt negotiation would turn on the attitude of the incoming administration. The European nations were anxiously listening for hints and rumors from the Roosevelt entourage at Albany and Hyde Park, hoping for a Democratic debt miracle.

Had the effort to secure cooperation with Roosevelt resulted only in a waste of time, this would have been bad enough. Hoover at the moment was a busy man, frantically seeking to keep the nation's economy afloat during the world economic hurricane. But in addition to a waste of time, Hoover's consultations with Roosevelt on the debt question helped engender such enmity between the two men that Roosevelt, for one, would never on any later occasion call upon Hoover's undoubted administrative talents, even during the crisis of a second World War. It doubtless is inaccurate to say that this sad state of affairs arose entirely out of the war-debt consultations at the end of Hoover's term of office; the personalities of the two men were in essence so different that conflict was almost inevitable. Certain it is, however, that discussions over the war debts in 1932 and early 1933 did not help matters. The debts were a complicated question and required thought and study, and Roosevelt gave them neither the one nor the other, but rather delegated the whole business to his adviser, Raymond Moley. From the outset Hoover, Stimson, and Mills disliked Moley, and moreover could never tell whether a particular suggestion came from Roosevelt or Moley. The president and his cabinet members disliked negotiating with a pretentious professor from Columbia University. Roosevelt on his part, with the ingrained suspicion of a professional politician, began to believe that Hoover was laying a trap, to commit him to a debt policy which would discredit the Democratic party in the eyes of the American people. There was not the slightest truth in this. Herbert Hoover was no person to set traps, especially if they involved the welfare of his country. He was struggling manfully with the debts and ten thousand other difficulties of a nation floundering in economic confusion. In December 1932 he was approaching the limit of his physical endurance. Tired out, sleepless, irritable, he began to believe that Roosevelt was being purposely and malevolently difficult, refusing to cooperate so that the country would fall down to the bottom of the economic scale: then the Republicans and Hoover would receive all the blame, and FDR upon taking office could grandly rescue the nation from the follies of his predecessor.

Hoover invited the president-elect to the White House on November 22, 1932, in an attempt to agree on a debt policy. At once the personalities of the two men collided. White House attendants brought in cigars and cigarettes and pitchers of orangeade and ice water, but these medicines were not strong enough to bring about a meeting of minds. At the conclusion of the conference the veteran head usher noticed that most of the cigars and cigarettes were gone, and all of the ice water. Afterward the president said, referring to Roosevelt's lack of understanding of the debt problem: "He did not get it at all." As for Moley, who had accompanied Roosevelt, Hoover suggested that the professor had been reading some magazine articles in the *Saturday Evening Post* which seemed to be his principal source of knowledge.[5]

At the meeting Hoover had asked that he and the president-elect confer at the White House next day with congressional leaders of both parties, where they jointly should urge resurrection of the old War Debt Commission to renegotiate the debt settlements. Roosevelt said that he would rather not attend such a meeting, but would communicate his approval to the Democratic congressional leaders. Hoover then suggested that after the White House meeting with the congressmen, he and FDR should draft a press communiqué on the debt question, which they would issue jointly, stating agreement. Roosevelt and Moley preferred that Hoover alone issue a statement. When Hoover duly met with the congressional leaders he was astonished to discover that Roosevelt had not gotten in touch with the Democratic members. FDR later told reporters that the debt question was "not his baby." [6]

5. Irwin H. Hoover, *Forty-Two Years in the White House,* p. 223. After Moley's apostasy from the New Deal he became friendly with Hoover, who ultimately appreciated Moley as "an able man with a mind quick to grasp public problems." *Memoirs of Herbert Hoover: The Great Depression,* p. 179. Moley likewise could praise Hoover's "immense talent for massive organization, his enlightened conception of the needs and capacities of the nation, his basic conviction that liberty and initiative are essential to our preservation and progress." Raymond Moley, *27 Masters of Politics: In a Personal Perspective* (New York, Funk and Wagnalls, 1949), p. 29.

6. *Memoirs of Herbert Hoover: The Great Depression,* pp. 178–84.

On December 15 Britain paid her pledged installment in full, $95,000,000 in gold, but in an accompanying note offered conditions of payment which made American acceptance difficult.[7] Italy, "cagey little Italy,"[8] paid after discovering that the British would pay. Poland defaulted; the Greek government deposited part payment in a blocked account; the French defaulted. Roosevelt may have sabotaged payment of the French installment by telling reporters at Warm Springs that he did not regard payment as a necessary condition for opening debt negotiations. The French press, according to the disgusted Hoover, "received this dispatch with elation and proceeded to eulogize Mr. Roosevelt as a great leader and to damn me a-plenty."[9] Hoover had reason to believe that the French could easily have made their payment of about $20,000,000, for French citizens at that time had over half a billion in dollar exchange in New York banks. A week after December 15, following a futile telegraphic exchange with Roosevelt, Hoover issued to the press his entire correspondence with FDR.[10] By the end of December 1932 the president and the president-elect of the United States were at loggerheads.

FDR while talking with Professor Felix Frankfurter one night in Albany suddenly made a proposal: "Why doesn't Harry Stimson come up here and talk with me, and settle this damn thing that nobody else seems to be able to."[11]

Frankfurter as a young lawyer twenty-five years before had worked under Stimson when the latter was United States attorney

7. The British stated that their payment of December 15 was "not to be regarded as a resumption of the annual payments." They had made the payment, rather, because time did not permit detailed discussions, but they wished the American government to know that without some debt adjustment they anticipated a "general breakdown of the existing inter-Governmental agreements" by June 15, 1933. British embassy to the Department of State, Dec. 11, 1932, *FR: 1932, I*, 776–8.

8. Stimson diary, Dec. 15, 1932.

9. F.D.R. later denied that the Warm Springs dispatch had any authority from him. *Memoirs of Herbert Hoover: The Great Depression*, pp. 184–5.

10. Hoover, Stimson thought, had conducted himself well in these debt negotiations. "His letters have been dignified and on a high plane of unselfishness. They made Roosevelt look like a peanut." Stimson diary, Dec. 21, 1932.

11. Stimson diary, Dec. 22, 1932.

for the southern district of New York, and during the World War he had become acquainted with Roosevelt on the old War Labor Board, of which he was chairman and FDR ex officio member as assistant secretary of the navy. Afterward, as a Harvard law professor and one of the most prolific letter-writers and telegram-senders of his generation, Frankfurter sedulously maintained his friendships and contacts. In 1932 he could help bridge a yawning gap between two presidential administrations. He hurried to a telephone and relayed Roosevelt's remark to his old chief in Washington.[12]

A few days later Roosevelt again intimated to one of Stimson's friends, this time Norman Davis, that it would be a mistake to put off the meeting.[13]

A talk with the president-elect was easily possible for Stimson, and given the disheartening stalemate in American Far Eastern diplomacy—and especially the secretary of state's desire to see Roosevelt continue the policy of firmness in Eastern Asia—it was eminently desirable. The only obstacle was that Stimson had to get the permission of President Hoover.

2

When the secretary of state on January 3, 1933, broached the subject at the White House, "H.H.," as Stimson expected, bristled with hostility. "He began by saying that he would never talk to him [Roosevelt] alone again. He said that Roosevelt was a very dangerous and contrary man and that he would never see him alone. I began by telling him, after I had recited the sequence of events, that what I wanted to do was to go and see Roosevelt myself and try to make arrangements so that Hoover could see him and see him alone when he went through Washington on his way to Warm Springs." Stimson courageously—and it took courage to stand up to Hoover when the latter was in an angry mood—told his chief that Roosevelt also should have information about

12. Diary, Dec. 22; *On Active Service,* pp. 289–90. On Dec. 24 Roosevelt sent a formal invitation to Stimson. Elliott Roosevelt and Joseph P. Lash, eds., *F.D.R. His Personal Letters: 1928–1945* (2 vols. New York, 1950), *I,* 314.

13. Norman Davis to Stimson, Dec. 28, 1932, Stimson MSS.

American foreign relations if he desired it, and that to refuse information was a serious responsibility.[14] Reluctantly Hoover agreed to think matters over.

Next day Stimson again conversed with the president, and with considerable effect cited a cable from Ambassador Edge in Paris who was proposing to resign on grounds that there was nothing left to do because of the Roosevelt-Hoover deadlock. Hoover finally yielded "and said that he was willing to have me go up there, provided that Roosevelt would ask him first. He is very doubtful about the possibility of success . . ." [15]

Stimson eagerly got in touch with Frankfurter, who talked to Roosevelt, and secured an immediate invitation to Hyde Park. The president-elect sent a formal letter to Hoover requesting the conference.[16]

From the outset the secretary intended to extend the conversation to include more than war debts, and Hoover and Roosevelt both understood this. Hoover expected nothing from the meeting, and had agreed to it in part because he believed that Stimson would better understand and appreciate Roosevelt's intransigence. The president hoped that, so far as concerned the general public, the meeting would give an appearance of cooperation between the outgoing and incoming administrations.

After some delay because of the death and funeral of former President Coolidge, Stimson on the morning of January 9, 1933, at last found himself taking a train up the Hudson from New York to Hyde Park. Roosevelt's chauffeur met him at a nearby station and drove him through snow, rain, and sleet three miles to the Roosevelt estate. Hyde Park, Stimson carefully observed, was a beautiful place with fine trees, but the rather stately old house, with its successive additions, suggested lack of orderliness. The interior amply corroborated this impression. The furnishings inspired a feeling of confusion. This was true even of the recently added large library room, of which the Roosevelt family evidently

14. Stimson diary, Jan. 3, 1933.

15. Ibid., Jan. 4, 1933.

16. Diary, Jan. 4. Roosevelt to Hoover, Jan. 4, 1933, in Elliott Roosevelt and Joseph P. Lash, eds., *F.D.R. His Personal Letters, 1*, 320–1.

were proud.[17] It was there at eleven o'clock of a cold January morning that the talk began, upon the outcome of which the secretary of state had placed his hopes not so much for an agreed debt policy as for a firm diplomatic policy in the Far East and any other area of the world where aggressors threatened the peace.

From the outset the president-elect did everything to make the interview pleasant. Stimson, who never had conversed with him before, had no difficulty getting on. The background of both men—their upbringing and experience—was not dissimilar. They were patrician New Yorkers, and party labels could hardly raise too much difference between them. Stimson beyond dispute was always something of the *grand seigneur,* as was Roosevelt, despite his more obviously democratic attitude. In international concerns both men were essentially liberals; and it is entirely possible that, if Stimson had ever undertaken to run for public office in the years after his gubernatorial defeat of 1910, he would have realized the growing social consciousness of Americans generally, the consciousness which Roosevelt helped improvise into federal legislation, and like Roosevelt he might have become a liberal in domestic politics. There were far more similarities than differences between Stimson and FDR.

As both men were by nature good talkers, their conversation never had a chance to lag. Roosevelt asked questions and Stimson answered. "I confined myself to giving him the information he asked for"—so Stimson later recalled, though one can well imagine that he did not limit his side of the conversation to objective answers, without adding personal views and opinions.[18] The talk ranged widely over many topics. War debts, the original purpose of the meeting, vied with Rooseveltian queries about Puerto Rico, Cuba, Haiti, recognition policy in Latin America, Philippine independence, the coming World Economic Conference, disarmament, recognition of Soviet Russia, and other matters, including the Far East. The latter subject lay closest to Stimson's heart, and

17. Diary, Jan. 9, 1933.

18. The following account of the conversation is from a State Department memorandum which Stimson placed in his diary.

it appears to have dominated the conversation, at least from his notes.[19]

Roosevelt fully approved the secretary's policy in the Far East; his only possible criticism was that it had not begun earlier. Stimson noted that Roosevelt possessed a personal interest in China—an ancestor once had held a position there, and indeed during the Civil War the *C.S.S. Alabama* nearly captured FDR's grandmother as she was voyaging out to China on a sailing vessel. The president-elect showed a "very lively" concern for Stimson's Asian policy. Japan's adventure in Manchuria he believed ultimately would fail because of economic pressure, and Stimson agreed, pointing out that this was the unanimous view of the Lytton Commission. The secretary mentioned the American fleet at Hawaii—how necessary it was there, and how Japan had sought to have the fleet withdrawn—and Roosevelt, firm friend of the navy ever since his service during the Wilson Administration, asked if it were possible that Japan had been rash enough to try to dictate the policy of the American fleet.[20]

FDR was completely charming that day at Hyde Park, and on no topic did he disagree with Stimson. The interview lasted through luncheon and during a long drive of the two men in Roosevelt's car back to New York. During this five-hour period they were entirely alone.

The effect of the conference, one must conclude, was not immediately discernible. To reporters Stimson afterward refused comment except that he and the governor had enjoyed a "delightful lunch." [21] To Undersecretary Castle he jubilantly telephoned that he had had a good talk with Roosevelt and that if

19. Stimson's memorandum filled eleven typescript pages. The Far East occupies two and one-half pages, and war debts fill almost two pages; these were the longest discussions.

20. For the fleet's appearance at Hawaii during the Shanghai Incident, see above, p. 210 n.

21. New York *Times,* Jan. 10, 1933. Raymond Moley thought that when Stimson told reporters that he had enjoyed a delightful lunch with FDR, it was only the gentle purr of the cat that had swallowed the canary. Raymond Moley, *After Seven Years* (New York, Harper, 1939), p. 94.

one could take at 100 per cent all he said, the future would look extremely hopeful. Castle was skeptical, as Roosevelt already had acquired a reputation for agreeing with the last man to whom he talked.[22] Hoover upon being told of the conversation remarked that it would be fortunate if Roosevelt's promises were worth 5 per cent.

Stimson himself returned to Washington with few doubts. He used the first opportunity to tell Ambassador Debuchi that March 4 would see no change in American policy. With considerable satisfaction he sent word to Sir John Simon that the American position remained as laid down in the Borah Letter.[23]

The secretary had in mind also to ask Sir John about the British attitude on Shanhaikwan; he telephoned Roosevelt what he wished to say, and Roosevelt gave authority to go ahead.[24] But when news of Stimson's assurances to London and Tokyo appeared in the press, reporters called upon Roosevelt for confirmation. This, obviously, was too important an augury for curious newspapermen to allow to pass. Roosevelt during his campaign had been highly equivocal—he had been almost silent—on foreign policy, and since his election the press had been curious about his plans. Confronted by reporters in the study of his New York City house at 49 East Sixty-fifth Street, the president-elect borrowed a pencil and wrote out a most interesting announcement. "Any statement relating to any particular foreign situation," he declared, "must, of course, come from the Secretary of State of the United States. I am, however, wholly willing to make it clear that American foreign policies must uphold the sanctity of international treaties. That is the cornerstone on which all relations between nations must rest." [25] Urged to explain his statement further, he refused.

Stimson in Washington dictated to his diary that this press statement "virtually affirmed his [Roosevelt's] alignment with our Far Eastern policy. It was a very good and timely statement and

22. Castle diary, Jan. 10, 1933.
23. Stimson diary, Jan. 12, 13, 1933.
24. Castle diary, Jan. 13.
25. New York *Times*, Jan. 18, 1933.

made me feel better than I have for a long time." [26] Perhaps this appraisal was correct. Roosevelt privately was telling two protesting advisers that "I have always had the deepest sympathy for the Chinese. How could you expect me not to go along with Stimson on Japan?" [27] But Roosevelt had not committed himself publicly to Stimson's policies; his press statement so pleasing to Stimson was a skillful equivocation, and did not in any sense accept the Stimson Doctrine or any other specific measure as future policy. To come out as FDR did for upholding the sanctity of international treaties was almost as innocuous a statement as anyone could possibly have made, as unexceptionable as his brief allusion to foreign policy in his first inaugural address: "In the field of world policy I would dedicate this nation to the policy of the good neighbor . . ." One must conclude that the Hyde Park colloquy did not immediately pin down the president-elect to anything important.[28]

Did the conference bear important future results? There is little reason to believe that it did. Certainly in the years immediately following the meeting of January 1933, FDR took no strong stand against Japanese aggression. American diplomacy in the Orient almost ceased while Roosevelt and the nation turned to grave domestic problems; the New Deal demanded and received all the national attention. When the historian Charles A. Beard looked into the index of Roosevelt's *Public Papers and Addresses,* he found that F.D.R. at least throughout 1933 failed to

26. Diary, Jan. 17, 1933; *On Active Service,* p. 293. In his memoirs Stimson remembered this press statement as having gone even farther in support of the administration's Far Eastern policy than the private talk at Hyde Park.

27. Raymond Moley, *After Seven Years,* p. 95. According to Moley, he and Rexford Guy Tugwell spent "hours" explaining to FDR why they felt it a tragic mistake to underwrite the Stimson policies in the Far East; but "We might as well have saved our breath. Roosevelt put an end to the discussion by looking up and recalling that his ancestors used to trade with China."

28. Raymond Moley believed then and later that Roosevelt's New York City statement, itself quite without significance, when read in connection with Stimson's statements marked a definite commitment to Stimson's Far Eastern policy. *After Seven Years,* p. 94.

show any interest at all in the Far East.[29] Later after the violent turn of events in Europe and the Orient in the latter 30's Roosevelt ultimately did carry out toward Japan a strong "Stimsonian" policy, of sharp diplomatic reprimand, economic embargoes, and, ultimately, a position risking and resulting in war. He even brought Stimson into the cabinet in 1940 as secretary of war. Still, these later developments bore almost no relation to the meeting at Hyde Park in 1933. FDR appointed Stimson to the cabinet in 1940 for perhaps two reasons, neither of them connected with the former secretary of state's well-known views on Far Eastern affairs. Roosevelt in June 1940, confronted by the appalling Franco-British military disaster in northern France, needed someone in his cabinet who could take a strong pro-British position; Stimson received a call to join the Roosevelt Administration the day after he made an outspokenly pro-British speech in New Haven. Then there was another exigency explaining Stimson's cabinet appointment under Roosevelt, namely, that in the summer of 1940, anticipating the campaign for a third term, FDR decided to entice into his cabinet some prominent Republicans, perhaps with the idea in mind of creating a sort of Union Party patterned on the party of that name during the Civil War. All

29. Beard discovered only three index references to Japan and none at all to Manchuria or Manchukuo. The first reference to Japan touched upon a visit of a Japanese representative as well as similar visits from agents of other governments in the spring of 1933 to discuss the world economic situation; the second reference listed Japan among the nations to which President Roosevelt sent an "Appeal for Peace by Disarmament"; and the third referred to a personal and unofficial conversation between Roosevelt and Viscount Ishii. *American Foreign Policy in the Making* (New Haven, 1947), pp. 143-4.

William L. Neumann in a most interesting article, "Franklin D. Roosevelt and Japan, 1913-33," *Pacific Historical Review,* 22 (1953), 143-53, contends that Roosevelt in 1933 began to assume a new and strong attitude toward Japan—much as he had had in his youth and as assistant secretary of the navy, and had moderated in the years after the Washington Conference. Neumann's principal evidence was a cabinet discussion on Mar. 7, 1933, when Roosevelt talked at length about the possibility of war with Japan (see James A. Farley, *Jim Farley's Story,* New York, 1948, p. 39). Yet this seems to have been an isolated expression of presidential opinion. There followed no public remarks of any sort..

this had little connection with the Hyde Park conference of 1933.[30]

One must say, in conclusion, of the meeting at Hyde Park on which Stimson had placed his last hopes as secretary of state, that the conference was notable for its lack of any kind of results. Two men of like mind had sat down together and talked about American policy in various parts of the world. Such a conversation, in 1933 fraught with possibilities for the future, in later years subject to exaggerative exegesis, really—and contrary of course to Stimson's hopes at the time—turned out to be an isolated incident of slight historical import.

3

Before the Hoover Administration came to its dreary end on March 4, 1933, there occurred a second futile meeting in Washington between Hoover and Roosevelt, over the war debt default and the possibility of using debt renegotiation as a lever to pry economic concessions out of the European nations. At the time of the French default, the premier of the moment, Edouard Herriot, courageously let it be known that he wished to pay the debt installment to the United States. The Chamber of Deputies turned him out of office by a vote of 402 to 187. As Stimson put it, their mouths were full of pickles,[31] and they would do nothing to

30. That Stimson could speak to Roosevelt about Far Eastern matters in 1933, become secretary of war in 1940, and be at the War Department when the attack came at Pearl Harbor in 1941, has seemed to some writers a suspicious circumstance. Charles A. Beard in his *American Foreign Policy in the Making,* p. 143, intimated a cause-and-effect relation, although in his philosophical writings on the processes of history he denied the possibility of such simple causality. *Theory and Practice in Historical Study,* Social Science Research Council Bulletin, *54* (1946), 136 n. According to Charles Callan Tansill, *Back Door to War* (Chicago, Regnery, 1952), p. viii, scholars have underestimated the importance of Roosevelt's "conversion to the explosive nonrecognition doctrine so strenuously advocated by Henry L. Stimson. This was a bomb whose long fuse sputtered dangerously for several years and finally burst into the flame of World War II. It was entirely fitting that Stimson became Secretary of War in 1940; no one deserved that title quite as well as he."

For the maneuvers to obtain a "coalition cabinet" in 1940 see Eliot Janeway, *The Struggle for Survival* (New Haven, 1951), pp. 125–45.

31. Diary, Dec. 16, 1932.

placate, let alone pay, their creditor across the Atlantic. Such was the situation when Roosevelt came to Washington in mid-January 1933.

Stimson met him on the afternoon of January 19 at the Mayflower. The first thing FDR said was (alluding to the Far Eastern situation), "We are getting so that we do pretty good teamwork, don't we?" Stimson laughed and answered "Yes." The two men discussed the French default, and Raymond Moley and Norman Davis joined in. Stimson left with the impression that he and FDR were in full agreement on the war debts as well as other matters.[32]

When Hoover and Roosevelt met at the White House the next day, agreement on the war debts was not in evidence. Seating arrangements for the conference in the Red Room were in diplomatic fashion—Hoover sat on a sofa with his back to the window; on his right was Roosevelt, in a chair; then came Stimson and Moley on the next sofa; and Norman Davis and Ogden Mills on chairs, making a circle.[33] Roosevelt and Moley insisted that debt settlement and assurances of economic cooperation should remain separate in all diplomatic negotiations: the American government should not attempt to gain general economic concessions in return for debt concessions. After interminable talk and no agreement the conferees composed an ambiguous communiqué, and Hoover gave up attempts to cooperate on the debt problem with his successor.[34]

It was after this meeting that there occurred a little set-to between Stimson and his chief which underlined in a peculiarly sharp manner the differing personalities of the two men. Their personal incompatibilities, as we have seen, did not have much effect upon the conduct of American diplomacy in the period 1929–33. The Hoover-Stimson differences were of less importance

32. Ibid., Jan. 19, 1933.

33. Ibid., Jan. 20.

34. Ibid. Hoover made a long memorandum of this meeting with the president-elect, which appears in Myers, *The Foreign Policies of Herbert Hoover*, pp. 229–36. There also is a memorandum by Stimson in the Stimson MSS.

than they later seemed. Difficulties nonetheless existed, and flourished in the tense atmosphere of January 1933. International trouble, the domestic economic crisis, defeat in the November election—all had combined to make Hoover at the end of his term a peevish and irritable, not to say despairing, individual. He now wished Stimson to send a note to France about the debts, and Stimson instantly assumed that Hoover was trying to do this out of party advantage and to keep the record straight. The secretary of state may have been right. In any event the two men had some "pretty hot words, the President getting more irritated than I had seen him for a long time. I spoke pretty freely myself." [35] Next day Stimson called up Hoover with a proposal to send notes to Italy and Czechoslovakia and other countries which had paid their installments, fixing a time when they could present their cases for debt readjustment. Hoover thought this a good idea, "but he would not take it in place of the French note . . . I must send the French note, too. We both again spoke pretty strongly to each other over the telephone. He told me that my views differed very largely from his. I told him that I recognized it, and that I was mighty glad of it. He then asked me if we were going to send the note . . . I said that I would if he directed it. Otherwise, my advice was against it. Well, he said that he requested it, and we hung up the telephones both mutually angry." Two days later, after a cabinet meeting, Hoover apologized in a rather embarrassed way.[36]

In early 1933 world events succeeded each other inexorably toward future disaster. At the League of Nations there was a long debate over the Lytton Report, which finally resulted in League acceptance of the report and Japanese retirement from the League. The report had been published on October 1, 1932.[37]

35. Diary, Jan. 21, 1933.

36. "After Cabinet today the President called me into his room, and in a rather embarrassed way told me that he regretted that he had blown up over the French note. He said that we were all tired and overworked and said things that we would not otherwise say." Stimson diary, Jan. 22, 24. See also Myers, *The Foreign Policies of Herbert Hoover,* pp. 236–9.

37. Two American experts who accompanied the commission, George H. Blakeslee and C. Walter Young, wrote the Lytton Report. So I am informed by Leon Hubbard Ellis, former second secretary of the American legation in

Watching the slow Geneva debate from the vantage point of Washington, Stimson suspected that the League was willing to publish a report but not adopt it—that the Geneva organization feared the withdrawal of Japan from the League. Stimson felt that the League should announce formally its verdict of guilt in the Manchuria case. "The whole question is whether or not the League will do its duty as to the principles before they start conciliation." [38] This would have been a logical consequence of the doctrine of nonrecognition of the fruits of aggression, which the League had adopted for Manchuria in the resolution of March 11, 1932. After much talk in the Committee of Nineteen, the League on February 24, 1933, adopted the Lytton Report. That same day, the first anniversary of publication of Stimson's letter to Senator Borah, the Japanese delegation made their dramatic exit from the Salle de la Reformation. Japan announced permanent withdrawal from the League, taking as a souvenir the Pacific islands held under League mandate. The chief Japanese delegate at Geneva, Yosuke Matsuoka, told the League that as Christ had been crucified on the cross, so was Japan being crucified by the nations of the League. Privately Matsuoka explained that the powers had taught Japan the game of poker but after they had acquired most of the chips they pronounced the game immoral and took up contract bridge.

In "Manchukuo" in early 1933 Japanese troops enlarged Manchukuoan territory by taking the entire province of Jehol up to the Great Wall. When the Manchurian puppet government proclaimed itself independent a year before, it had included Jehol as Manchukuoan territory, and the new nation somewhat confusedly announced that it was taking what it all the while possessed. Jehol contained some old Chinese imperial palaces, and much coal, and the strategic mountain passes leading into North China. The Japanese had no trouble in occupying them, for the

---

China, who occupied an office in Peking with General McCoy during the summer of 1932 when the report was being written, and was in a position to observe the inner workings of the commission.

38. "Simon has taken a very weak position . . ." Stimson diary, Dec. 15, 1932.

Chinese put up almost no defense. Admiral Montgomery Meigs Taylor, U.S.N., at that time commander of the Asiatic Squadron, set down in a private letter to the chief of naval operations a piquant description of the campaign. It was, he wrote, a "sad thing to realize that after all the oratory about defending our sacred land to the last drop of blood . . . Chengtu was taken by two armored cars and 125 infantry in trucks. . . . Tang Yu Lin [the local governor] showed himself in his true light as a rapacious, selfish warlord of the worst type. Intent only on his own enrichment he cared only to get his property away, it being said that he emptied trucks of munitions and supplies en route to the front to fill them with his loot and take it to a safe place. It is reported that when the Japanese were near Chengtu, he had to be wakened from an opium sleep to give orders." [39]

The Japanese occupied Chengtu (usually known as Chengteh) on March 4, the day President Roosevelt took the oath of office. Japanese and Chinese representatives on May 31, 1933, signed a truce at Tangku, a little town near the Great Wall, temporarily ending hostilities.

At the time of the Jehol campaign, court circles in Tokyo buzzed with excitement that the army authorities might follow capture of the province by an excursion into the Peking-Tientsin area. This, they feared, might have had serious consequences, not merely complaints by the League of Nations but decisive action by the great powers. Foreign Minister Count Yasuya Uchida told Prince Saionji's private secretary, Baron Kumao Harada, that he would instruct the war minister to move in such a manner as to limit the affair; but Harada and Saionji were not certain that the army would show any such restraint. War Minister Araki favored finishing off matters in the shortest possible time, by sending in a large force as the army had done at Shanghai. He had heard much talk, he said to Harada, concerning Japan's situation in international politics, but no matter what Japan did the Western

39. Taylor to Admiral William V. Pratt, Shanghai, Apr. 14, 1933, Taylor MSS. Nelson Johnson sent a most discouraging dispatch to the Department on Mar. 29, 1933, relating the farcical defense of Jehol and the impotence of the Nanking government. 793.94/6218.

nations would not speak well of her, and it was hence of no use to behave. Harada replied that it was not a question of behaving so much as avoiding things which were not profitable. The navy minister and the naval general staff appear to have sided with the Foreign Office against the army, and by a narrow margin carried the day for nonextension.[40]

With this decision affirmed by the Tangku truce, there remained only a few personnel matters for settlement in China. There had to be some provision for displaced persons such as Chang Hsueh-liang. The latter was still young, but no longer marshal of Manchuria. Chang came to an agreement with Chiang Kai-shek, handed over to Chiang the remnants of his Manchurian troops, and went off to Shanghai. There his still-loyal adviser, W. H. Donald, had him cured of the drug habit, after which Chang departed on a grand tour of Europe.[41] The erstwhile marshal, one should add, left for Europe under a cloud, for at the last moment and to obtain money for his trip he sold the Chinese Naval Hospital in the French Concession in Tientsin.[42] Undaunted by criticism which raged around him for this indiscretion, Chang went on his way. He began his vacation by flirting on the boat with Edda Ciano, Mussolini's daughter, who with her husband was en route home from China to Italy.[43]

Count Ciano had not yet achieved his European and world reputation, but already in Europe the New Order was casting a shadow ahead. Hitler at the end of January 1933 had succeeded General Kurt von Schleicher as chancellor of Germany. The garish pomp of the new regime quickly captured the hearts of large masses of the German people, just as it disgusted and nauseated foreign observers. There was a long-remembered scene on the night of January 30 when a huge torchlight parade was held in Berlin to acclaim the new chancellor. Torches flamed and hissed,

40. Saionji-Harada diary, Dec. 26, 1932, Jan. 16, 21, 25, Feb. 17, 1933; Kido diary, Mar. 18, May 19, 1933.

41. Selle, *Donald of China,* pp. 282–5.

42. Admiral Montgomery Meigs Taylor to his brother, Col. J. R. M. Taylor, U.S.A., May 19, 1933, Taylor MSS.

43. Count Ciano had been serving as Italian minister to China.

tossing grotesque shadows over marchers and onlookers. Thousands after thousands of Storm Troopers paraded past Hitler and President von Hindenburg, the bands playing tunes and airs of imperial days and the World War. Hitler followed the celebration with great glee from an open window of the Reich Chancellery, laughing, gesticulating, at times dancing up and down. A few yards away at another window stood *Der alte Herr,* old Hindenburg, whom liberal Germans had mistaken as the protector of the Republic. The old man looked on with childish enjoyment; persons nearby noticed that he occasionally beat time with his crooked stick to the familiar military marches that resounded from below.[44]

In America the Hoover Administration was ending its four years of office at a time when the Great Depression touched its lowest point. The banking system of the country, wobbling since 1930–31, propped by the RFC in 1932 and by FDR's campaign promises not to desert the gold standard, collapsed in early 1933, and by March 4 almost every bank in the country had closed, many states having declared "bank holidays." Most members of Hoover's administration departed with feelings of bitterness, believing that they had lost the election to the Depression and the obscurantist campaigning of a political opportunist. "We are at the end of our string," Hoover admitted privately on inauguration day. "There is nothing more we can do." [45] Press pictures taken on March 4 showed Hoover riding grimly alongside Roosevelt on the way to the inaugural; the retiring president's dour face well represented his feelings.

The inaugural of course turned out to be a stirring affair, in which Roosevelt gave one of the great speeches of his generation. His fellow countrymen took hope in the prospect, in part eventually realized, of a New Deal in American politics and society.

In foreign relations Roosevelt's first administration would mark time during the domestic reform. The Italo-Ethiopian War of 1935–36 jarred on the nation's sensibilities, but it took more than the conquest of Abyssinia and the challenge of the Rhineland

44. Konrad Heiden, *Der Fuehrer* (Boston, 1944), p. 540.
45. Joslin, *Hoover Off the Record,* p. 366.

crisis and the beginning of the Spanish Civil War and even resumption of war in China in 1937 to give Americans a sense of disaster. Not until the Munich crisis of 1938 did they begin to awaken to the fact that they had lost the peace of Versailles, so dearly won in 1917–18. Until the summer of 1940 the United States continued to adhere to the old policy of isolation. In 1940, when it was too late, people began to realize that signs of disaster had first appeared in the last two years of the Hoover Administration.

For Stimson in January, February, and early March 1933 the routine of the State Department had gone on from day to day. Perhaps the greatest disappointment of this period was the Philippine Independence Bill, which passed Congress "with a whoop" over Hoover's veto; on January 13, 1933, in the House, 274 to 94, and on January 17 in the Senate, 66 to 26. "We are in a pitiful position," the president said, commenting on the vote. "Whatever the subject, there are not thirty senators we can depend upon. It's a rout." [46] Voting for Philippine independence, Congress nonetheless was only registering the feelings of the American people, who had found the Islands too heavy a strategical burden, and were sick of accusations of imperialism. Philippine independence was incidentally helpful to a number of business firms, who in 1933 congratulated one another that the competition of Philippine exports with domestic and Caribbean products would end. The Filipino leaders themselves did not wish independence, knowing that it would bring economic difficulty. Sergio Osmena and Manuel Quezon, visiting in Washington at the time, went to the White House and asked Hoover personally to veto the independence bill, explaining that they were lobbying for independence merely because their people forced them to. Hoover, astonished at such irresponsibility, threatened to call in the press, whereupon the Filipino leaders blandly replied that they would deny their statements. Hoover told them he hoped they would never come into the White House again.[47]

46. Ibid., p. 339.

47. *Memoirs of Herbert Hoover: The Cabinet and the Presidency,* p. 361.

Stimson had had a special program of his own for the Philippines, a dominion status similar to that of Canada with Britain, but the forces for independence were almost irresistible, especially after they obtained the support of several former American administrators in the islands, including Cameron Forbes. The lamentable results of premature Philippine independence would not become evident for many years afterward. In 1933 passage of the bill through Congress only served further to impress the Japanese that the United States cared little for the affairs of the Far Pacific. True, the Philippines had long been the Achilles' heel of American Far Eastern policy, but to cast the islands loose at the particular moment that Congress chose—while the secretary of state was attempting vigorous diplomacy in the Far East—was, to put it mildly, inopportune.[48]

Stimson in anticipation of early departure from office could set aside his disappointment. Washington after all was a long way from Jehol and the Philippines, and as for developments in Europe he could not hear the music of the bands in distant Germany or see the baleful flare of the torches and their grotesque shadows. One evening in February 1933 he and Mrs. Stimson went to a meeting of the Oxford Movement in a Washington hotel, where they listened quietly, impressed by the hymns and sincerity of the participants. When the day of departure at last approached, it came as a day of deliverance. Stimson in all his years of public office had never known so hectic and unenjoyable a time as the months since September 1931. On inauguration day he turned over his duties to Senator Cordell Hull, and that evening he and his wife went out to dinner with some friends and close associates, and "had really the best time we have had in Washington. . . . After dinner we talked a little . . . but not very long and then when the ladies came down we gathered around the piano and

48. The grant of independence in the Hawes-Cutting Act was conditional upon Filipino approval, which was not forthcoming because of the act's tariff provisions. In 1934 the Filipinos accepted the Tydings-McDuffie Act containing slight modifications. It provided for a "commonwealth" government until 1946 and then independence.

had singing until well after midnight . . . the spirit was perfectly lovely and we enjoyed it more than anything that had happened to us here."[49]

With music, with friendly singing around a piano, four difficult years of American diplomacy came to an end, at least for Henry L. Stimson—and for his chief, President Herbert Hoover.

49. Diary, Mar. 4, 1933, *On Active Service,* p. 296.

Chapter Fifteen: THE WORLD ECONOMIC CONFERENCE

On March 4, 1933, a new president came into office, with a new secretary of state, just after Adolf Hitler became chancellor of Germany. One may ask if Franklin D. Roosevelt, whose views on foreign policy and diplomacy later became so pronounced, was able in his first months in office—or for that matter his first years—to do any better in foreign relations than had his predecessor. FDR's perfunctory invocation, in his inaugural, of the good neighbor in world policy was a signal of his personal absorption in domestic problems. It fell to a new secretary of state to fashion foreign policy: Cordell Hull, bereft of diplomatic experience, an idealist who believed that high tariffs rather than high politics was the basic cause of wars. Thus equipped, would the Roosevelt Administration find it possible to move American diplomacy off dead center, as it had come to rest at the end of the Hoover-Stimson era?

The test of the Roosevelt Administration as a maker of foreign policy—and proof that FDR and Hull, like Hoover and Stimson, found diplomacy extremely difficult and even impossible in the midst of the Great Depression—came shortly after the Democrats took office, in the summer of 1933 when the World Economic Conference convened in London. Here was an opportunity for some arrangement that could improve both world economic relations and the prospects for world peace. With the appearance of Hitler in Germany, and military domination of the Japanese government since 1931, the future of peace was becoming clouded. Perhaps, it might have been assumed, a forward-looking Administration would manage to find some economic formula during the

London Conference that could improve the economic picture throughout the world and, thereby, strengthen the supports of world peace. But as Roosevelt discovered after the World Economic Conference had already begun its sessions, to improve the world's economy involved certain sacrifices in the American domestic economy, and these he was unwilling to make. The London Conference of 1933 was in a sense the culmination, the high point, of American efforts after 1929 to maintain international peace. This was the conference at which statesmen openly recognized the importance of economic arrangements to save the world from war. That the chance to underwrite peace economically was lost in the summer of 1933 was some indication of the appalling domestic economic problems faced by the American government during the Great Depression.[1]

1

The Roosevelt Administration started off with an explosive surge of legislation the like of which had never before been seen in the history of the United States. In the spring of 1933—the famous Hundred Days—there followed in quick succession a series of legislative acts which gave hope of economic recovery to the entire nation, and which historians have long since set down as one of the greatest psychological boosts ever given by a newly elected government to a discouraged people. The nation's economic life was almost at a standstill when Roosevelt took office.

1. The only published study of the World Economic Conference is Jeannette P. Nichols, "Roosevelt's Monetary Diplomacy in 1933," *American Historical Review, 56* (1950–51), 295–317. See also the unpublished study by John O. Gallagher, "American Economic Foreign Policy and the Failure of the 1933 World Economic Conference," a doctoral thesis at the Fletcher School, 1953. I am indebted to William Kamman for use of his unpublished thesis, "The United States and the London Economic Conference of 1933," Indiana University, 1956.

Seeking manuscript materials for this present chapter, I made a fruitless search through the main archival file in the Department of State records, 550.S1/1–1446, together with ancillary files. The Cordell Hull MSS are at present (1957) closed to research for this period. Fortunately the Roosevelt MSS at Hyde Park contained interesting material on the conference.

Estimates of unemployment ranged between 13,000,000 and 18,000,000, with the number of persons in actual distress approaching 75 per cent of the unemployed. The New Deal in its initial hundred days of reform gave encouragement to these Americans for almost the first time since they had entered the depths in 1931 and 1932. As for international accomplishment during that time, the record is likewise clear: there was practically none. In actual fact, the diplomacy of the United States stopped almost completely while the country fastened its attention on domestic reform.

Secretary of State Cordell Hull was not himself inactive during this springtime of the New Deal. As the various Administration measures were being drawn up in the executive offices, sent to Capitol Hill, and passed by an enthusiastic Democratic Congress, Hull in the impressive secretary of state's office in the State, War, and Navy Building prepared for the World Economic Conference which, he hoped, would reform international trade in the same manner that his chief was renovating the country's domestic economy. Hull had never forgotten the tariff accomplishment of the Wilson Administration, Democratic precursor of the Administration of 1933. As a young Tennessee congressman he had voted for the Underwood Tariff of 1913 and had hoped along with other idealists that it would ease the path of international relations. The first World War ruined such hopes; and after the war came the two Republican high tariff acts of 1922 and 1930. Hull held to his hope that sometime the world would find its senses, lower tariffs, and ease the economic path to international tranquillity. Little did he realize then that in 1933 he would himself have some chance of returning the world to freer trade.

The secretary was no zealot in his anti-tariff views. He was no free trader. He had no intention of turning the economic clock back to the days of the Manchester School of Great Britain at the time of the repeal of the Corn Laws. He knew that many rigidities had developed in the international exchange of goods, that creation of other workshops of the world in America, Germany, and elsewhere had made quite impossible the laissez-faire conditions of nearly a hundred years before. Former President Hoover has written humorously of Hull that FDR's secretary of state was a "fanatic" on the trade question: "He apparently believed that reduction of tariffs would cure all domestic and foreign ills, including chilblains." [2] This was not quite true, for Hull believed that the economic doctors of his day had developed other remedies for the world's economic ailments besides reduction of tariffs. Still he held that there were many unnecessary tariffs—that the walls with which so many nations had surrounded their trade had, many of them, no rational foundations—and that a careful, common-sense approach to tariffs might make for freer trade, freer domestic economies, more efficient use of national resources, better life for peoples of all nations, more disposition on their part to be satisfied with their national boundaries rather than wanting the territory of their neighbors.

Whether Franklin D. Roosevelt, that "most complicated human being," [3] went along with these views on world trade is difficult to say. One might well hazard the guess that Roosevelt had never thought out his position on international trade, had never felt that it was necessary to think about the subject until some concrete action in regard to commerce was presented to him for his approval or rejection.

The president did have some convictions on monetary matters; during his first months in office he was determined to raise price levels in the United States. To prevent private hoarding of gold during the banking crisis, Roosevelt on April 5, 1933, under the Emergency Banking Act had ordered that all gold and gold certificates be turned in at the Federal Reserve Banks by May 1, and by an executive order of April 20 he laid a prohibition on gold exports, thus taking the country off the gold standard. The dollar began to fluctuate in relation to the gold countries (France, Belgium, Holland, Switzerland, and Italy) and the sterling bloc (Britain, the Dominions, and Scandinavia). What this meant for the prospects of the World Economic Conference was at the moment unclear. It could have been argued, though foreign nations

2. *The Great Depression,* p. 364.

3. "He was the most complicated human being I ever knew . . ." Frances Perkins, *The Roosevelt I Knew* (New York, Viking, 1946), p. 3.

did not believe this, that it was the domestic banking crisis alone which drove Roosevelt to abandon the gold standard, and that he actually had no desire to participate in a currency war. It could be argued that his continuing intention to take part in the World Conference at London was a clear indication of his willingness to conclude there some arrangement for pound-dollar-franc stability. On April 19, the day before prohibition of gold exports, Roosevelt in his press conference said: "One of the things we hope to do is to get the world as a whole back on some form of the gold standard." Presumably this could be done without conflicting with the president's intention to raise domestic price levels.

The World Economic Conference had been planned, of course, for almost a year before FDR took office, long before the domestic economic crisis of the spring of 1933. The exact antecedents of the conference are difficult to trace until more archives are opened up, but one is on fairly safe ground in saying that the conference came out of the continuingly difficult diplomatic situation between the United States, on the one hand, and the debtor nations of Europe on the other. The Hoover Moratorium expired on December 15, 1932, and the debtors had met at Lausanne in June 1932 and virtually repudiated both their obligations to the United States and the reparation payments owed them by Germany under the Young Plan. In the uneasy atmosphere of this tacit European agreement—that debts and reparations would be written off—it was wise to make a gesture toward the powerful creditor across the Atlantic. Even before the Lausanne Conference met, overtures were made in Washington for a special economic conference to discuss all sorts of economic questions, presumably including debts; and this was the genesis of the World Economic Conference of 1933. President Hoover suggested in May 1932 that Prime Minister MacDonald convene such a meeting in January 1933, for two major purposes—world currency stabilization and reduction of trade barriers.[4] MacDonald agreed, doubtless hoping

4. Hoover, *The Great Depression,* p. 363. Hoover had suggested a conference to Premier Laval during the latter's visit to Washington in November 1931. The premier felt that the time was not yet ripe for such a meeting. Ibid., p. 130. The British ambassador in Washington on May 13, 1932, asked

that the debts-reparations difficulties might somehow come under discussion at the same time, even if not specifically included in the agenda. Officially four topics were excluded from discussion at the conference: disarmament, specific tariff rates, debts, and reparations. Disarmament already was under discussion at the World Disarmament Conference at Geneva, but as for the other topics, it seemed impossible that world economy could come under debate without reference to such important international realities.

Organization for the Economic Conference went on apace during the summer, autumn, and early winter of 1932. Never, it would seem, was American participation in a great international conference more thoroughly prepared for. A preparatory committee of experts met at Geneva in November 1932 and included two Americans, John H. Williams, professor of economics at Harvard, and Edmund E. Day, an economist who at the moment was director of the division of social sciences of the Rockefeller Foundation.[5] Simultaneously an organizing committee established itself, including on the American side Norman H. Davis and the United States ambassador in Berlin, Frederic M. Sackett. The latter would soon, with the change of administrations, disappear from the scene. Norman Davis, "sniffing a conference from afar like a battle horse," [6] was ready to do anything necessary to ensure that the meeting would deal authoritatively with major questions of world economics. There was no let-up in the activities of Davis and Sackett, and of Day and Williams, but after defeat of the Hoover Administration in November 1932 the new president-elect preferred postponement for some months of the opening of the World Economic Conference. Day and Williams and Davis continued to go back and forth across the Atlantic from meetings in Europe to discussions in Washington. There were additional conversations at Hyde Park and in New York with the president-elect. It was virtually agreed to open the conference as soon as

---

the Department of State, presumably under instructions, whether the time had not come for convocation of an international monetary and economic conference. *FR: 1932, I*, 808.

5. Day later (1937–49) served as president of Cornell University.

6. Hooker, ed., *The Moffat Papers*, p. 155 (diary entry of Oct. 7, 1937).

the Roosevelt Administration had entered office and pushed through Congress its first major acts of domestic legislation. The conference took on a sort of complementary aspect to the New Deal—it would be the New Deal in international economics. It might be noted that Roosevelt had warned in his inaugural that "Our international trade relations, though vastly important, are, in point of time and necessity, secondary to the establishment of a sound national economy. I favor as a practical policy the putting of first things first. I shall spare no effort to restore world trade by international economic readjustment, but the emergency at home cannot wait on that accomplishment." Even so, this did not seem to augur any drastic reservations for the World Economic Conference.

Secretary Hull watched anxiously the reactions of his chief to the preliminaries of the World Conference—the visits to Washington of such foreign statesmen as Prime Minister MacDonald of Britain, Edouard Herriot of France, Viscount Ishii of Japan. The president met statesman after statesman, with unflagging interest and even enthusiasm; and the secretary of state concluded hopefully that the London meeting enjoyed Roosevelt's fullest support and approval.

Judging from the communiqués issued after each of the preliminary visits by important foreign statesmen—MacDonald, Herriot, Ishii, Hjalmar Schacht of Germany, Guido Jung of Italy, Richard Bennett of Canada, Tomás A. LeBreton of Argentina, T. V. Soong of China, Alberto Pani of Mexico, J. F. de Assis Brasil of Brazil, Pedro A. Torres of Chile—a cynic might have thought that the World Conference's high-level exploratory conversations had not been fruitful. There were the usual banalities of international discourse, in which statements of vigor were followed by small but efficient words which sapped out all the vigor. Still, there could be no doubt that the hearty MacDonald, for instance, left Washington feeling that he was taking back some kind of pledge about monetary stabilization, so that at London the pound sterling might be tied down to the dollar. Likewise Herriot of France found FDR most cordial, and came to believe, if one can attach importance to Herriot's public statements, that the American president was willing to do something for gold-standard countries and that perhaps the American delegation at London would prove friendly toward the franc and toward France's defaulted war debt to the United States. After Herriot's visit Schacht of Germany arrived, and he was received with pomp and cordiality equal to that accorded Herriot and MacDonald. He heard the Marine Band play "Deutschland, Deutschland über Alles" as he entered the White House for a formal luncheon. If in conversation with officials at the State Department he encountered some plain speaking about the belligerent tone of the new Hitler government of which he was a representative, he found the president willing to show to Germany some measure of good will in advance of the London Conference; perhaps, Schacht felt, Germany's case at London would get a friendly hearing from the Americans. After Schacht came other foreign representatives—special envoys from the countries with which American trade was of considerable importance. There also were specially arranged conversations with forty-two ambassadors and ministers of additional countries accredited to Washington. Presumably, since there was so much discussion (so any reasonable observer might have thought), there must have been much interest and not just barren conversation.

The dossiers of pourparlers for the World Economic Conference grew to startlingly large proportions. The president of the United States continued to show his good humor and interest in the conference. The secretary of state carefully put together all his favorite projects for reduction of world trade barriers, and discussed them at length among his intimate advisers. It was at this time that Hull placed on the president's desk a proposal for a reciprocal trade agreements act, exactly like the act that Congress passed in 1934 except that the proposed act of 1933 contained a clause whereby Congress could disavow within sixty days any tariff-reduction agreement negotiated by the Department. Roosevelt at the moment said nothing against this proposal to Secretary Hull.

It became necessary to appoint the delegation to the conference. The final date for the meeting in London had been set during the MacDonald visit. Raymond Moley later would write facetiously that the date of June 12, 1933, was arrived at by FDR and Mac-

Donald because the president did not want to convene a world conference at the same time that Congress was in session and because MacDonald didn't want the conference in session during the grouse season in England which came later in the summer.[7] For whatever reason, June 12 was the date; and late in May the president announced the members of the American delegation. The chairman was Secretary of State Hull. Assisting him as vice chairman was Roosevelt's old running mate in the Democratic campaign of 1920, James M. Cox. The other delegates were Key Pittman, president pro tempore of the Senate; James Couzens, reputedly the only Republican senator willing to go to London; Samuel D. McReynolds, chairman of the House foreign affairs committee; and Ralph W. Morrison, a wealthy San Antonio Democrat, retired banker and cotton dealer, a kind of "dark horse" delegate whom FDR chose at the very last moment. Reporters saw some confusion in the choice of these men. Hull, Cox, and McReynolds were low tariff. Couzens and Pittman were high tariff. No one, not even the president, knew the tariff views of Morrison.[8] Secretary Hull, let it be added, was not consulted on any of the appointments to his delegation.[9] Perhaps he could have felt satisfied that the president had at least refused to heed the advice of eighty-five members of Congress, including ten senators, who petitioned FDR to appoint as the delegation's economic adviser Father Charles E. Coughlin of Detroit, the radical "radio priest." The adviser was, instead, James P. Warburg of New York, a fairly conservative banker and idealistic student of international affairs.

2

"The proceedings prior to the conference," Secretary Hull later wrote, "grew increasingly unstable and almost chaotic. It

7. "What with Congress on the one side and grouse on the other, agreement on June 12th was a triumph of diplomacy." *After Seven Years,* p. 206.

8. Morrison was unbelievably ignorant of international affairs. At a press conference in London he inquired of newspapermen, "Who *is* Beneš?" Harold B. Hinton, *Cordell Hull: A Biography* (Garden City, N.Y., 1942), p. 228.

9. *Memoirs of Cordell Hull, I,* 249.

was in this state of turmoil, cross-purposes, and frequent changes of positions by Governments that the Conference was to meet." There followed "indescribable confusion." "Never in my life have I witnessed such bewildering movements and utterances containing the most surprising changes of opinion without a moment's notice to anyone. There was never so much milling around and tugging and pulling as characterized this conference. It seemed to be moving and operating most of the time in a dense fog." [10]

Whence came the confusion? Who at least was responsible on the American side? The American delegation consisted of high and low tariff men. The purposes of the delegation were uncertain, for Roosevelt would not allow his delegates to talk about currency stabilization, either temporary or permanent, a matter that naturally went hand-in-hand with tariff measures. Permanent stabilization he would not consider at all. Temporary stabilization, for the duration only of the World Economic Conference, he delegated as a special task to Professor Oliver M. W. Sprague of Harvard, acting for Secretary of the Treasury William H. Woodin, and to George L. Harrison, governor of the New York Federal Reserve Bank. Sprague and Harrison were to talk with French and British central bank and treasury officials. Confusion deepened when Secretary Hull, en route to the conference, received a cable from the president advising that it was impossible to get a reciprocal trade agreement act through Congress, then in the last throes of its session; hence Hull would have nothing in the way of concrete tariff reduction to offer the representatives of other nations at London. [11] Roosevelt advised the secretary that he could negotiate bilateral trade agreements which the Senate

10. *Memoirs of Cordell Hull, 1,* 248, 254.

11. In London on May 12 representatives of the United States, Britain, France, and five other powers had signed a tariff truce, agreeing not to sharpen their "measures of all kinds which at the present time misdirect and paralyze international trade" nor to adopt new ones, before July 31. There was some question about whether the truce would last until the end of July, for Section 3 (e) of Title I of the National Recovery Act authorized the president to limit imports and to license importers and to permit the entry of specified articles on terms and conditions and limitations as to quantities. The Agricultural Adjustment Act also had tariff provisions.

could then ratify in its autumn session, but Hull knew only too well that it was impossible to get such special treaties through the Senate, particularly when the Senate had not authorized them. When Hull at last arrived in London he encountered further confusion when he sought to get President Roosevelt to approve his opening speech to the conference. The president had his desk stacked high with last-minute business from Congress, and delayed so long in reading Hull's speech that the secretary had to put off the address for two days, a fact that was misinterpreted in London as studied American impoliteness.

Hull at London had absolutely nothing to offer the representatives of sixty-three other nations gathered imposingly at the Geological Museum in South Kensington. Everything was highly organized, ready for international action. There was a Monetary and Financial Commission, with two subcommissions and two subcommittees; and an Economic Commission, with four subcommissions and seven subcommittees. At the beginning of the conference the delegates limited themselves to short opening statements, to avoid the speech making fiasco of the World Disarmament Conference. Preliminaries thus were dispatched in a few days. Everyone was ready to get down to business. The French were asking what the United States would do about stabilizing the dollar, the British were asking for a pound-dollar-franc agreement, smaller countries wanted reduced American tariffs, there was muffled talk about debt adjustments (following the universal default, save for Finland, on the semiannual debt payments due the United States on June 15, 1933.[12] Hull had nothing to offer, other than homilies about freer trade and the moral willingness of the American government to do as much as possible to increase the world's commerce. He could not talk about temporary stabilization; that was the task of Sprague and Harrison. He could not talk about permanent stabilization; that was forbidden to any American delegates in London. He could make no tariff offers under a general reciprocal trade agreements act, for Roosevelt at the moment would not send in such a bill to Congress. It was

12. Britain, Italy, and Latvia made token payments totaling $11,154,592.20. Finland paid in full, $148,592.

futile to negotiate bilateral agreements, which the Senate in its wisdom would only reject. As for the disarmament question, that was the business of the Geneva conference. War debts and reparations were beyond the secretary of state's instructions. It was a painfully embarrassing personal situation to be head of a helpless delegation, and almost a tragic situation for an individual who for twenty years since the Underwood Act of 1913 had waited to do something important for all-round reduction of American and world tariffs.

Secretary Hull fidgeted and squirmed with embarrassment, alternating between hope and despair, mothering his discordant delegation through interminable private and conference sessions, openly acknowledging his inability to prevent individual delegates from talking pessimistically about the conference or giving to the press their own private views on currency and tariffs.

The Sprague-Harrison faction of the delegation—if these two special emissaries could be described as a delegational faction—made a cautious proposal to Roosevelt by cable on June 16, suggesting temporary stabilization of exchanges by the United States, France, and Britain. There was a proviso that allowed the American government full liberty of action if in the interest of the domestic recovery program it should desire to terminate the arrangement. Roosevelt vetoed the proposal. Harrison left for New York in disgust. In hope of some other formula on stabilization agreeable to Roosevelt, Sprague continued on, working with Warburg and Cox. Cox at about this time cabled his former vice-presidential running mate the undiplomatic plea, "If you love us at all don't give us another week like this one." [13]

The president answered by cable that he was delighted the way things were going.[14]

3

At this juncture there came the strangely planned appearance at the World Economic Conference of Assistant Secretary of State Raymond Moley. This trip has occasioned much comment

13. Cable of June 22, 1933, *FR: 1933, I,* 654.
14. Roosevelt to Hull and Cox, June 24, *FR: 1933, I,* 655.

and speculation, and all one can say about it, with retrospect of nearly twenty-five years, is that nobody to this day knows what President Roosevelt had in mind in sending Moley. If the World Conference was confused before he arrived, it was doubly perplexed thereafter; and what FDR was planning to do must remain a very large question mark. Moley in his *After Seven Years* had the impression that Roosevelt had used him in some vague way or other.[15] At the time he thought that he was being sent to communicate to the American delegation the president's thinking on the purposes of the conference.

Whatever the reason for dispatching Raymond Moley to London in June 1933, the result was, for a week before Moley arrived, the wildest speculation on the purposes of his mission, a speculation that Moley did little to dispel. Despite disclaimers in his later book, he at the moment regarded his mission as important enough to warrant personal press statements and press conferences. Everyone knew that he was a sort of "Man Friday" of the president, and his press encounters, together with the fact of his dashing flight by navy plane and destroyer to the president's schooner *Amberjack* off Nantucket prior to leaving for London,[16] the immediate departure for Europe aboard the liner *Manhattan*, and the special plane sent from London to Cobh to bring him quickly to the waiting Economic Conference: all this had a dramatic effect. Perhaps Moley could not have avoided sensational newspaper reporting regardless of how he behaved. If he had adopted a policy of no press contacts and quiet journeying to London, he might only have received publicity as a "man of mystery"—his situation would have been like that of General Dawes at Paris in November–December 1931. Surely Roosevelt, who understood the mechanics of public relations, knew the cumulative effect of his assistant's publicized movements, and could have arranged for some deflation of the mission to its proper proportions. Perhaps the president instead wished to give the impression in the United States that he was taking large interest in the desultory conference

15. *After Seven Years*, p. 198.

16. Roosevelt in June 1933 was sailing the *Amberjack* along the New England coast to his summer house at Campobello Island.

at London; perhaps he felt that a little high drama would prod the delegations to action.

Secretary Hull, quite naturally, was furious at this disavowal of his leadership in London. Moley already had ruffled him by having been put on the State Department payroll without any Department responsibilities. Moley in the spring of 1933 moved in and out of the reaches of the government on various missions for the president, and Hull could do nothing to stop such free-wheeling by his nominal subordinate.

The assistant secretary had managed to commit one indiscretion after another. Two days after his appointment to the State Department he held a press conference in Washington in which he roundly berated the press for referring to him as the president's Man Friday, and then proceeded to say that he would not be able to receive them frequently because he would be running back and forth to the White House.[17] Later in the spring he came to Hull's apartment one morning. "His face was serious, and he proceeded to say to me that he did not seek my position as Secretary of State, contrary to any rumors to that effect. After he left I remarked to another visitor, 'Moley at least has the subject on his mind.' "[18]

Then there was the Leith-Ross affair. After Prime Minister MacDonald's visit to the White House, Roosevelt commissioned his special assistant to carry on secretly some war debt negotiations with the economic adviser of the British Foreign Office then in Washington, Sir Frederick Leith-Ross; some time later the British ambassador inadvertently let the cat out of the bag to Hull, to the latter's intense displeasure.[19] Again there was the national radio address which Roosevelt allowed Moley to make on May 20, in which the assistant secretary of state undiplomatically said that foreign trade was of little importance to the United States, that "Our domestic policy is of paramount importance," and that the American people should not raise their

17. Hooker, ed., *The Moffat Papers,* pp. 89–90 (diary entry of Mar. 6, 1933).
18. *Memoirs of Cordell Hull, 1,* 247.
19. *After Seven Years,* pp. 203, 210–12.

hopes too high for the World Economic Conference.[20] Naturally undertook a special mission to the London Conference, Hull was so mad he could hardly contain himself. Recovering his temper, the secretary decided, according to the account in his memoirs, to give the young man enough rope and see what would happen.

Incident after incident continued to "rawhide" the secretary of state in London. The press announced that the secretary was old, inefficient, and inept. Moley was described as "the man who controlled presidents." Upon arrival the special delegate held a press conference, with the secretary of state standing obediently to one side, ignored by the shouting newspapermen. All the statesmen of Europe wished to see Moley. "Can you send Moley over to me? I'd like to talk to him," MacDonald said to Hull, adding as an afterthought, "And you can come too, if you like." [21] "Moley, Moley, Moley, Lord God Almighty," chanted some of the newspapers.

The assistant secretary entered into the negotiations then being carried on by Sprague, Warburg, and Cox, and drew up a careful but innocuous statement, to be made by Britain, the United States, and the gold bloc countries, that they would do their best, as their individual situations permitted, to stabilize currencies. Hull carefully refused to have anything to do with this proposal, saying that as a delegate to the London Conference he had no authority to handle stabilization. Moley went ahead, and on June 30 cabled the proposal to the president.[22]

when this bumptious professorial presidential representative

20. Ibid., p. 209: "there's nothing in my public career about which I have less regret." But see *Memoirs of Cordell Hull, I,* 249: "In the circumstances Moley deserved a severe call-down from the President, but unfortunately Mr. Roosevelt sometimes gave his intimates undue liberties over his other friends." When Hull's memoirs appeared in serial form in 1948, Moley wrote a letter to the New York *Times,* published on Feb. 2, 1948, in which he gave a justification of this incident, repeating the points made in his *After Seven Years.*

21. *Memoirs of Cordell Hull, I,* 259–60. For Moley at London see Hull's remarks in *The Secret Diary of Harold L. Ickes: the First Thousand Days, 1933–1936* (New York, 1953), pp. 75–7.

22. For the "Joint Declaration by the Countries on the Gold Standard and by Those Which Are Not on the Gold Standard," see *FR: 1933, I,* 670–1.

Hull's great moment now came: Roosevelt on July 1 turned down Moley's proposal.

When word of Moley's humiliation arrived in London, the secretary of state was starting to leave for Cliveden to attend a garden party given by Lady Astor. He was walking from Claridge's to a waiting limousine when Moley rushed up, saying "We've just got to do something about it." Hull joyously proceeded to rawhide Moley: "You had better get back home. You had no business over here in the first place." Utilizing his choicest Tennessee expressions, the secretary set his assistant secretary straight on a number of matters.[23]

This finished Moley at London. The president's special representative shortly thereafter took ship back to the United States.

On the following Monday came the grand climax of the World Economic Conference, an event of far larger proportions than any personal mishap to an assistant secretary of state. Curiously, Moley's humiliation had occasioned it. Roosevelt's quondam representative had gone to considerable trouble to negotiate the currency proposal that FDR turned down, and acting on the impulse of this move against temporary stabilization the president went further and sent a message to Hull, received on July 2 and released to the press on July 3, in which he blew up the entire conference:

> I would regard it as a catastrophe amounting to a world tragedy if the great Conference of Nations, called to bring about a more real and permanent financial stability and a greater prosperity to the masses of all nations, should, in advance of any serious effort to consider these broader problems, allow itself to be diverted by the proposal of a purely artificial and temporary experiment affecting the monetary exchange of a few nations only. Such action, such diversion, shows a singular lack of proportion and a failure to remember the larger pur-

23. *Memoirs of Cordell Hull, I*, 261. Moley in *After Seven Years*, p. 255, said that Hull "received the news coldly." Charles Michelson, who was press officer of the American delegation, has written that "I was not there, but my information is that it was anything but a cold meeting; in fact, I gathered that the comments of the Secretary of State—not on the message but on the messenger—were about the hottest in our modern diplomatic history." *The Ghost Talks*, p. 111.

poses for which the Economic Conference originally was called together.

I do not relish the thought that insistence on such action should be made an excuse for the continuance of the basic economic errors that underlie so much of the present world wide depression.

The world will not long be lulled by the specious fallacy of achieving a temporary and probably an artificial stability in foreign exchange on the part of a few large countries only.

The sound internal economic system of a nation is a greater factor in its well being than the price of its currency in changing terms of the currencies of other nations.

It is for this reason that reduced cost of government, adequate government income, and ability to service government debts are all so important to ultimate stability. So too, old fetishes of so-called international bankers are being replaced by efforts to plan national currencies with the objective of giving to those currencies a continuing purchasing power which does not greatly vary in terms of the commodities and need of modern civilization. Let me be frank in saying that the United States seeks the kind of a dollar which a generation hence will have the same purchasing and debt paying power as the dollar value we hope to attain in the near future. That objective means more to the good of other nations than a fixed ratio for a month or two in terms of the pound or franc.

Our broad purpose is the permanent stabilization of every nation's currency. Gold or gold and silver can well continue to be a metallic reserve behind currencies but this is not the time to dissipate gold reserves. When the world works out concerted policies in the majority of nations to produce balanced budgets and living within their means, then we can properly discuss a better distribution of the world's gold and silver supply to act as a reserve base of national currencies. Restoration of world trade is an important partner, both in the means and in the result. Here also temporary exchange fixing is not the true answer. We must rather mitigate existing embargoes to make easier the exchange of products which one nation has and the other nation has not.

The Conference was called to better and perhaps to cure fundamental economic ills. It must not be diverted from that effort.[23a]

In this message the president, for the first time during the London meetings, made his views perfectly clear. He had decided, he virtually said, to place domestic economic recovery above any international measures.

After this torpedoing of the purposes of the London meeting, the conference's remaining sessions were an anticlimax. Confusion at last had come to an end, albeit in a manner scarcely anticipated by the idealistic Hull at the beginning of the world meeting. The secretary's dreams of another New Freedom throughout the world had disappeared with one blast of the New Deal trumpet. After Roosevelt's message of July 3 there was little to do but go home.

Hull cabled a diplomatic congratulation to the president about a "very able and courageous statement" which, he carefully added, had received some criticism for "harshness and untimeliness" of language.[24] Moley more heartily congratulated the president, and sent an outrageous report, quickly communicated to Hull and other members of the delegation, criticizing the Americans in London for inability to follow FDR's instructions.[25] Meanwhile Hull waged a valiant fight to keep the conference in session for a few days or a week or so, to prevent delegates of other countries from claiming that the United States had killed the world meeting. Almost everyone was up in arms. The British delegation was incensed. MacDonald, fearing loss of his cherished position as prime minister, spoke of Roosevelt as "that person" and couldn't understand what had gotten into him; [26] Neville Chamberlain as chancellor of the exchequer wrote in his diary that the American

23a. *FR: 1933, 1,* 673–4.

24. Hull to Roosevelt, July 3, 1933, *FR: 1933, 1,* 679.

25. Ibid., p. 680; *Memoirs of Cordell Hull, 1,* 266; *After Seven Years,* pp. 262–3; Michelson, *The Ghost Talks,* pp. 106–8.

26. Ernest K. Lindley, *The Roosevelt Revolution: First Phase* (New York, Viking, 1933), p. 211. Hull and MacDonald had several written and oral clashes during this time, and the secretary of state became quite blunt with the prime minister. See Hull's correspondence in the Roosevelt Library, P.S.F., Box 32, *London Economic Conference* Folder, MacDonald to Hull, July 5, 1933; Hull to MacDonald, July 11; Hull to Roosevelt, July 12.

president's "effusion" had "completely declared his intention to go his own way," and that it was "useless" to continue the conference.[27] The French delegation went from hotel to hotel, in imitation of American political procedure, lining up delegates to vote the conference out of existence and denounce the American president. Hull somehow kept the conference's steering committee from voting against the United States, but for several days it was touch and go before the French and British quieted down. The conference thereafter went on "twitching," to use the word of Warburg,[28] for three weeks, until it rolled over lifeless on June 27, 1933.

4

Why did FDR torpedo the World Economic Conference? Raymond Moley in a letter to the New York *Times* in 1948 confessed that he had never learned the reason. Moley's colleague at London, Oliver M. W. Sprague, who helped negotiate the temporary stabilization proposal which brought on the bombshell message, concluded that Roosevelt's motives were "obscure." [29] James A. Farley in his memoirs has set down a curious conversation in which FDR raised the specter of an international plot against him, led by the bankers whom he had castigated in his inaugural address in 1933. The president told Farley that Thomas W. Lamont of J. P. Morgan and Company had arranged for Herbert Bayard Swope to assist Moley during the latter's mission to the conference, and that Lamont had also placed someone on the *Manhattan* to contact Swope and Moley during the voyage to London.[30] He may have been so aroused by discovery of this alleged plot that he vetoed the stabilization proposal and then sent the bombshell that broke up the conference.

27. Keith Feiling, *The Life of Neville Chamberlain* (London, 1946), p. 223 (diary entry of July 4, 1933).

28. James P. Warburg, *The Money Muddle* (New York, Knopf, 1934), p. 121. Warburg on July 6 resigned as financial adviser to the American delegation.

29. Oliver M. W. Sprague, *Recovery and Common Sense* (Boston, 1934), p. 49.

30. *Jim Farley's Story*, pp. 40–1.

Roosevelt's logic seems to have been neither melodramatic nor obscure. The president's immediate problem in July 1933 was the structure of domestic prices in America. After the stock-market crash of 1929, prices had fallen drastically, until by the spring of 1933 the Bureau of Labor Statistics' general index of wholesale prices stood at 59.6 of the level of 1926. Farm prices were 40.6. The early New Deal measures sought to push prices to higher levels. Attempts to stabilize currencies even temporarily, FDR evidently believed, would result in a "stronger" dollar, a fall in domestic price levels as the international value of the dollar rose; and this he would not allow. There had been startling improvements in prices in the United States during the early New Deal months. The BLS general index had moved to 69.7 on July 22, and farm products rose during the same period to 62.7—increases of 17 per cent and 54 per cent. So long as this movement continued, there was every reason to leave well enough alone and not to attempt currency stabilization—regardless of how harmless the proposal might appear—for even a temporary period. As Roosevelt himself explained in 1934 in *On Our Way*, "we were engaged at home in a great program of rehabilitation—a program which called for the raising of values—and . . . no human being could, at that moment, determine exactly where even a temporary stabilization point should be fixed for the dollar, franc and pound." [31]

What lay behind the encouraging rise in prices within the United States during the New Deal's first months is difficult to

31. *On Our Way* (New York, John Day, 1934), pp. 123–4. Professor George F. Warren of Cornell, who in the early days of the New Deal had a considerable influence over Roosevelt's monetary thinking, wrote a memorandum on July 12, 1933, stating the importance of avoiding any agreement at London that would take away "our freedom to change the dollar any day." Roosevelt Library, P.S.F., Box 32, *London Economic Conference* Folder.

Raymond Moley in his memoirs has written that the two advisers present with Roosevelt on July 2, 1933, when FDR sent his destructive cable to London, were Henry Morgenthau, Jr., and Louis Howe. Presumably Morgenthau as farm administrator was interested in raising farm prices. Louis Howe may have been jealous of Moley's influence with the president (so Moley believed). It is true that the first draft of the "bombshell" message is in

say.[32] Perhaps the mere fact of prohibiting private holdings or exports of gold lent uncertainty to prices in the country and stimulated speculation in basic commodities, thus raising their prices. Certainly there was much talk about inflation in the spring of 1933. Senator Burton K. Wheeler sponsored a bill to coin silver at the old 19th-century ratio of 16-to-1. Then Senator Elbert D. Thomas had offered an amendment to the Emergency Farm Relief Bill, which passed Congress, giving the president almost unlimited power to inflate the currency by printing greenbacks, to depreciate the currency by reducing its gold content, to resort to bimetallism, or to any other scheme he saw fit to use. Such permissive legislation had itself an inflationary effect. Further inflationary factors were the prospects for smaller farm crops under the agricultural program, and hopes for increased exports to be made possible by currency depreciation.

Domestic prices in the United States, for some reason or reasons, were rising; the World Economic Conference had the misfortune of convening at this delicate moment; out of this situation apparently came Roosevelt's decision to forbid any currency stabilization at London. This in itself, one might have supposed, would not have been enough to end the conference. Actually, however, a temporary agreement on stabilization was just about all that the United States had come to London to offer—debts and tariffs having previously been excluded from negotiation—and when the president in admittedly sharp language [33] dismissed even the prospect of temporary stabilization, he destroyed the conference's last small reason for existence. Already the nations of Europe, especially Britain and France, were touchy because of the debt

---

Howe's handwriting, and that Roosevelt then edited this draft. See Roosevelt Library, P.S.F., Box 32, *London Economic Conference* Folder. Nonetheless there are no traces of any "intrigue" by Howe in the Howe MSS at the Roosevelt Library.

32. In late July 1933 the prices of farm products broke sharply, the rise in wholesale prices tapered off, industrial production slackened, the dollar showed strength on the foreign exchanges.

33. Roosevelt cabled Hull on July 4, 1933, that "I purposely made language of my message a bit harsh." *FR: 1933, 1,* 681.

question, which had arisen briefly on June 15. To this dissatisfaction had been added the nationalistic tariff policy of the Americans. The United States representatives at London continued to act as though they had something to negotiate, perhaps a temporary currency stabilization. All the world had watched breathlessly as Raymond Moley flew to Nantucket and sailed in haste for London. When Roosevelt disavowed Moley and sent the conference his pronouncement of July 3, it was too much.

Upon return to the United States, Secretary and Mrs. Hull stopped off for a week end at Hyde Park and visited President and Mrs. Roosevelt. Apart from expressing surprise at Moley's activity during the conference, the president had no explanation of his lack of support of the American delegation. Secretary Hull, a courteous Southern gentleman, could not bring himself to demand an explanation. Perhaps the secretary should have resigned at this first in a long series of personal humiliations that he was to suffer from his famous chief.[34] Perhaps, on the other hand, there would have been no Reciprocal Trade Agreements Act of 1934 had the secretary offered his resignation in that initial summer of his secretaryship. It is always difficult to know what to do when one has achieved a long-sought position of responsibility and then sees his authority undermined; perhaps the sensible thing is to hope that the first time will be the only time. On the second occasion, perchance, the proper way of procedure would appear more clearly.

Secretary Hull's personal course after the World Economic Conference was altogether unclear. What was not unclear was that President Roosevelt had decided to give his attention to domestic problems—a decision that characterized his public

34. James M. Cox later wrote that after the presidential message of July 3, 1933, Hull was close to resigning, and would have done so "if Mrs. Hull and I had not induced the Secretary to spend a week end in the country in this trying time." *Journey Through My Years* (New York, Simon and Schuster, 1946), p. 370. Shortly after the delegates arrived, and apparently because Roosevelt delayed so long in passing upon Hull's opening speech to the conference, the secretary was on the verge of resigning. Roosevelt Library, P.S.F., Box 32, *London Economic Conference* Folder, Warren Delano Robbins to Roosevelt, June 15, 1933.

actions until, really, the summer of 1940. After the World Economic Conference there were no more large international assemblages outside the Western Hemisphere at which the United States sought seriously to assist in European and world problems.[35] In 1935 a second London Naval Conference met for a few short and ineffective sessions. It was an isolated, inconsequential meeting. In 1937 upon Japan's revival of war with China and invasion of China proper, signatories of the Nine-Power Treaty engaged in small talk at a Brussels Conference. Again nothing happened, for none of the participating governments, especially the United States, was willing to do anything substantial for world peace.[36] In reality, with the Economic Conference of the summer of 1933 the American contribution to world peace came to an end, not to be resumed with any effectiveness until time had run out, the second World War had begun, France had met defeat, Britain was going down, and President Roosevelt in the summer of 1940 proposed the sale of fifty over-age destroyers in return for American bases on British possessions in the New World. This action, little more than a gesture, he coupled with a move of substance in the spring of 1941: the Lend-Lease Act. By that time defeat in Europe seemed certain unless America entered the second World War.

35. Peace in the New World was strengthened by such meetings as the Inter-American Conferences at Montevideo in 1933 and Buenos Aires in 1936.

36. For this saddening conference see Hooker, ed., *The Moffat Papers,* pp. 154–88.

Chapter Sixteen: CONCLUSION

What can one say, in conclusion, about American diplomacy during the Hoover-Stimson years? Are there any "lessons" from the record of those years?

Diplomacy in the Great Depression, as we have seen, succeeded or failed in its grand purpose, the preservation of peace, because of the combination in each diplomatic instance of four factors. In each problem of international relations from 1929 to 1933 there was, first, the ever-present Depression itself, which from the autumn of 1930 onward became the first factor in the calculations of statesmen everywhere in the world. Secondly, there was the peculiar heritage of diplomatic assumptions and policies with which American diplomatists confronted international problems. There were also the personal qualities of American statesmen. And last, there was the nature of diplomatic problems: some problems responded quickly to statesmanlike measures; others were so complicated or obscure that perhaps no amount of human wisdom could have availed for their solution.

The Great Depression was the overriding event of the times. Never was an economic catastrophe so evident in the actions of American diplomacy. It palsied the hands of American statesmen and sent them searching for formulas and phrases in which to settle, so they hoped, the difficulty of the moment. The spirit of twenty-five years ago is difficult to recapture today, for Americans now are living in an era of unprecedented prosperity. The Golden Twenties that preceded the Great Depression were, economically speaking, days of privation compared to the Fabulous Fifties of our days. Memory of the Depression has grown very dim. It was not dim in the years 1929 to 1933. "Too deep for the average citizen to fathom, the floods of disaster had rolled in to erase ancient tide marks and tug at the moorings of inherited wisdom. This era brought a questioning into American life deeper than any other since the Civil War. Stereotypes of thought, traditional saws, the tribal wisdom of the elders, all were challenged in books, magazines and private talk. Perhaps, after all, the promise of American life would turn out merely to be propaganda, the tyranny of words or the folklore of capitalism." [1] In the darkest years of the Depression, the years that coincided in the United States with the second half of the Hoover Administration, it seemed to some intelligent men that Western civilization was breaking down, that it was falling with as great a shock as had the civilization of Rome in the 5th century A.D. If such fears of the Depression era were, as we now can see, unfounded, it still is true that the catastrophic turn of international relations after 1929 marked—as Spengler had so somberly predicted—a "historical change of phase." When world peace, like economic prosperity, disappeared in the Great Depression, there entered a new era of tumult, upheaval, revolution, and war, which in the 1950's shows no sign of departure. How, at the sudden beginning of such a time of trouble, could one fairly reproach American or European statesmen for uncertainty and timidity?

The Great Depression explains, if it does not justify, many of the acts of diplomatists in the difficult years after 1929; but when one comes to the second element of American diplomacy in those years, diplomatic assumptions and policies, there is more room for debate. Here the problem is not whether the American assumptions and policies of 1929 were adequate for the years that followed—they were, beyond doubt, inadequate. The question is, rather, why American diplomatists clung to their assumptions and policies after events had proved those tenets and procedures useless. There had been no postwar trial of American diplomacy, prior to 1929. In that year came the test of the Kellogg-Briand Pact in Manchuria, which was somewhat inconclusive; the Pact

1. Dixon Wecter, *The Age of the Great Depression* (New York, Macmillan, 1948), p. 34. See also Arthur M. Schlesinger, Jr., *The Age of Roosevelt: The Crisis of the Old Order*, Boston, 1957.

lived on, to be invoked on another occasion. But beginning in 1931 with the Far Eastern Crisis, American policies invoked from the paralysis of the Great Depression—the Kellogg Pact and the Nine-Power Treaty and that diplomatic embodiment of American good intentions, the Stimson Doctrine—proved completely ineffective. Even the assumptions on which they had been built collapsed. International equilibrium disappeared in Eastern Asia, despite the largest amount of advice-giving and plain speaking that the United States had ever administered to recalcitrant Asians. Likewise international equilibrium disappeared in Europe (although this was not so immediately apparent) when Hitler came to power in January 1933. Should there not have been realization, by responsible American officials, that American diplomacy required new assumptions and policies?

Only a few individuals during the Great Depression were willing to try a diplomacy based on force rather than moral suasion and legal admonition. In the midst of the Shanghai Incident, Winston Churchill, then in America for a lecture tour, visited Stimson at the State Department and offered some advice. Churchill approached the Shanghai matter from his usual standpoint. "There is not much idealism in him," Stimson commented. The secretary's visitor was "very anxious that our two countries should stand together, and thought that our two fleets, while either one of them would have trouble alone, would have no difficulty in having our way in the China question." [2] Such views were not Stimson's, or those of other responsible statesmen of the time. American diplomatists continued to hope for the future; they sought to preserve American rights in theory, rather than announce the destruction of those rights in fact and attempt—however unsuccessful such an attempt might have been—to set in motion a new policy.

Then there was the third factor in American diplomacy during the Great Depression: American diplomatists themselves—their personal abilities or lack thereof. Here one must at the outset make the rather threadbare observation (for it has been made so many times before, in regard to other eras of American diplo-

2. Stimson diary, Feb. 13, 1932.

macy) that American diplomacy during the Great Depression suffered from too much knowledge of law. Secretaries of state almost without exception have been lawyers; and while no one will deny that the law is an estimable occupation, legal learning does not always make for the suppleness of thought necessary for the best diplomacy, for willingness to accept approximations in lieu of complete statutory performance. There is the ever-present danger that a lawyer–secretary of state will rely too much on international law for the security of a position. On several occasions Secretary Stimson might have found his path easier if he had concerned himself less with the "juridical tidiness of international life."

As far as concerns the ability of other American diplomatists during the Hoover years, the record is fairly plain: ability was high, with several notable exceptions such as the absent-minded ambassador in Tokyo. One has only to make a list of a few of the leading diplomatic representatives of the United States during the Depression years to observe the general level of excellence. When was the United States in later years any better staffed? This, one may say again, is a surprising fact—the abilities of American diplomatists—in view of the attractions of the business world during the 1920's and the disinterest of the American people in foreign affairs.

Lastly, there is the problem of events themselves. Little is inevitable in diplomacy, but it is sometimes true that events become so difficult that human intelligence at the moment finds itself unable to look into them, and can observe only outside appearance. During his last two years of office, Stimson afterward recalled, he was "the servant of events, and not their master." [3] Nowhere, of course, was the triumph of events over intelligence so obvious as in the problem of understanding the Great Depression; the inadequacy of professional economic knowledge of the time was manifest in the economists' perplexity as to the Depression's cause and cure. And their lack of knowledge extended to foreign affairs. Diplomatists, accepting the advice of the professional men of learning, believed that the Japanese government would bankrupt itself because of the Far Eastern Crisis—that, as President-

3. *On Active Service,* p. 191.

elect Roosevelt told Stimson at Hyde Park, the military adventure in Manchuria would place such grave charges on the already over-burdened Japanese fiscal structure that there would follow a complete collapse. This was the unanimous opinion of the Lytton Commission. No one in the early 1930's understood how by expert "managing" of national debts and by other precarious measures all kinds of stimulants could be applied to national economies, with results that defied some of the basic tenets of orthodox economics. Japan did not "go broke" because of the Manchurian affair. Exports increased and industry began to expand. Similar measures later were taken, with great success, in supposedly bankrupt Germany.

In the triumph of events over intelligence in Washington during the early years of the Great Depression there was also, as we have seen, the failure of political, not merely economic, knowledge. Few individuals at the moment understood the implications of the Far Eastern Crisis or, in Europe, the significance of Hitler's power. For several years afterward diplomacy moved uncertainly around the edges of reality. Achievement of power by Hitler, like the seizure of power by the Japanese militarists, was an event with only one precedent in the world of the 20th century, the Bolshevik Revolution of 1917. The Russian Revolution had not yet turned outward in the early 1930's. No one knew, at the beginning of the Depression years, what could happen when the machinery of great modern governments passed under control of individuals with little or no appreciation of the values and traditions of Western civilization. American diplomatists, like their European counterparts, found themselves overwhelmed by the events of the Great Depression.

Bibliographical Essay

The enormous multiplication of 20th-century historical records, in both printed and written forms, makes it difficult to compile a bibliography on a historical topic of any scope. One must reckon with the problem of selection—including only the most important titles.

The following printed sources are more fragmentary than they would be if students of the 20th century had not ignored much of the history of diplomacy, both American and European, in the interwar period. There are wide gaps in the literature of general works, monographs, and biographies for the period 1919–39. One may hope that the rich historical source materials, printed and manuscript, now available for these years, will be more fully exploited in the years to come.

1. Bibliographical Aids

For the era 1929–33 in American diplomacy the best guides remain the volumes published by the Council on Foreign Relations under the title, *Foreign Affairs Bibliography*. More recent publication must be searched out in the quarterly and annual lists of such periodicals as the *American Historical Review*, the *Journal of Modern History*, *Foreign Affairs*, and the *Far Eastern Quarterly*. There are, one should add, excellent sections on foreign affairs in Oscar Handlin *et al.*, *Harvard Guide to American History*, Cambridge, Mass., 1954. In a sense bibliographical aids, because they deal with problems of historical study in the 20th century, are the articles by Max Beloff, "Historians in a Revolutionary Age," *Foreign Affairs*, *29* (1950–51), 248–62; and Raymond J. Sontag, "On the Study of Diplomatic History," *Pacific Historical Review*, *15* (1946), 207–13.

2. General Works

Excellent introductions to American foreign policy in the 20th century are Edward Mead Earle's "A Half-Century of American Foreign Policy: Our Stake in Europe, 1898–1948," *Political Science Quarterly, 64* (1949), 168–88; and Samuel Flagg Bemis, "The Shifting Strategy of American Defense and Diplomacy," in Dwight E. Lee and George E. McReynolds, eds., *Essays in History and International Relations in Honor of George Hubbard Blakeslee* (Worcester, Mass., 1949), pp. 1–14. Also helpful is George F. Kennan's interpretive *American Diplomacy: 1900–1950,* Chicago, 1951. For diplomacy after the first World War and through the 1920's there is no better guide than Allan Nevins' *The United States in a Chaotic World: A Chronicle of International Affairs, 1918–1933,* New Haven, 1950. Denna Frank Fleming has written a useful account, *The United States and World Organization: 1920–1933* (New York, 1938), which may be accompanied by Dwight E. Lee's *Ten Years: The World on the Way to War, 1930–1940,* Boston, 1942. Drew Pearson and Constantine Brown, *The American Diplomatic Game* (Garden City, N.Y., 1935) is a slangy journalistic account containing—in view of its date of publication—a surprising amount of "inside" information, unfortunately mingled with surmise and innuendo. Charles A. Beard's *American Foreign Policy in the Making, 1932–1940: A Study in Responsibilities* (New Haven, 1946) has an interesting section on the Stimson-FDR interview of January 1933. One should also consult Arthur M. Schlesinger, Jr.'s *The Crisis of the Old Order: 1919–1933,* Boston, 1957; while predominantly domestic history, there is considerable discussion of foreign affairs. Charles Callan Tansill in *Back Door to War: The Roosevelt Foreign Policy, 1933–1941* (Chicago, 1952) has some seventy pages concerning Henry L. Stimson's tenure at the State Department. The first study to make use of unpublished State Department material, *Back Door to War* is a haphazard piece of research dominated by a retrospective thesis. Tansill's conclusions find little support in the random materials he has chosen to illustrate Stimson's secretaryship of state.

The bulk of American diplomacy in the period 1929–33 concerned Far Eastern affairs, and the best guide to American diplomacy toward that part of the world in the 20th century is A. Whitney Griswold's *Far Eastern Policy of the United States,* New York, 1938; despite its inability to use the now-available records of the Department of State, this beautifully written and argued book remains a classic treatment of its subject. There are a number of general books on the Far East, concerning the internal affairs and external relations of that area of the world. Paul H. Clyde, *The Far East* (2d ed. New York, 1952) is the best general work in this field. H. B. Morse and Harley F. MacNair, *Far Eastern International Relations* (Boston, 1931) is an excellent treatment of its subject. A shorter book is G. F. Hudson's *The Far East in World Politics: A Study in Recent History,* Oxford, 1937. Leisurely, measured, a thoughtful volume, in few words it brings many complex events and ideas into clear focus. Useful for its special subject is F. C. Jones, *Manchuria since 1931,* London, 1949.

On the general subject of Japanese foreign relations in the 20th century there are many volumes, some of which are of merit. A well-written and well-organized survey of Japan's foreign relations from 1542 to 1936 is Roy H. Akagi, *Japan's Foreign Relations,* Tokyo, 1936. This volume presents the Japanese side on crucial and debatable matters, but otherwise is a fairly dispassionate account. Another survey is Seiji Hishida, *Japan among the Great Powers,* New York, 1940. A helpful book, rather oddly organized, at times intensely detailed, nonetheless informative and useful, is S. Tatsuji Takeuchi, *War and Diplomacy in the Japanese Empire,* Chicago, 1935. The best account of Japanese history of the past hundred years, a book that contains much information on diplomacy and foreign policy, is Chitoshi Yanaga's *Japan since Perry,* New York, 1949. This textbook is an extraordinary tour de force, embodying the latest Western and Japanese scholarship.

For the mainsprings of Japanese diplomacy during the Hoover-Stimson era, the best sources are Harry Emerson Wildes, *Japan in Crisis* (New York, 1934) and Arthur M. Young, *Imperial Japan: 1926–1938,* New York, 1938. Both these books give convincing reasons why Japan became an aggressive state during the 1930's. A more journalistic and sensational account appears in Hugh Byas' *Government by Assassination,* New York, 1942. Viscount Kikujiro Ishii, "The Permanent Bases of Japanese Foreign Policy," *Foreign Affairs, 11* (1932–33), 220–9, is a reasonable and plausible statement of Japan's aims and problems in foreign policy—if one does not see that it is completely one-sided. Viscount Ishii's lack of perspective was not uncommon in Japan. As for economic factors in Japan's expansive foreign policy during the 1930's and early 1940's, there is much information in G. C. Allen's *Japan: The Hungry Guest* (London, 1938), *Japanese Industry* (New York, 1940), and *A Short Economic History of Modern Japan,* London, 1946.

General works on China's foreign relations, like those on Japan, are extremely numerous. One can single out for American-Chinese relations Foster Rhea Dulles' survey, *China and America: The Story of Their Relations since 1784,* Princeton, 1946. Sir John Pratt has written a sharply analytical account in *War and Politics in China* (London, 1943), which can be read together with the same author's *Expansion of Europe into the Far East,* London, 1947. Formerly adviser to the British Foreign Office, Sir John often deals with 20th-century events in which he took a considerable part. His opinions, usually convincing, are never in doubt. One should also mention the masterly book by Harley F. MacNair, *China in Revolution: An Analysis of Politics and Militarism under the Republic* (Chicago, 1931), which not merely chronicles the twists and turns of Chinese politics from the revolution of 1911–12 to the springtime of 1931 but often interprets these domestic political convolutions in terms of Chinese foreign relations.

Books on the policies of the various European powers are too numerous to mention in detail. The first volume of Max Beloff's *Foreign Policy of Soviet Russia: 1929–1941* (2 vols. Oxford, 1947–49) is the best treatment of Russian policy during the Hoover-Stimson years. Louis Fischer's *The Soviets in World Affairs: 1917–1929* (2 vols. New York, 1930; reprinted, Princeton, 1951) is still best for its period. For Russian policy in the Far East, there are David J. Dallin's *Rise of Russia in Asia* (New Haven, 1949) and *Soviet Russia and the Far East,* New Haven, 1948. For British foreign policy, see William N. Medlicott, *British Foreign Policy since Versailles,* London, 1940; P. A. Reynolds, *British Foreign Policy in the Inter-War Years,* London, 1954; Charles L. Mowat, *Britain between the Wars,* Chicago, 1955. French policy appears plainly, for the first decade after the Paris Peace Conference, in Raymond Poincaré, "Since Versailles," *Foreign Affairs,* 7 (1928–29), 519–31. There is no acceptable treatment of German foreign policy in the interwar period. For the larger problem of German relations in Europe, one may consult Arnold Wolfers, *Britain and France between Two Wars: Conflicting Strategies of Peace since Versailles* (New York, 1940), and W. M. Jordan, *Great Britain, France, and the German Problem: 1918–1939,* London, 1943. The latter volume contains many keen insights, although—because it is written in a topical, "international relations" style—it is more a series of essays than a coherent work on its subject. Louis Aldo DeSanti, "U.S. Relations with Italy under Mussolini: 1922–1941," a doctoral thesis at Columbia, 1951, is a capable piece of research in the Department of State files in Washington, D.C. For the broad course of European international relations in the interwar years there is no better source than the superb little volume by Hajo Holborn, *The Political Collapse of Europe,* New York, 1951.

In concluding this section on general works it is impossible to avoid listing some titles concerned with the Great Depression in the United States. Here there is a tremendously large literature, of which Dixon Wecter's *Age of the Great Depression: 1929–1941* (New York, 1948) is outstanding. Jonathan N. Leonard, *Three Years Down* (New York, 1939) chronicles the depressing movement of wages, prices, and hopes after the market crash of 1929. John K. Galbraith's *The Great Crash* (Boston, 1955) is a witty and informed account. The classic description of the market disaster is Frederick Lewis Allen's *Only Yesterday* (New York, 1931), supplemented by the same author's *Lords of Creation,* New York, 1935; *Since Yesterday: The Nineteen-Thirties in America,* New York, 1939; and *The Big Change: 1900–1950,* New York, 1952.

3. Special Works

A. Monographs

The only published book on the Hoover-Stimson policies is William Starr Myers' *The Foreign Policies of Herbert Hoover: 1929–1933,* New York, 1940. Myers used the Hoover papers and enjoyed the full confidence of the former president, but his book is far from satisfactory. Laudatory, uncritical, it has also become badly outdated by the masses of historical materials on the Hoover-Stimson era now available. Two short accounts of American diplomacy from 1929 to 1933 are Henry L. Stimson, "Bases of American Foreign Policy during the Past Four Years," *Foreign Affairs, 11* (1932–33), 383–96; and especially William R. Castle, "Recent American Policy in the Far East," *Annals of the American Academy, 168* (1933), 46–53. Stimson later set down a detailed narrative in his memoirs, written with McGeorge Bundy, *On Active Service in Peace and War,* New York, 1948. In preparing this present book I was privileged to use a manuscript on American foreign relations written by Undersecretary of State William R. Castle that deals, in part, with the years 1929–33; this thoughtful work presents the course of American diplomacy far more frankly than did Stimson either in his article or in his memoirs.

For yearly descriptions and analyses of international relations, see the series published by the Council on Foreign Relations—the *Survey of American Foreign Relations,* prepared for 1929, 1930, and 1931 by Charles P. Howland; and *The United States in World Affairs,* prepared for 1931, 1932, and 1933 by Walter Lippmann and the research staff of the Council. There is also, of course, the Royal Institute's annual *Survey of International Affairs,* edited by Arnold J. Toynbee.

Aspects of the Hoover-Stimson policies appear in various volumes. Invocations of the Kellogg Pact, through consultation and other methods, are set forth in Russell M. Cooper, *American Consultation in World Affairs,* New York, 1934; James C. Charlesworth, "Implementation of the Pact of Paris," a doctoral thesis at the University of Pittsburgh, 1933; and Manley O. Hudson, *By Pacific Means: The Implementation of Article Two of the*

Pact of Paris, New Haven, 1935. Robert Langer, *Seizure of Territory: The Stimson Doctrine and Related Principles in Legal Theory and Diplomatic Practice* (Princeton, 1947) is a legal study.

On Latin American affairs the only special volume, apart from articles and books dealing in brief with events of 1929–33, is Alexander DeConde, *Herbert Hoover's Latin-American Policy* (Stanford, 1951), in which the author has set down in quite interesting form the elaboration of Hoover's good neighbor policy.

On the Chinese Eastern Railway affair of 1929, one should consult Tao-hsing Chang, *International Controversies over the Chinese Eastern Railway* (Shanghai, 1936), and, especially, Herbert Spielman, "Henry L. Stimson and American Policy toward the Chinese Eastern Railway Dispute of 1929," a useful doctoral thesis at the University of Chicago, 1949; together with the article by K. K. Kawakami, "The Russo-Chinese Conflict in Manchuria," *Foreign Affairs, 8* (1929–30), 52–68. The Far Eastern adviser of the Department of State, Stanley K. Hornbeck, wrote an analysis, "American Policy and the Chinese-Russian Dispute," *Chinese Social and Political Science Review, 14* (1930), 41–60. There are pertinent chapters in Eugene Lyons, *Assignment in Utopia* (New York, 1937), and Aitchen K. Wu, *China and the Soviet Union,* New York, 1950. Probably the best treatment of all is in Pauline Tompkins, *American-Russian Relations in the Far East,* New York, 1949; this detailed study, well-written and provocatively argued, is based on material in the Department of State files.

As for the principal American international effort of 1930, the London Naval Conference, there are a number of general volumes on problems of naval disarmament. One of the ingredients of American naval policy and of the naval rivalry of the 1920's, appears in George T. Davis' excellent *A Navy Second to None,* New York, 1940. Helpful in tracing the various disarmament moves during the 1920's is the short and lucidly nontechnical book by Henry Wilson Harris, *Naval Disarmament,* London, 1930. Less helpful are Rolland A. Chaput, *Disarmament in British Foreign Policy* (London, 1935), and Giovanni Engely, *The Politics of Naval Disarmament,* London, 1932. Each of these latter books falls short in its special way—Chaput seeks to be "scientific" and becomes dull and superficial; Engely has to argue the flimsy logic of Mussolini's naval policy, and often indulges in quotations from the Duce's speeches. It is indeed strange that so important a subject as naval disarmament, which often stood at the front of European and American politics during the interwar period, has received scholarly treatment only in the United States. Benjamin H. Williams, *The United States and Disarmament* (New York, 1931) was a pioneer treatment. The leading American student of disarmament is Merze Tate, whose *The United States and Armaments* (Cambridge, Mass., 1948) is the first broad, scholarly study, emphasizing the naval conferences from 1921–22 to 1935–36. An important facet of naval disarmament is dealt with by George V. Fagan, "Anglo-American Naval Relations, 1927–37," a doctoral thesis at the University of Pennsylvania, 1954.

For preliminaries of the London Naval Conference of 1930, see Raymond Leslie Buell, "Anglo-American Naval Understanding," *Foreign Policy Reports, 5* (1929–30), 175–92; John W. Davis, "Anglo-American Relations and Sea Power," *Foreign Affairs, 7* (1928–29), 345–55; and James L. Godfrey, "Anglo-American Naval Considerations preliminary to the London Naval Conference of 1930," *South Atlantic Quarterly, 49* (1950), 303–16. The latter article is a pedestrian survey based on the American and British documentary collections published after the second World War; the former two articles are typical of many that appeared in contemporary magazines and journals. For the London Conference, rather than its pourparlers, the two best analyses remain the contemporary articles in *Foreign Affairs, 8* (1929–30), 499–532, by André Géraud ("Pertinax") and Walter Lippmann. Both represent journalistic reporting at its best. Pertinax and Lippmann had a knack of reducing diplomatic complexities to their essential parts and then presenting them, often, in a brilliant manner. Secretary Stimson and Prime Minister J. Ramsay MacDonald have their own joint article, "The London Naval Conference, 1930," in *Encyclopaedia Britannica, 14,* 373–4. A factual survey of the conference's activities, it is complemented by William T. Stone's "The London Naval Conference," *Foreign Policy Reports, 6*

(1930–31), 101–30. With publication of the British and American documents after the second World War, Conyers Read undertook two surveys, "Recent United States and British Government Publication on the London Naval Conference of 1930," *American Historical Review, 54* (1948–49), 307–14; and "More Light on the London Naval Treaty of 1930," *American Philosophical Society Proceedings, 93* (1949), 490–508.

For the Hoover Moratorium there is much scattered contemporary publication but no scholarly monograph. A helpful nontechnical approach to the reparations-debts imbroglio is C. R. S. Harris, *Germany's Foreign Indebtedness,* Oxford, 1935. On the difficulties in the summer of 1931 and thereafter, see Mildred S. Wertheimer, "The Financial Crisis in Germany," *Foreign Policy Reports, 7* (1931–32), 455–75. Of special interest because they represented President Hoover's own views were four articles by Mark Sullivan for the *Saturday Evening Post, 205,* running from March through May 1933. Such particular accounts must be supplemented by the memoirs of Stimson and of Hoover, wherein there are fairly detailed analyses, and by the extremely valuable "inside" account in Undersecretary Castle's diary.

The Far Eastern Crisis has been dealt with in several detailed volumes, of which the first was Westel W. Willoughby, *The Sino-Japanese Controversy and the League of Nations* (Baltimore, 1935), an exhaustive account in which "the reader may have assurance that he will find . . . every significant statement that was made, or argument that was advanced, during the progress of the controversy before the League." There followed Stimson's own *The Far Eastern Crisis: Recollections and Observations,* New York, 1936. Although something of an apologia, it is a first-rate piece of work, well-written and cogently argued. That Stimson in this book stepped lightly appears from the more frank narrative of the Far Eastern Crisis in *On Active Service;* as he explained in the latter volume, "what required circumspection then can be discussed more freely now." Studies based on State Department documents published in the 1940's in the series *Foreign Relations of the United States* are Samuel Hsuan Wang, "The Sino-Japanese War and the American Far Eastern Policy, 1931–1941," a doctoral thesis at Cornell, 1947; I-kua Chou, "The American Policy in China: From 1929 to 1939," a thesis at the Fletcher School of Law and Diplomacy, 1949; Richard Grigg, "Japanese-American Relations, 1931–1937," a thesis at Georgetown University, 1950; and Keith S. Petersen, "The United States, Great Britain, and the Far Eastern Crisis of 1931–1933," a thesis at the University of Chicago, 1949. James W. Christopher has published *Conflict in the Far East: American Diplomacy in China from 1928–1933* (Leiden, 1950), written from the American published documents. There remains the careful monograph by Sara R. Smith, *The Manchurian Crisis 1931–1932: A Tragedy in International Relations,* New York, 1948. Miss Smith wrote without benefit of the American documents but used to advantage many other materials, including published documents of the League of Nations.

Background for the Manchurian Incident of 1931 appears in various publications dealing with the politico-economic structure of Sino-Japanese rivalries and of Western interests in China. C. Walter Young, *Japan's Special Position in Manchuria* (Baltimore, 1931), *The International Legal Status of the Kwang-Tung Leased Area* (Baltimore, 1931), *Japanese Jurisdiction in the South Manchuria Railway* (Baltimore, 1931) are definitive. George H. Blakeslee, "The Foreign Stake in China," *Foreign Affairs, 10* (1931–32), 81–91, is a fine summary, which may be supplemented by Charles F. Remer, *Foreign Investments in China,* New York, 1933. Also interesting are John R. Stewart, "Is Manchuria Vital to Japan?" *Bulletin of the Geographical Society of Philadelphia, 30* (1932), 88–108, which points out that Manchuria was not especially important to the Japanese economy; H. F. Bain, *Ores and Industry in the Far East* (New York, 1933), a careful work based on several years of research in China; and C. Walter Young, "Economic Factors in Manchuria Diplomacy," *Annals of the American Academy of Political and Social Science, 125* (1930), 293–307, a first-rate survey of Manchurian economics. Complicating factors of high importance in Sino-Japanese relations are dealt with in C. F. Remer and William B. Palmer, *A Study of Chinese Boycotts with Special Reference to Their Economic Effectiveness,* Baltimore, 1933; Harry L. Kingman, *Effects of Chinese National-*

ism upon Manchurian Railway Developments, 1925–1931 (Berkeley, 1932), a most useful monograph based on extensive research in contemporary materials, by a person who spent ten years in the Orient; and a more general treatment of the same subject by T. A. Bisson, "Railway Rivalries in Manchuria between China and Japan," *Foreign Policy Reports, 8* (1932–33), 29–42.

On the Mukden Incident of 1931 there is the well-done article by Ben Dorfman in *Harper's, 169* (1934), 449–62, which because of availability of quantities of new material from the Tokyo war crimes trial has been largely superseded by my own article, "The Mukden Incident: September 18–19, 1931," *Journal of Modern History, 27* (1955), 66–72. See also the useful work by Irving I. Kramer, "A Study of the Reasons Advanced by Japan to Justify the Manchurian Incident of 1931," a thesis at Columbia in 1950. These interpretations of Japanese motives in Manchuria find amplification in such studies as Paul S. Dull's brilliant "The Assassination of Chang Tso-lin," *Far Eastern Quarterly, 11* (1952), 453–63; Royal Wald's "The Young Officers Movement in Japan, ca. 1925–1937: Ideology and Actions," University of California doctoral thesis, 1949; and Delmer M. Brown's *Nationalism in Japan*, Berkeley, 1955. There is considerable literature in English on nationalism in Japan, of which the following are representative: Kenneth W. Colegrove, *Militarism in Japan*, Boston, 1936; E. E. N. Causton, *Militarism and Foreign Policy in Japan*, London, 1936; Hillis Lory, *Japan's Military Masters: The Army in Japanese Life*, New York, 1943; John M. Maki, *Japanese Militarism*, New York, 1945; Hilary Conroy, "Government Versus 'Patriot': The Background of Japan's Asiatic Expansion," *Pacific Historical Review, 20* (1951), 31–42; and Robert A. Scalapino, *Democracy and the Party Movement in Prewar Japan: The Failure of the First Attempt*, Berkeley, 1953.

American diplomacy toward the Mukden Incident appears in Paul H. Clyde, "The Diplomacy of 'Playing No Favorites': Secretary Stimson and Manchuria, 1931," *Mississippi Valley Historical Review, 35* (1948), 187–202. In this article Clyde aptly characterizes Stimson's policy of inaction during the first weeks of the crisis. Another somewhat similar study is Benjamin B. Wallace,

"How the United States 'Led the League' in 1931," *American Political Science Review, 39* (1945), 101–16. For the Stimson Doctrine there is Moong-bau Chang, "The Stimson Doctrine of Non-Recognition," a well-written thesis at Columbia, 1949. Another unpublished study on nonrecognition, of a more general nature, is Ross N. Berkes, "The Use of the Power of Recognition as an Instrument of Diplomacy," a doctoral thesis at the University of Southern California, 1942. Ernest R. Perkins, "The Nonapplication of Sanctions against Japan, 1931–32," in D. E. Lee and G. E. McReynolds, eds., *Essays in History and International Relations,* pp. 215–32, concludes that at no time was the United States willing to use economic or military sanctions against Japan. Richard N. Current's "The Stimson Doctrine and the Hoover Doctrine," *American Historical Review, 59* (1953–54), 513–42, contends that there were two doctrines of nonrecognition and that the doctrine of Hoover, which prevailed in 1932–33, did not presume sanctions of any sort other than moral.

The Shanghai Incident has an interesting though controversial review by Payson J. Treat, "Shanghai: January 28, 1932," *Pacific Historical Review, 9* (1940), 337–43. Treat believes that its beginning on the night of January 28, 1932, was an accident, not a willful act of the Japanese naval commander in Shanghai. Thomas T. Hamilton, "The Impact of the Shanghai Incident of 1932 upon the United States and the League of Nations," a doctoral thesis at Duke, 1953, covers the Shanghai affair from the perspective of the published American diplomatic documents, with some use of the Washington archives.

There were a large number of contemporary articles and essays on the Lytton Report of 1932, representative of which are Arthur E. Kuhn, "The Lytton Report on the Manchurian Crisis," *American Journal of International Law, 27* (1933), 96–100; and George H. Blakeslee and Nathaniel Peffer, *The Lytton Report,* Foreign Policy Association Pamphlets, 86, December 1932. A sprightly discussion of some of the problems and their solutions during the drafting of the Lytton Report appears in C. Walter Young, "Legal Aspects of the Lytton Report," in John M. Mathews and James Hart, eds., *Essays in Political Science in Honor of Westel Wood-*

bury Willoughby (Baltimore, 1937), pp. 306–38. The German member of the Lytton Commission, Heinrich Schnee, recorded his experiences in *Völker und Mächte im Fernen Osten,* Berlin, 1933.

Fluctuations of public opinion during the Sino-Japanese crisis have been set down by Eleanor Tupper and George E. McReynolds, *Japan in American Public Opinion* (New York, 1937), a general work dealing in part with the Far Eastern Crisis; Reginald Bassett, *Democracy and Foreign Policy, A Case History: The Sino-Japanese Dispute, 1931–33* (London, 1952), a brilliant political science study showing that there was no support for sanctions in Britain during the troubles in the Orient; and T. J. Betts, "Chinese Public Opinion," *Foreign Affairs, 11* (1932–33), 470–7, stressing the traditionalism and passivity of Chinese opinion.

For the World Disarmament Conference of 1932–34 there is no monograph, and one must search through such volumes as Alfred Zimmern, *The League of Nations and the Rule of Law,* London, 1936; Charles K. Webster, *The League of Nations in Theory and Practice,* London, 1933; F. P. Walters, *A History of the League of Nations,* 2 vols. London, 1952; John W. Wheeler-Bennett, *Disarmament and Security since Locarno: 1925–1931,* London, 1932; J. W. Wheeler-Bennett, *The Pipe Dream of Peace: The Story of the Collapse of Disarmament,* New York, 1935; A. C. Temperley, *The Whispering Gallery of Europe* (London, 1939), by a British representative at the conference; Norman Hillson, *Geneva Scene* (London, 1936), a colorful account of the conference and successive events; and John T. Whitaker, *And Fear Came* (New York, 1936), a journalist's interesting record of Geneva and the breakdown of peace.

For the World Economic Conference the only published study is Jeannette P. Nichols, "Roosevelt's Monetary Diplomacy in 1933," *American Historical Review, 56* (1950–51), 295–317. Unpublished accounts are John O. Gallagher, "American Economic Foreign Policy and the Failure of the 1933 World Economic Conference," a doctoral thesis at the Fletcher School, 1953; and especially the careful thesis by William Kamman, "The United States and the London Economic Conference of 1933," Indiana University, 1956. There is some information on the Economic Conference in James P. Warburg's *The Money Muddle,* New York, 1934.

B. Biographies and Autobiographies

Of first importance for any study of the Hoover-Stimson era in American diplomacy is the three-volume autobiography of former President Hoover: *Years of Adventure: 1874–1920,* New York, 1951; *The Cabinet and the Presidency: 1920–1933,* New York, 1951; and *The Great Depression: 1929–1941,* New York, 1952. This memoir was written at various times, and sets forth in considerable detail Hoover's background and actions in private and public life. Demonstrating in full measure the extraordinary abilities of its author, it is a memoir that could have been written by no other American president except John Quincy Adams. Hoover's *American Individualism* (New York, 1922) is a kind of economic autobiography. A useful biography is Eugene Lyons, *Our Unknown Ex-President* (Garden City, N.Y., 1948), a eulogistic book that can in some respects be profitably compared with Thomas L. Stokes' unfriendly account of Hoover in *Chip off My Shoulder,* Princeton, 1940. Helpful for White House detail are Theodore G. Joslin, *Hoover Off the Record* (Garden City, N.Y., 1934), by Hoover's press secretary; and Irwin Hood ("Ike") Hoover, *Forty-Two Years in the White House* (Boston and New York, 1934), by the veteran head usher. See also Ray Lyman Wilbur and Arthur Mastick Hyde, *The Hoover Policies,* New York, 1937; William Starr Myers, ed., *The State Papers and Other Public Writings of Herbert Hoover,* 2 vols. Garden City, N.Y., 1934; William Starr Myers and Walter H. Newton, *The Hoover Administration,* New York, 1936.

Secretary of State Stimson together with McGeorge Bundy produced *On Active Service in Peace and War,* an extremely well-written and thoughtful book, of course friendly to its senior author, accurate and convincing in most of its generalization and detail. Stimson's views appear elsewhere in his *American Policy in Nicaragua* (New York, 1927); *Democracy and Nationalism in Europe* (Princeton, 1934), a set of lectures on European problems; and *My Vacations* (privately printed, 1949), a delightful little book about the author's many vacations, from his younger days in the West to experiences in the Philippines, including an account of life as a country squire at the Long Island estate of Highhold. A capable unpublished sketch of Stimson is John Anthony Brown, Jr., "The Public Life of Henry L. Stimson," a thesis at the University of Chicago, 1945. The only biography of Stimson presently in print is Richard N. Current, *Secretary Stimson: A Study in Statecraft,* New Brunswick, N.J., 1954. An unfriendly study, it brings together many of the unpleasant aspects of Stimson's personality.

American ambassadors in the years 1929–33 later produced several memoirs or became subjects of biographies. The most colorful ambassador of the time, Charles G. Dawes, published his *Journal as Ambassador to Great Britain,* New York, 1939. The volume, unfortunately, is a curious production from the point of view of editing, for Dawes expurgated some of his more lively phrases and also other personal material. There seems to have been some literary editing. Students should consult the manuscript diary, presently in the Northwestern University Library. There are two formal biographies of Dawes, both of them collections of anecdote, quotation, conversation, reminiscence, and surmise: Paul R. Leach, *That Man Dawes: The Story of a Man Who Has Placed His Name High among the Great of the World in This Generation because He Ruled His Life by Common Sense,* Chicago, 1930; and Bascom N. Timmons, *Portrait of an American: Charles G. Dawes,* New York, 1953. A scholarly study, using the Dawes papers and diaries at Northwestern, is John E. Pixton, Jr., "The Early Career of Charles G. Dawes," a doctoral thesis at the University of Chicago, 1952. Pixton has finished a full-dress biography which will be of much value to the world of scholarship.

Other accounts of American representatives abroad are Hugh R. Wilson, *Diplomat between Wars,* New York, 1941; during the Hoover-Stimson years Wilson did not hold leading diplomatic appointments abroad, but he is so charming a writer and so acute an observer that his memoirs are always interesting. Of similar value is Nancy Harvison Hooker, ed., *The Moffat Papers: Selections from the Diplomatic Journals of Jay Pierrepont Moffat,*

Cambridge, Mass., 1956; Moffat assisted at the State Department in preparation for the World Disarmament Conference. Harold Nicolson's *Dwight Morrow* (New York, 1935) is an able work. George Rublee, one of Morrow's staff assistants at the London Naval Conference, undertook a reminiscence twenty years later for the Columbia University oral history project; the results were not too happy, for Rublee's memory was shaky; the twelve dictated pages on the London Conference are of little or no value to the historical student. Walter E. Edge, *A Jerseyman's Journal: Fifty Years of American Business and Politics* (Princeton, 1948) records the memories of Hoover's ambassador to France. Joseph C. Grew has set down his diary entries in *Ten Years in Japan* (New York, 1944), and later published other writings and recollections in Walter Johnson, ed., *Turbulent Era: A Diplomatic Record of Forty Years, 1904–1945,* 2 vols. Boston, 1952. Of value for its point of view on the World Disarmament Conference is Jeannette Marks, *Life and Letters of Mary Emma Woolley,* Washington, 1955. For the World Economic Conference one should consult James M. Cox, *Journey Through My Years,* New York, 1946; Charles Michelson, *The Ghost Talks,* New York, 1944; Raymond Moley, *After Seven Years,* New York, 1939; and *The Memoirs of Cordell Hull,* 2 vols. New York, 1948.

There are biographies and autobiographies of some European and Asiatic statesmen of the time. Sir John Simon's *Retrospect* (London, 1952) contains little on his relations with Stimson as foreign secretary. Carl E. B. Roberts, *Sir John Simon* (London, 1938) fails to fill in where Simon in *Retrospect* passed over lightly. Robert Cecil's *A Great Experiment* (London, 1941) is a kindly autobiography, containing much wisdom. Benjamin Sacks, *J. Ramsay MacDonald in Thought and Action: An Architect for a Better World* (Albuquerque, New Mexico, 1952) used the MacDonald papers, which unfortunately seem not to have amounted to much; the biography contains little novel information on MacDonald's relations with Hoover and Stimson. Sir Esme Howard's *Theatre of Life* (2 vols. Boston, 1935–36) is a most attractive memoir, by the British ambassador in Washington during the early part of the Hoover-Stimson era. The British ambassador in

Tokyo, Sir John Tilley, published his reminiscence, *London to Tokyo,* London, 1942. He was ambassador in Tokyo from 1926 to 1930.

The German ambassador in Washington, Friedrich W. von Prittwitz und Gaffron published his diplomatic memoir, *Zwischen Petersburg und Washington: Ein Diplomatenleben* (Munich, 1952) after years of eclipse during the Nazi era. It contains nothing new about the Hoover-Stimson period. Georges Suarez, *L'Artisan de la paix* (Paris, 1952), Vol. 6 of *Briand: Sa Vie, son oeuvre avec son journal et de nombreux documents inédits* (6 vols. Paris, 1938–52), has little on the London Naval Conference or the Far Eastern Crisis, perhaps indicating that these matters did not bulk large to Frenchmen.

For Far Eastern history there is Hollington K. Tong, *Chiang Kai-shek: Soldier and Statesman* (2 vols. London, 1938), written by the well-known newspaperman and diplomat. One has the distinct feeling about this inordinately fulsome biography that its author knew he was abridging history. The work is far too skillful to have been written by an undiscerning person. Hallett Abend, *My Life in China: 1926–1941* (New York, 1943), is by the New York *Times* correspondent. Well-written, frank, provocative, it seems a model piece of journalism. Two interesting books about "old China hands" are the reminiscences of John B. Powell, *My Twenty-Five Years in China,* New York, 1945; and Earl Albert Selle's *Donald of China,* New York, 1948. Both volumes contain occasional errors of detail, but in the main they are convincing.

4. Newspapers and Periodicals

The New York *Times* is indispensable for students of 20th-century history, both because of that newspaper's coverage and because of its admirable index. No other paper in the United States, and perhaps in the world, prints so much news each day. With its index the *Times* is ideal for the historian's research. One must, of course, beware of certain biases in the *Times*' coverage —emphasis on New York local news and New England news, and perhaps an undue interest in foreign affairs. Even so, there is no substitute source for the news printed in its columns.

Of less value is the London *Times,* which although indexed has far fewer column-inches of news.

For this present study I did not undertake the large task of searching through files of Continental newspapers. On important occasions the London *Times* or the New York *Times* or the State Department made systematic surveys of foreign press opinion.

Useful periodicals are the *American Journal of International Law,* the *British Year Book of International Law, Foreign Affairs,* and its British counterpart, *International Affairs.*

5. Printed Sources

Two collections of documents relative to general diplomatic history of the era 1929–33 are the documentary annexes to the Royal Institute's annual *Survey of International Affairs* and the Carnegie Endowment's monthly *International Conciliation.*

The printed diplomatic documents of the Department of State, *Foreign Relations of the United States,* are voluminous for the period 1929–33, with three volumes (Washington, 1943–44) for the year 1929, three (Washington, 1945) for 1930, three (Washington, 1946) for 1931, five (Washington, 1947–48) for 1932, five (Washington, 1949–52) for 1933. A special two-volume supplement of *Foreign Relations* for Japan 1931–41 appeared in 1943; documents printed in the supplement do not appear in the regular series.

The second series of *Documents on British Foreign Policy: 1919–1939* (London, 1946–), edited by Sir Llewellyn Woodward and Rohan Butler, is in process of publication. I have not used the second-series volume on the Far Eastern Crisis, which Sir Llewellyn informs me is now (1957) in press.

There has been no regular documentary publication for the period 1929–33 by governments other than the United States and Great Britain. *Documents on German Foreign Policy: 1918–1945* (Washington, 1949–), published by the Department of State, is apparently going to be limited to the projected Series D (1937–45).

For the London Naval Conference there was some contemporary publication that supplements *Foreign Relations* and the *British*

Documents—London Naval Conference: Speeches and Press Statements by Members of the American Delegation, Washington, 1930; and *Proceedings of the London Naval Conference of 1930,* Washington, 1931.

The League of Nations issued a series of reports, inquiries, and appeals pertaining to the Far Eastern Crisis. There was, first of all, the Lytton Report, *Appeal by the Chinese Government: Report of the Commission of Enquiry,* Geneva, 1932. The Report was accompanied by a number of special studies, printed separately under title of *Supplementary Documents to the Report of the Commission of Enquiry,* Geneva, 1932. There followed *Observations of the Japanese Government on the Report of the Commission of Enquiry* (Geneva, 1932), a smoothly written and well-argued statement; and *Communication from the Chinese Delegation* (Geneva, 1932), a railing and intemperate reply. Because the Lytton Commission did not investigate at Shanghai, there is a separate literature: *Reports of the Committee of Enquiry Set Up at Shanghai under Article 15, Paragraph 1, of the Covenant* (Geneva, 1932), factual reports on the political and military situation; *Appeal from the Chinese Government in Virtue of Article 15 of the Covenant: Report by the Secretary-General on the Action Taken by the League on the Sino-Japanese Dispute* (Geneva, 1932), a recital of League resolutions and appeals from September 1931 to February 1932; and *Explanatory Note Communicated by the Japanese Government* (Geneva, 1932), the Japanese case at Shanghai.

An unusual sort of documentary publication, because it is mimeographed, is the large corpus of material that appeared during the Tokyo war crimes trial. This material is mostly in the form of proceedings and exhibits, covering Japanese history from 1928 to 1945. Almost all of it has been released to a number of the larger libraries in the United States. The Tokyo records divide into several groups: (1), the transcript of proceedings, which totals 48,288 pages; (2), the exhibits, some 30,000 pages; (3), certain documents not used in the trial; (4), pretrial interrogations; (5), Japanese records gathered by the prosecutor of the trial; (6), certain diaries and memoirs. Judgment of the International Military Tribunal, delivered in 1948, required eight mimeograph volumes—three for majority judgment and five for special opinions and dissent. The best way to approach this mass of material is through several available guides: James T. C. Liu, "The Tokyo Trial: Source Materials," *Far Eastern Survey, 17* (July 28, 1948), 168–70; Solis Horwitz, "The Tokyo Trial," *International Conciliation, 465* (November 1950), 473–584; Delmer M. Brown, "Recent Japanese Political and Historical Materials," *American Political Science Review, 43* (1949), 1010–17; A. S. Comyns-Carr, "The Tokyo War Crimes Trial," *Far Eastern Survey, 18* (May 18, 1949), 109–14; A. S. Comyns-Carr, "The Judgment of the International Military Tribunal for the Far East," *Transactions of the Grotius Society, 34* (1948), 141–51. Paul S. Dull of the University of Oregon has published *The Tokyo Trials: A Functional Index to the Proceedings of the International Military Tribunal for the Far East,* Center for Japanese Studies Occasional Papers, 6, Ann Arbor, Michigan, 1957.

6. Manuscript Sources

A. Archives

All archival material of the Department of State dating beyond the year 1939 is deposited in the Department archives, in a special building in Washington. Material through 1939 is in the National Archives building. The "open period" for researchers presently (1957) includes archival material prior to January 1, 1930; the "limited-access" period is from January 1, 1930 to January 1, 1942; thereafter the archives are closed. Research in the limited-access period involves, one should add, a most liberal policy by the Department in the review of notes. In my own case I saw anything that I wished, took notes on anything that seemed of importance, and had only a few minor details—pertaining to personalities still living—blue-penciled.

There are available in Washington two large groups of materials from the Japanese archives. One is the "World War II collection of seized enemy records: Japan," and may be approached through the article by James W. Morley, "Check List of Seized Japanese Records in the National Archives," *Far Eastern Quar-*

terly, *9* (1950), 306–33. These volumes are in physical existence at the Federal Records Center, Region 3, Alexandria, Virginia; they were formerly housed in the National Archives, where they occupied some 3,450 cubic feet of space. They are in excellent condition, and access to them is unrestricted. Unfortunately their return to Japan is imminent. A little less than half of the records appear to be those of the Japanese Navy Ministry, and the remainder those of the War Ministry. There is a "startling paucity" (according to Morley) of materials relating to the Manchurian Incident, the China Incident, and the Great East Asia War. Probably some records were destroyed in the fire-bomb raids on Tokyo. Some may have been purposely destroyed. Moreover, when during the recent war the business of record-keeping in Tokyo got completely out of hand, many records were lost through failure to record them properly, storage in the wrong building, etc.

A second large collection of Japanese archival material is held by the Library of Congress. This consists of microfilms made in Japan in 1949–51. The library has 2,116 reels of negative microfilm, over two million pages, of selected foreign office documents, covering the period 1868–1945. As funds have permitted, positive film reproductions of these documents have been made. At present (1957) approximately 1,320 reels of positive film have been printed, and are available for use in the library or for interlibrary loan. The remainder of the film, in the original negative, is available only if researchers are willing to purchase positive prints from the library's photoduplication service. The Division of Orientalia under direction of Edwin G. Beal and Cecil H. Uyehara has compiled a *Checklist of Archives in the Japanese Ministry of Foreign Affairs*, Washington, 1954.

In connection with these holdings of Japanese foreign office material by the United States, one should mention how difficult it really is for a defeated nation to destroy all traces of its international double-dealing. The Japanese had many foreign adventures and maneuvers in domestic politics of which they justly could have been ashamed. At the end of the second World War there was a considerable effort to destroy compromising material, and it was being burned at the very time that General MacArthur's occupying troops were entering Tokyo. Yet two factors prevented the destruction of all evidence: (1), there was simply too much of it, scattered through the archives in the necessarily confused organization to which all archives, sooner or later, succumb; and (2), a certain Japanese minister who had access to most if not all Japanese foreign office material had a habit of taking copies of important documents and secreting them in his house, and this material was uncovered soon after the war by Allied investigators for the Tokyo war crimes trial.

German foreign office documents for 1920–33, captured by the Western Allies at the end of the second World War, are now (1957) being microfilmed. As copies are received, they are being deposited in the National Archives in Washington and made available to the public. The physical records meanwhile are being returned to West German control.

British, French, and other diplomatic documents for the interwar years are apparently beyond hope of examination by historical students. The British diplomatic archives are presently open through the year 1902. The archives of the Quai d'Orsay are closed beyond the year 1896.

B. Personal Papers: Manuscript Collections

Herbert Hoover MSS. Hoover Institution on War, Revolution, and Peace, Stanford University. The papers of President Hoover are a vast collection, some 5,000,000 items. They presently are being organized and are not yet open to historical students. Through the kindness of Mr. Hoover, and with the assistance of his able archivists in the Hoover Collection, I was able to check through the card file for the presidential years and to utilize information from the material on foreign relations.

Stimson MSS. Yale University Library. The material for Stimson's years as secretary of state has been indexed by the indefatigable John Beverley Riggs, and is in the best physical condition of any manuscript collection I have seen anywhere. The index is a marvel of clarity and helpfulness. See J. B. Riggs, "The Henry

L. Stimson Collection," *Yale University Library Gazette,* 27 (1952), 55–65.

Frank R. McCoy MSS. Library of Congress. A somewhat disappointing collection with few revealing letters for the period when McCoy was a member of the Lytton Commission.

Montgomery Meigs Taylor MSS. Library of Congress (Naval Historical Foundation Collection). As commander of the Asiatic Squadron, Taylor carried on an interesting correspondence with the chief of naval operations, Admiral William V. Pratt.

Franklin D. Roosevelt MSS. Franklin D. Roosevelt Library, Hyde Park. There appears to be no material here of importance on the Stimson-FDR meeting of January 1933. There is, however, interesting correspondence on the World Economic Conference.

Elihu Root MSS. Library of Congress. Root was Stimson's confidant and the most esteemed Republican elder statesman. Occasionally Stimson sought his advice.

Hilary P. Jones MSS. Library of Congress (Naval Historical Foundation Collection). A disappointing collection—only one boxful of papers, containing one folder. Nothing of interest on the London Naval Conference.

Charles G. Dawes MSS. Northwestern University Library. Valuable for Dawes' views, which often had importance in the making of American policy. Dawes' views are not infrequently expressed in strong midwestern phrases.

Edward Price Bell MSS. Newberry Library. A careful collection, excellently arranged, lacking in value because Bell was further from the seats of power than he imagined.

William E. Borah MSS. Library of Congress. A vast collection, of much importance for diplomatic history of the interwar years.

Nelson T. Johnson MSS. Library of Congress. Valuable collection, by the minister to China during the Hoover-Stimson years.

Joseph C. Grew MSS. Houghton Library at Harvard. A large collection with not much of immediate interest during the Hoover-Stimson period.

Nicholas Murray Butler MSS. Columbia University Library. A large collection with important information about public figures.

Frank B. Kellogg MSS. Minnesota State Historical Society. Coolidge's secretary of state.

Jane Addams MSS; Emily Green Balch MSS; William I. Hull MSS. Swarthmore College Peace Collection. These collections, together with the private records of numerous peace organizations in the United States and Europe during the interwar years, give much insight to pacifist and near-pacifist activity and its occasional influence in the conduct of diplomacy. The Swarthmore College Peace Collection is an unrivaled depository for records of private organizations for world peace.

Louis McHenry Howe MSS. Franklin D. Roosevelt Library, Hyde Park. Although Howe was with FDR when the latter sent the "bombshell" message to the World Economic Conference, and although the original draft of Roosevelt's cable is in Howe's handwriting, there is nothing about this crucial document in the Howe MSS.

Jay Pierrepont Moffat MSS. Houghton Library at Harvard. Moffat was an interesting correspondent.

Edmund E. Day MSS. Collection of Regional History at Cornell. Day was a member of the Commission of Experts for the World Economic Conference. There is a large but not too revealing folder of correspondence pertaining to his work on this commission.

Jacob Gould Schurman MSS. Collection of Regional History at Cornell. Schurman resigned as ambassador to Berlin in December 1929. His papers for his ambassadorship contain little except newspaper clippings and formal letters of congratulations and felicitation such as take so much of the time of any envoy.

Dwight W. Morrow MSS. Amherst College Memorabilia. At the London Conference of 1930, Morrow compiled a little notebook of naval statistics, with which he confounded his fellow diplomats and even the "experts" of the various delegations. The notebook is in the Morrow MSS. This is a well arranged collection, from which Sir Harold Nicolson appears to have skimmed the best material. I could not find in the papers the memoranda of conversations at London, copies of which are in the Stimson MSS. The originals are not in the State Department files.

Salmon O. Levinson MSS. University of Chicago Library. A huge collection by an indefatigable letter writer. No student of American diplomacy during the interwar years can afford to overlook the Levinson papers, for they contain many—albeit scattered—letters of interest. Levinson corresponded with everyone of importance who would write to him, and many who would not.

Norman H. Davis MSS. Library of Congress. The difficulty with the Davis MSS is that Davis almost always was on the periphery of decisions on foreign policy. The collection nonetheless contains many useful items.

Ogden Mills MSS. Library of Congress. Mills was undersecretary of the treasury from 1927 to 1932, and secretary from February 1932 to the end of the Hoover Administration. The color of his personality sometimes emerges from his correspondence, but he usually failed to set down his intimate thoughts in writing.

C. Personal Papers: Diaries

William R. Castle diary. Washington, D.C. This diary contains an extraordinarily interesting account of diplomacy in the Hoover-Stimson years. Beautifully written, acute in judgment, it is of the highest historical importance.

Journal of W. Cameron Forbes. Library of Congress. This diary is not yet available for citation or publication. It is a most interesting work.

Koichi Kido diary. Purchasable on microfilm from the Library of Congress. This diary, presently available in a rough English translation (of certain parts of the diary used at the Tokyo trial), begins in 1931 and runs to 1945. A high Japanese court official, Kido throughout his career picked up Tokyo gossip and set it down in his diary.

Saionji-Harada memoirs. Purchasable on microfilm from the Library of Congress. Prince Kimmochi Saionji was last of the eight Genro, the elder statesmen who acted as highest councilors and advisers to the throne. From 1924 until his death in 1940 at the age of 92, Saionji was the sole supreme adviser to the Emperors Taisho and Hirohito. He was consulted by the throne on all critical state affairs, particularly on the choice of succeeding premiers. Baron Kumao Harada, Saionji's private secretary, acted as liaison between the prince and important Japanese statesmen, politicians, and other individuals, meeting them to obtain information on current behind-the-scenes political activities. He reported his activities to the prince each week. Each week he also dictated notes of his findings, which he turned over to the prince for correction and addition. There are some 3,600 pages of this material, covering the years 1930–40.

Charles G. Dawes diary. Northwestern University Library. There are numerous discrepancies between this manuscript diary and the published version.

Joseph C. Grew diary. Houghton Library at Harvard. Detailed and most interesting diary, only a fraction of which was published in *Ten Years in Japan*.

Jay Pierrepont Moffat diary. Houghton Library at Harvard. A brilliantly written diary, setting down for this period its author's work in the Department on preparation for the Disarmament Conference. Only a small part of the diary was published in Hooker, ed., *The Moffat Papers*.

Henry L. Stimson diary. Yale University Library. Stimson kept a diary during various phases of his public and military career. As secretary of state he began his diary in 1930, dictating each day's events into a dictaphone on the following morning. Sometimes dictations ran to ten or twelve pages. Stimson had no intention that the diary should soon become available to students. On September 25, 1931, Walter Lippmann "dropped the remark that that book would carry all the history of that time, or rather that the history of that time would be written out of that book. I told him that I was not writing any Archie Butt book and that no historian would get the book until long after everybody was dead."

INDEX

AMERICAN HISTORY TITLES IN THE NORTON LIBRARY

Samuel Flagg Bemis *The Latin American Policy of the United States* N412

Ray Allen Billington, Ed. *The Reinterpretation of Early American History* N446

Fawn Brodie *Thaddeus Stevens* N331

Robert E. Brown *Charles Beard and the Constitution* N296

Edmund Cody Burnett *The Continental Congress* N278

George W. Cable *The Negro Question: A Selection of Writings on Civil Rights in the South* N420

Dudley T. Cornish *The Sable Arm: Negro Troops in the Union Army, 1861-1865* N334

John Paton Davies, Jr. *Foreign and Other Affairs* N330

Dwight Lowell Dumond *Antislavery* N370

Herbert Feis *Contest Over Japan* N466

Herbert Feis *The Diplomacy of the Dollar* N333

Herbert Feis *The Spanish Story* N339

Herbert Feis *Three International Episodes: Seen from E. A.* N351

Robert H. Ferrell *Peace in Their Time: The Origins of the Kellogg-Briand Pact* N491

Dewey W. Grantham *The Democratic South* N299

Fletcher Green *Constitutional Development in the South Atlantic States, 1776-1860* N348

Michael Garibaldi Hall *Edward Randolph and the American Colonies, 1676-1703* N480

Holman Hamilton *Prologue to Conflict: The Crisis and Compromise of 1850* N345

Pendleton Herring *The Politics of Democracy* N306

Preston J. Hubbard *Origins of the TVA: The Muscle Shoals Controversy, 1920-1932* N467

Rufus Jones *The Quakers in the American Colonies* N356

George F. Kennan *Realities of American Foreign Policy* N320

Howard Roberts Lamar *The Far Southwest, 1846-1912: A Territorial History* N522

William L. Langer *Our Vichy Gamble* N379

Douglas Edward Leach *Flintlock and Tomahawk: New England in King Philip's War* N340

James Madison *Notes of Debates in the Federal Convention of 1787 Reported by James Madison* N485

C. Peter Magrath *Yazoo: The Case of Fletcher v. Peck* N418

Alpheus T. Mason *The Supreme Court from Taft to Warren* N257

Burl Noggle *Teapot Dome* N297

Douglass C. North *The Economic Growth of the United States, 1790-1860* N346

Norman Pollack *The Populist Response to Industrial America* N295

Robert E. Quirk *An Affair of Honor: Woodrow Wilson and the Occupation of Veracruz* N390

Robert E. Quirk *The Mexican Revolution, 1914-1915* N507

Eric Robson *The American Revolution, In Its Political and Military Aspects: 1763-1783* N382

James W. Silver *Confederate Morale and Church Propaganda* N422

John W. Spanier *The Truman-MacArthur Controversy and the Korean War* N279

Ida M. Tarbell *History of the Standard Oil Company* (David Chalmers, Ed.) N496

Frederick B. Tolles *Meeting House and Counting House* N211

Arthur B. Tourtellot *Lexington and Concord* N194

Frederick Jackson Turner *The United States 1830-1850* N308

Harris Gaylord Warren *Herbert Hoover and the Great Depression* N394

Arthur P. Whitaker *The United States and the Independence of Latin America* N271

Bryce Wood *The Making of the Good Neighbor Policy* N401

C. Vann Woodward *The Battle for Leyte Gulf* N312

Benjamin Fletcher Wright *Consensus and Continuity, 1776-1787* N402

Howard Zinn *LaGuardia in Congress* N488

EUROPEAN HISTORY TITLES IN NORTON PAPERBOUND EDITIONS

Aron, Raymond. *On War.* N107

Aron, Raymond. *The Opium of the Intellectuals.* N106

Benda, Julien. *The Treason of the Intellectuals.* N470

Bloch, Marc. *Strange Defeat: A Statement of Evidence Written in 1940.* N371

Brandt, Conrad. *Stalin's Failure in China.* N352

Brinton, Crane. *The Lives of Talleyrand.* N188

Butterfield, Herbert. *The Whig Interpretation of History.* N318

Burn, W. L. *The Age of Equipoise.* N319

Calleo, David P. *Europe's Future: The Grand Alternatives.* N406

Dehio, Ludwig. *Germany and World Politics in the Twentieth Century.* N391

East, W. Gordon. *The Geography Behind History.* N419

Eyck, Erich. *Bismarck and the German Empire.* N235

Ferrero, Guglielmo. *The Reconstruction of Europe.* N208

Feis, Herbert. *Contest Over Japan.* N466

Feis, Herbert. *Europe: The World's Banker 1870-1914.* N327

Feis, Herbert. *The Spanish Story.* N339

Feis, Herbert. *Three International Episodes:* Seen from E. A. N351

Fischer, Fritz. *Germany's Aims in the First World War.*

Gatzke, Hans W. *Stresemann and the Rearmament of Germany.* N486

Gulick, Edward Vose. *Europe's Classical Balance of Power.* N413

Halperin, S. William. *Germany Tried Democracy.* N280

Hobsbawm, E. J. *Primitive Rebels.* N328

Langer, William L. *Our Vichy Gamble.* N379

May, Arthur J. *The Hapsburg Monarchy: 1867-1914.* N460

Menéndez Pidal, Ramón. *The Spaniards in Their History.* N353

Newhouse, John. *Collision in Brussels: The Common Market Crisis of 30 June 1965.*

Nichols, J. Alden. *Germany After Bismarck: The Caprivi Era, 1890-1894.* N463

Rowse, A. L. *Appeasement.* N139

Russell, Bertrand. *Freedom versus Organization: 1814-1914.* N136

Thompson, J. M. *Louis Napoleon and the Second Empire.* N403

Waite, Robert G. L. *Vanguard of Nazism: The Free Corps Movement in Postwar Germany, 1918-1923.* N181

Whyte, A. J. *The Evolution of Modern Italy.* N298

Wolfers, Arnold. *Britain and France between Two Wars.* N343

Wolf, John B. *Louis XIV.*

Wolff, Robert Lee. *The Balkans in Our Time.* N395